The Macedonian Resurrection

The Story of the Internal Macedonian Revolutionary Organization

Victor Sinadinoski

Copyright © 2017 by Victor Sinadinoski
All rights reserved. This book or any portion thereof may not be reproduced or used in any manner whatsoever without the express written permission of the publisher except for the use of brief quotations.

Printed in the United States of America

ISBN: 978-1542961349

"Macedonia's peculiar atmosphere of tense deadly hatred, combined with the chivalrous spirit which dictates that a man's hands must be clean, so that he may die clean, and that one's life must be sacrificed, as a matter of course for a friend, cannot be duplicated." —*Arthur D. Howden Smith, 1908*

(This page intentionally left blank)

For my beautiful and remarkable wife, Svetlana, who, besides being the love of my life, loves a good story; and the Macedonian liberation movement is filled with a bottomless trove of characters that make for a fascinating tale.

(This page intentionally left blank)

Table of Contents

1. Welcome to Macedonia ... 9
2. IMRO: For the People, By the People ... 24
3. The Intrusion of SMAC ... 49
4. Financing the Revolution ... 68
5. 1903: They Year of the Uprising ... 85
6. Macedonia Between Left and Right ... 107
7. Aleksandrov and a Divided Macedonia ...131
8. Mihajlov's Reign and IMRO's Demise ... 155

   Endnotes ... 182

(This page intentionally left blank)

I.

Welcome to Macedonia

The Internal Macedonian Revolutionary Organization (IMRO) sprouted in 1893 as a resistance movement to Turkish oppression. It eventually evolved into a governing enterprise of its own – complete with courts, taxes and soldiers – and was welcomed enthusiastically by the Macedonian peasants. Espousing the view of a Macedonia for the Macedonians, IMRO's founders navigated through several obstacles in order to win a significant following among the destitute peasantry, as well as an uncomfortable notoriety in regional and international circles. For several decades, IMRO was synonymous with the Macedonian liberation movement.

Before the IMRO rocketed to prominence, however, the Macedonian masses had been lingering in an uninterrupted hypnotic state. They accepted Turkish rule as a fixed reality; they believed that they were powerless to alter their conditions; and they could not envision a society where peace and liberty supplanted Ottoman brutality and injustice. Still, many Macedonians refused to flaccidly absorb Turkish abuses and misdeeds or the tenacious infiltrations into their lives by the Bulgarian, Greek and Serbian propaganda. They organized a small-scale but meaningful resistance.

One of these early notorious rebel leaders was Dimitar Popgeorgiev-Berovski, born in Berovo in 1840. Berovski had a wide and varied education and career: he attended a Greek high school in Solun; in 1858 he studied at the Theological Academy in Odessa, Ukraine; and in 1861 he began studying at the Belgrade Military School in Serbia, where upon finishing he enlisted as an officer in the Serbian army. Afterwards, he returned to his native Berovo to teach, as well as to fight against the domination of the Macedonians by the Greek Church and to reestablish the Macedonian Orthodox Church in Ohrid. When the Bulgarian Church formed in 1870 and Turkey opened her doors to it, Berovski began opposing Bulgaria's usurpation of Macedonian communities. By 1874, six Macedonian towns – Dojran, Kukush, Maleshevo, Solun, Strumica and Voden –

abandoned the Bulgarian and Greek Churches and instead allied with the Roman Catholic Church (Uniates). Berovski was elected by Maleshevo residents as the president of the Uniate church-school community there. The next year he led Strumica's Macedonians in expelling the Greek bishop from the town.[1]

In April of 1876, Berovski was chosen to lead the Razlog Uprising. The Uprising was supposed to extend to Maleshevo, Strumica, Petrich and Melnik, but unforeseen circumstances caused it to erupt prematurely in May. The rebels managed to extend their activity to Kochani, but the Turks swiftly quelled the revolution. Still, Berovski did not relinquish his efforts. Instead, when Bosnia and Hercegovina was granted autonomy within the Ottoman Empire, he continued agitating the Turkish authorities. Soon, the Russians and Turks found themselves at war in 1877, and Berovski joined Dedo Ilyo Markov-Maleshevski (born in 1805, also in Berovo) leading Macedonian volunteers in the Russian army.[2] The Turks lost this war and the Treaty of San Stefano gave much of Macedonia autonomy as a unit within Bulgaria. But the Powers were not satisfied with these conditions and revoked Macedonia's autonomy, and they warned Turkey to instead initiate reforms within Macedonia.

Dedo Ilyo was present in San Stefano, Bulgaria when the Treaty was signed in March of 1878. Being one of the most revered Macedonian leaders of his time – he was known as 'the last Macedonian outlaw' – there could be no better representation of the Macedonian spirit in attendance. He had spent the better half of his life fighting for freedom. While revolutionary activity had gone back several generations in his lineage (his grandfather, for example, died in a battle with Bashibazouks), his personal campaign against the Ottomans intensified in 1850, when he fled into the mountains after killing a Turk who had wounded his brother in an attack. In the 1850s, he recruited a band of several dozen Macedonian outlaws that roamed the mountains protecting Macedonian peasants from Turkish attacks in Maleshevo, Pijanec and Osogovo. His band included many Macedonians in similar situations, like Kocho Georgiev Ljutov, who after killing a Turk out of revenge, was jailed and then escaped. But the Turks chased Dedo Ilyo and his followers out of the region and by the 1860s, he had found refuge in Solun and Mt. Athos. The authorities then destroyed his home, kidnapped his wife and children and took them to Kyustendil (in Bulgaria), and killed a dozen of his fellow outlaws who had returned to their homes, four of whom were hanged in Nish (in Serbia).[3]

Seeking justice in 1860, Dedo Ilyo crossed into Serbia with his band of remaining outlaws and joined forces with the notorious Bulgarian rebel Georgi Rakovski. In 1862, at Belgrade, Dedo Ilyo's revolutionaries – alongside Serbians and Bulgarians – clashed in a major battle with Turks, and he eventually received honors from Serbia's Prince Mihailo Obrenovich for his bravery. He also led 300 of his volunteers in battles against the Ottomans in the Serbian-Turkish War of 1876. He was disappointed in the Serbs' efforts during the war; and in public he claimed that the Serbs were good at flaunting their weapons in the streets but were quick to flee from the Turks in the battlefield. A Serbian soldier retaliated and wounded him for his remarks, but Dedo Ilyo again received official Serbian honors for his war efforts. He then returned to Macedonia in 1878 and led a battalion of volunteers against the Turks, claiming victory in Pijanec.[4]

Immediately after the Berlin Congress of 1878 chucked the Macedonians back into Ottoman privation, the Macedonians ignited several more rebellions meant to flush out the Ottoman yoke, and they manufactured assassination plots to counter the aggression emanating from their neighbors. That these trials failed to secure the Macedonians' primary objective – the establishment of an independent Macedonia for the Macedonians – does not mean that the plots were without benefit. As a matter of fact, these local and relatively isolated deeds were the precursors to the organized Macedonian liberation movement structured under IMRO. In a nutshell, these outmatched yet courageous heroes inspired younger generations to continue shouldering the resistance movement.

The first major uprising after the Berlin Congress materialized in Kresna shortly after the Berlin Congress reversed the results of the San Stefano Treaty from a few months prior. The Macedonian Bishop Nathaniel of Ohrid began organizing the revolution in summer and autumn of 1878. He summoned Dedo Ilyo and Berovski, along with other rebel leaders from eastern Macedonia, to the Rila Monastery in Bulgaria (just outside of Macedonia) in late September, and Stojan Karastoilov was elected commander of the Kresna Uprising.[5]

Karastoilov had led rebel bands in Nevrekop and Drama throughout the 1870s; and during the Russo-Turkish war in 1877-

1878, he operated around Melnik and Serres. Like many Macedonian fighters of his time, he was drawn into battling the Turks after Ottoman authorities unleashed havoc on his village. When the Macedonian April Uprising failed in 1876, Karastoilov's village and region was ravaged – peasants were massacred, women were raped and villages were burned. Karastoilov, his brother and other peasants from Starchishta went to the island of Thasos to pick olives. There, they acquired arms and swore to avenge Turkish reprisals and atrocities.[6]

Hence, with respected and passionate leaders at the helm, in early October, Karastoilov and Stefan Karchev's band of 400 Macedonians attacked and captured a Turkish garrison in Kresna. After this initial success, the Macedonian fighters dispatched a letter to a Macedonian Committee in Gorna Djumaja, the nearest large town. In part, it proclaimed:

> **We Macedonian insurgents keep following our cause. Tonight, we led an 18-hour battle with two herds from the regular Turkish army. We suffered losses such as one person killed and three people wounded, while 9 Turkish soldiers were killed, 11 were wounded, and 119 soldiers and 2 officers have been captured.**[7]

Many villages around Kresna and in eastern Macedonia were thus liberated by 1879. Among the first villages to be freed was Vlahi, and it was here that the rebels established their headquarters. Berovski was elected the movement's Chief of Staff,[8] and revolutionary bands continued to successfully recapture several villages and ultimately assembled "local administrative organs in each village that they controlled." One of these local bodies even proclaimed an "independent Republic of Macedonia."[9] A constitution and rules of the Macedonian Revolutionary Committee were also established.[10]

But the leaders of the Macedonian insurgency soon came into conflict with Bulgarian leaders. The Macedonians' objective for the uprising was to liberate Macedonia from the Ottoman Empire. The Bulgarians, on the other hand, wanted to exploit these rebel successes as an instrument for reinstating the details of the Treaty of San Stefano, which proposed to attach Macedonia to Bulgaria. Western European powers were wary of a Great Bulgaria in the Balkans and what it could mean for promoting Russian interests in the region. The Macedonia fighters were beginning to realize that union with Bulgaria was no longer practical nor desirable and that only initiatives for an independent Macedonia or a larger Balkan Confederation would offer the best chance for freedom and security.

The Bulgarian leaders eventually succeeded in assuming control over the greater part of the Macedonian revolution. The Bulgarian Unity Committee's soldiers, steered by Louis Vojtkevich and Adam Kalmikov, stopped at no crime in preventing the Macedonians from succeeding. Most devastating to the Macedonian movement was the ousting of Berovski and the murder of Karastoilov and two important rebels, Georgi Cholakov and Ivan Trendafilov.[11]

Vojtkevich was particularly known for engaging in outlandish conflicts,[12] and was thus a reliable figure to interfere with the internal Macedonian uprising. There is scant information on where and when he was born, but he hailed from the Russian Empire and had Polish origins.[13] He participated in several rebellions and uprisings, such as the January Uprising in Poland against the Russian Empire.[14] Vojtkevich moved to Macedonia in 1870 and settled in Veles. He taught French at the Bulgarian school there and eventually married the daughter of Dimitar Karamfilovich, an important public figure.[15] Vojtkevich then rose to arms against the Turks in the Bosnian Uprising of 1875, the Serbian-Turkish war in 1876, and the Russo-Turkish War in 1877-1878, for which he served as a commander in northern Macedonia.[16]

The Sofia-based Bulgarian Unity Committee noticed him and appointed him as a leader of a volunteer detachment of Bulgarian fighters that tried to enter into Macedonia by the way of Kyustendil in order to begin an uprising. However, after that attempt failed, the Bulgarian Unity Committee put him in charge of 250 Bulgarian volunteers to join the Kresna-Razlog Uprising.[17] In November of that Uprising, the Bulgarian Unity Committee settled him in Bansko as the military head after the leader of the band that helped secure victory there, Banjo Marinov, was severely wounded. One writer noted that he arrived "to feast, not to fight." He soon clashed with the Macedonian leader, Karastoilov, who insisted on strengthening the rebel forces and administration in the victorious villages before extending the Uprising. Vojtkevich, however, was in no mood to be challenged on his desire to spread the war as soon as possible.[18]

It was also here that Vojtkevich came into a leadership struggle – temporarily – with another Bulgarian Unity Committee leader, Kalmikov. Like Vojtkevich, Kalmikov was from Russia and participated in both the Serbian-Turkish and Russo-Turkish Wars of the late 1870s.[19] Like Vojtkevich, he also tried to penetrate into Macedonia before the Kresna-Razlog Uprising began.[20] But before their competitive personalities could come to a collision, Berovski, Karastoilov and other Macedonian leaders had them removed from their commanding roles.[21] The Bulgarian Unity Committee, however, supported these foreign commanders in usurping command from the local Macedonians. Vojtkevich and Kalmikov arrested Berovski and killed Karastoilov and two of his trusted rebels.[22] Immediately, the Macedonians wanted revenge. Gorna Djumaja's commander, for example, ordered twenty Cossacks to capture the killers dead or alive.[23]

Even though Karastoilov's followers managed to chase Kalmikov out of the revolutionary area,[24] this takeover by the Bulgarians caused an unhealthy fracturing of the rebellions, and most Macedonian fighters withdrew their efforts. George Zimbilev was the sole local Macedonian leader remaining and could not continue the fight with a disintegrated force.[25] He abandoned his efforts, leading to the uprising's defeat in May of 1879.[26] Moreover, the Bulgarian interference fueled Macedonian disdain for Bulgarian leaders such as Stefan Stambolov, who had an active role in the uprising and would proceed to have an even greater role in subverting and coveting the Macedonian Cause. The injection of Bulgarian fighters and interests in the local uprising squashed any chances of the European Powers favorably examining the notion of an independent Macedonia.

The Kresna Uprising was by no means the only localized rebellion, and Turkish victory there did not conclude Macedonian revolutionary activity around the country. From 1878 through 1881, Macedonians in the western regions formed armed bands that determinedly attacked the Turkish authorities. These attacks were frequent in the regions surrounding Prilep, Kichevo, Bitola, Ohrid and Resen.[27] In the late summer of 1878, one of these rebellions' leaders was Commander Vasil. He and his two-thousand followers harassed and attacked Turkish regular and irregular soldiers:

> Vassil Voyvoda [captain], who is famous in our lands and operates with his men between the Kostour, Bitolya and Ohrid mountains...He selected from among them only the brave, who are able to handle arms, and enlists them as members of his band, which number no fewer than 2,000 men and is divided into five chetas [bands], each of them headed by its own honest voyvoda. The peasants look upon Vassil's band as their savior, which they most hospitably welcome, offering all available means for the attainment of the goal. In this way it has triumphed in several clashes with Albanian bashibazouk bands which, scattered all over the country, act unpunished, without recognizing any superior authority.[28]

On June 2, 1880, Macedonians hailing from all regions formed a government atop Mt. Gramos. The president of this assembly was Stefan Nikolov, the head of government was Vasil Simon, and military leaders were the experienced Leonidas Voulgaris and Konstantin Trpkov-Bufski. A protocol was signed by over thirty representatives who insisted that the nature of their movement was strictly Macedonian and that future maneuvers should be "inspired strictly by Macedonian interests and rights." Simultaneously, eight former Macedonian commanders formed the Macedonian League in Bulgaria as the "Temporary Administration of Macedonia." They created a constitution with over one-hundred articles and their slogan was "Freedom for Macedonia or Death!" They aimed to start out as a military organization and wrote instructions on how to establish and structure a Macedonian army in an eventual autonomous Macedonia. They even sent a declaration to Macedonians around the entire country on how to respond if the European Powers did not react favorably to their goal of an autonomous Macedonia.[29]

The next year, on March 23, 1881, the provisional Macedonian government delivered a manifesto to representatives around the country. It was addressed to the "true Macedonians, faithful to the homeland" and stated:

> Our dear Macedonia, our dear homeland is calling: You, who are my faithful children; you, who like Aristotle and Alexander the Great, are my heirs; you, in whose veins Macedonian blood

flows, do not leave me to die, help me. What a sad sight, real Macedonians, it would be if you were to witness my burial.[30]

Through the 1880s, western Macedonian bands continued employing guerrilla tactics against the Turkish authorities. Spiro Crne's band operated in the Prilep area; Mijale Todorov's band controlled Macedonian actions in the Kichevo region; and in Mariovo, Selechka and Krushevo, the brothers Dime and Mijaile Chakrev unleashed mayhem on the Turks.

Crne was a well-known rebel during his time. Before he took up arms, he made a living by smuggling tobacco and other goods, upsetting the Turkish monopoly.[31] After the Serbo-Turkish War in 1876, Turkish assaults on the native Prilep population exploded. This bothered Crne, but it was not until his sister was insulted by a local Turk that he decided to do something about the Macedonians' conditions. The Turk went into hiding and Crne let the Turk's friends know that he and his criminal brethren would be slaughtered. Crne and his friend Mojsil Djordjevich armed themselves and organized in a monastery outside of Prilep, where his friends Tode Bachvar, Pecko Bale and Dime Cincarin joined them. From there they met up with Petar Ristich, who had already been operating in the mountains seeking to eliminate a Turkish band led by Kuchuk Seleyman. Rather quickly, the Macedonians were confronted by a contingent of Turkish troops – Ristich was killed and Crne was wounded, so he abandoned his efforts and returned home to recover.[32]

Crne reorganized, however, this time with financing from Christian leaders and joined by two friends, Crni Djordje and Stevan Karanfiolvich-Popadika. Crne and his friends set up an ambush on the road to Trojaci on which he knew Seleyman would be traveling, thanks to information he received from peasants. After waiting for two days, Seleyman finally arrived. Caught by surprise, he and six of his party were killed, with Crne having fired the shot that killed Seleyman.[33]

Crne then escaped into Vranje, Serbia and began organizing a band of Macedonians for an eventual clash with the Turks. Along with dozens of other rebel leaders from Macedonia and Old Serbia, he appealed to the Serbian government for thousands of weapons and ammunition. The government heeded their call, and Crne began training his volunteer rebel detachment of Macedonians in Vranje.

His and Micko Krstich's bands crossed into Macedonia in the spring of 1880. Krstich's band was immediately destroyed around Kriva Palanka, so Krstich and his remaining comrade joined with Stevan Petrovich-Porechanin's band in Poreche. Meanwhile, Crne's band entered into a fierce battle with Ottoman soldiers near Ovche Pole. While 40 Turks and Albanians were killed, only Crne and three others from his band survived, so they retreated into Serbia.[34,35,36]

Then the Brsjak Revolt erupted in Poreche on October 14, 1880. It was organized by Micko Krstich, Ilija Delija, Rista Kostadinovich, and Andjelko Tanasovich, and was in some ways a continuation of the Kumanovo Uprising that transpired in 1878, when armed Albanians and Turks began raiding many Macedonian and southern Serbian villages, committing unavoidable atrocities. The Russian government eventually pressured the Serbian government to withdraw its support for the Macedonian revolt, and Macedonians were then left to their own devices once again during the Brsjak Revolt. In April of 1881, Crne's band of a dozen rebels left Serbia and began battling with Turkish troops. Within a couple of weeks, Crne's band was eliminated, and the Turks publicly displayed Crne's severed head as a point of pride and warning to the Macedonian population.[37] The Brsjak Revolt fizzled away and by the summer of 1881 many of these western Macedonian leaders had been summarily eliminated. Crne had lost his life near Kumanovo, while the Chakrev brothers died in a house set alight by the Turks. Todorov was eventually killed on the battlefield.[38]

Meanwhile, George Zimbilev and his band were swirling in a feud with Greeks (specifically, Macedonians aligned to the Greek Church) and Circassian horsemen in eastern Macedonia. In 1880, Zimbilev's band retaliated against the Greek Church in Gorno Brodi by burning all of its books in the Greek language because the local Greeks opposed the Macedonian language being used in church services.[39] The village Greeks reported this to the Turkish authorities, who then commissioned a Circassian named Hadji Jusuf and 70 of his horsemen to eliminate Zimbilev's band. To intimidate Zimbilev, Jusuf detained his entire family – plus many women related to members in his band – and threw in jail for several months and up to three years.[40] Zimbilev's band descended on Jusuf's band in April of 1882 and killed him along with twelve others from his horde.[41]

Being hotly pursued by more soldiers and police, Zimbilev's band sought safety in Bulgaria. The Ottoman authorities rounded up hundreds of Macedonians – many not connected to Zimbilev's band – in villages around Serres and Demir Hisar, and sentenced them to lengthy prison sentences.[42] But Zimbilev returned in the summer of 1873 with a force of 33 rebels to settle accounts with the authorities. However, a 500-strong contingent of Turkish soldiers and Bashibazouks nearly wiped out the band. Zimbilev was one of five that survived and escaped, but he had lost his brother.[43]

Up until the 1880s, Turks and Greeks had been the Macedonians' main opponents. Serbians and Bulgarians were generally looked to as brethren; a people who spoke a similar language and practiced a similar faith. But Macedonia was tempting to official Serbian and Bulgarian designs. One of the non-Macedonians who had injected himself into this Macedonian resistance was upcoming Bulgarian leader, Stefan Stambolov. After the Treaty of San Stefano was renounced by the European Powers at the Berlin Congress, Stambolov helped create revolutionary committees in Bulgaria and Macedonia to stir agitation among the dejected peasants. Many of these committees chose Stambolov as their representative, and he thus ventured into Macedonia in November of 1878 to join Macedonians who had already initiated the struggle for Macedonian freedom. Just inside the eastern Macedonian border, Stambolov formed a governing body resembling a small kingdom where he temporarily reigned along with the Bulgarian Bishop, Michael of Plovdiv. These two men organized and disseminated bands across many parts of Macedonia, but were hastily defeated by the Ottoman army, who eventually put out a price for Stambolov's head.[44]

Just as quickly as the Turks suppressed the Bulgarian intrusion into Macedonia did Stambolov then began to detest the Macedonians "for their treachery." He could not trust the Macedonians and the Macedonians felt the same toward him. Stambolov knew that the Macedonians did not possess any "real sense" of Bulgarian patriotism, and he was never sure that "when he lay down at night whether he would rise next morning...being aware, that almost any Macedonian, if he found the chance, would murder him in order to secure the reward on his head." At the same time, many Macedonians did not believe Stambolov was working toward Macedonian interests and was instead inflicting more harm to the

Macedonian Cause than good. Contrary to his original expectations, Stambolov was not greeted as a hero or savior by the Macedonians. These reasons thus fueled Stambolov's relentless effort to emphasize only Bulgarian interests in his Macedonian agenda. From that point forward "he always retained a strong contempt and antipathy" for the Macedonian people.[45] By 1889 Stambolov had wiped out all Macedonian revolutionary bands operating throughout Bulgaria, of which most consisted of Macedonian natives or Macedonian sympathizers working to obtain funds for the Macedonian Cause. This is how Stambolov secured the hatred of the Macedonian agitators and their friends.[46]

Throughout the period between 1878 and the formation of IMRO in 1893, many Macedonian-initiated and localized rebellions sparked and faded. When rebellions were crushed and the Macedonians were defeated by the Turks, Macedonian factions took direct aim at Bulgaria's Prince Ferdinand and Stambolov, who had become Prime Minister of Bulgaria in 1887. One of the first significant, organized assassination plots by Macedonians after the Kresna-Razlog Uprising in 1878/1879 occurred in Bulgaria. After Prince Ferdinand assumed control of Bulgaria also in 1887, several Macedonians organized small bands of cutthroats that would become instruments of this new system of political assassinations. One band originally plotted to assassinate the Prince but then later altered its plans, selecting instead Prime Minister Stambolov as their target. They hoped that a murdered Stambolov would scare Prince Ferdinand into abdicating from his throne. Stambolov was certainly not ignorant of these plots, but he doubted their seriousness and could not believe that anyone would be bold enough to make an attempt on his life.[47]

In 1890, Stambolov discovered a concrete plot to kidnap and assassinate him along with Prince Ferdinand. The leaders of the plot were arrested, one of them being Kosta Panica, an army major with Macedonian ancestry.[48] Panica, who had a varied career in Bulgaria as an original member of the Eastern Rumelian Revolutionary Committee and as the Sofia Court Martial in the 1880s, gained the admiration of many Macedonians. He opposed Prince Ferdinand's rule and lambasted Stambolov as tyrannical, over-confident and authoritarian. Moreover, Stambolov believed in a gradual approach to acquiring Macedonia for Bulgaria while Panica believed that revolution against the Turks was the only option to free Macedonia. Panica managed to recruit many Macedonians in his campaign against Stambolov and Prince Ferdinand, who was not a native Bulgarian, which made him an enemy of the Panslavist movement raging through Eastern Europe.[49]

Panica's original plan was to kidnap Prince Ferdinand in November of 1889 on his return trip to Sofia from a European tour. Panica had also wanted to capture several Bulgarian government ministers and execute them publicly. But because most ministers were absent at Prince Ferdinand's homecoming to Sofia, Panica postponed the assassination until February of the next year.[50] Stambolov, however, discovered the plot after intercepting Panica's mail, and one of Panica's personal attendants also leaked details of the assassination plot to him.[51] Stambolov then sent a police officer to inform Panica that he knew about the plot and offered to ignore his misdeeds if he abandoned the plot. This infuriated Panica, who was determined to fulfill his mission. Being that Panica's house had already become a hotbed for revolutionary activity, Stambolov thus decided to arrest Panica the day before the planned assassination.[52]

Panica "was court-martialed and executed, further intensifying the anti-Stambolov feelings among Macedonian activists."[53] At trial, Panica proclaimed "he wished to secure Russian intervention in the favor of the Macedonian liberation from the Turkish yoke[.]"[54] In a demonstration of power and wickedness, Stambolov ordered a squad of Panica's Macedonians to carry out the execution.[55] However, in response and as a warning to the Bulgarian leaders, Macedonian nationalists placed a sign in the spot where Panica was executed, which read: "This is where Stambolov and Prince Ferdinand will be shot."[56]

Panica's Macedonians and others were determined to follow through with their threats. On the night of March 27, 1891, Stambolov had been chatting with the new Minister of Finance, Hristo Belchev, at a café in Sofia when Stambolov decided that they should walk and talk. The two men resembled each other, as they were of the same build and wore similar clothing; and while Stambolov was darker, the difference in complexion was not noticeable at night. As they were walking along the street, a pistol shot rang out and Stambolov fled, shouting for Belchev to follow him. He eventually made it to a guard house when he heard exclamations that "Stambolov [was] dead!" He returned to the scene with a handful of guards only to discover that Belchev, who decided upon hearing the first shot to run into a public garden and hide behind trees, lay dead with a bullet in his heart.[57]

The Macedonian assassins planned the murder in Belgrade. Naum Tiufekchiev, from Resen, organized the group in Serbia, which included his two brothers, Nikola and Dimitar, Mihail Stavrev (also from Resen's surroundings), Krsto Nozharov, and Dimitar Rizov, from Bitola.[58] Five assassins were involved in committing the deed. The youngest of the Tiufekchiev brothers, eighteen-year-old Dimitri, died during a preliminary inquiry by officials, after being beaten and cruelly tortured. Stavrev was accidentally shot in the hand by Naum during the struggle with Belchev. The hole in his hand prevented him from leaving the country, so he stayed in the house of a friend for a month until his hand healed and he then fled to Serbia. The fourth accomplice was Nozharov, and the last was Georgi Velikov. At his trial, the court could not find sufficient proof to convict him of first degree murder; instead, he was sentenced to eighteen years of penal servitude. After the regime changed in 1895, Velikov was released and became part of the new government.[59]

Stambolov punished many more Macedonians and Macedonian sympathizers for the murder and attempt on his life. Arrests, trials, imprisonments and executions – deserved or not – followed. Trajko Kitanchev, from the village of Podmochani near Resen, for example, was sentenced to three years in prison simply because he was a central figure in the Macedonian movement and had opposed Stambolov's platform on Macedonia.[60] Also arrested were Bulgarian political opponents to Stambolov, such as the former Prime Minister, Petko Karavelov, who had contested Stambolov's warming attitude toward the Ottoman regime. Karavelov was accused of instigating the plot to instill a pro-Russian regime in Bulgaria and was almost executed for it.[61]

However, the Macedonian assassins did not let a failed assassination attempt foil their ambitions. In November of 1891, Stambolov intercepted a letter from Naum Tiufekchiev and his brother, Nikola, outlining their plans to kill Georgi Vulkovich, who was Bulgaria's diplomatic agent in Istanbul, as well as a close friend to Stambolov. Stambolov asked the Ottoman authorities to increase protection for Vulkovich and warned him that Macedonians were plotting to murder him. Vulkovich shrugged off the notion that such a thing could happen, thinking that no one would want to kill him.[62]

Meanwhile, in late December, Naum had boarded a ship in Odessa and traveled to Istanbul, accompanied by Hristo and Vladimir Shismanov, who were acting with government support from Russia, and Georgi Vulkov, a professional killer who went by the nick-name "Merdzhan". On a crisp February evening, as Vulkovich was returning to the Bulgarian Diplomatic Agency in Istanbul, he turned around to footsteps rushing toward him and saw a man wielding a knife. He screamed for help, but it was too late – the next day he succumbed to several stab wounds. Another version of the murder suggest that he was stalked by two men during a street carnival. Either way, he was dead.[63]

Two men were arrested for the murder – Hristo Stefan Popeto from Resen and Georgi Vulkov-Merdzhan. The Shismanovs and Tiufekchievs managed to escape with the help of the Russian Embassy. While they were still on Turkish territory, Stambolov demanded from Ottoman authorities that they catch the Macedonians and extradite them to Bulgaria to face trial, but the Sultan did not want to anger Russia. The trial proceeded without several defendants present and all were found guilty. Popeto and Merdzhan were sentenced to death.[64]

By 1895, in addition to losing two close friends, Stambolov had lost his position as Prime Minister due to circumstances in Bulgaria's political arena. In July, he wrote an article critical of Prince Ferdinand and the Macedonian agitation, and advocated for closer ties with the Ottoman leaders. The Macedonians residing in Bulgaria found this particularly traitorous.[65] They unleashed their opposition to Stambolov and his policies by stabbing him to death in the streets of Sofia:

> **He was stabbed, shot, hacked and beaten in a most terrible manner...Both of the ex-premier's hands were chopped; one wrist was almost severed from the arm; he was repeatedly stabbed about the body and shot in the head. After he fell the assassins continued stabbing and hacking him until compelled to run away.[66]**

Stambolov lived for two days after the attacks. The attackers' knives struck him 23 times on the face and head, and all unprotected parts of his body were slashed. For those two days, Stambolov waded in and out of consciousness, occasionally blaming Prince Ferdinand for the attack, as Prince Ferdinand had seemed to now be appeasing the Macedonian attitude for a Bulgarian-backed revolution as the only means for securing Macedonian freedom.[67]

The assassin who orchestrated and carried out the murder of Stambolov was the familiar Naum Tiufekchiev. Joining him were Stavrev, a Macedonian named Atzov and a Bulgarian named Boni Georgiev;[68] and together with about a dozen other men, they had been quartering in a hotel owned by the Ivanov brothers (who were well-known gun merchants) plotting the crime.[69] Atzov, being a coachman, drove Stambolov to the scene of the crime, while Tiufekchiev had been working for the ministry of public works as means to get close to his victim.[70] In the encounter, Stavrev was shot in the neck by Stambolov's bodyguard. The few police officers present took the bodyguard into custody because he had fired a weapon. By the time they realized the facts, Stavrev had escaped into the woods.[71] During their trial (of which many, again, were not present), the prosecutors read a letter written by Stambolov, which suggested that he had been aware of the plots to assassinate him and that he knew Naum Tiufekchiev would be responsible.[72]

After several small rebellions and a high-profile assassination, the Macedonians proved that they had the ability to organize and resist Turkish injustices and Balkan chauvinism. However, if the Macedonians were to have any real shot at success, they would need a movement that awakened and organized the peasant masses. This movement was already in its infancy by the time Stambolov was killed, but it would fester throughout the Balkan landscape for several decades. This book takes the reader on a journey from the inception of the notorious IMRO revolutionary struggle in the 1890s and 1900s and through the period of Macedonian gangsterdom that deepened the Macedonians' division and panicked Macedonia's neighbors in the 1920s and 1930s. This is the story of the Macedonian resurrection.

II.

IMRO: For the People, By the People

By the 1890s, the Macedonian peasants were in a desperate position. First, the economic condition of the Empire was pitiful and the peasants were drowning in poverty. Second, faithfulness to the Christian identity subjected the Macedonians to daily crimes and abuses by the authorities, and justice was not a worthwhile pursuit. Third, brigands and bandits roamed the land, extracting money, valuables and blood from every village through which they passed. Fourth, a steadily growing agitation by her neighbors put Macedonia in a peculiar position with no one to trust and no one to help them.[73] Therefore, any change in their conditions – any prospect of freedom, justice and economic opportunity – had to come from within Macedonia and specifically from the peasant class. The initial difficulty was getting organized in a chaotic and poverty-ridden atmosphere. Fortunately, there were many Macedonians – intellectuals, tradesmen and peasants alike – who possessed the will and found the means to organize the Macedonian population into a bastion of resistance.

In the late 1880s and early 1890s, a number of educated Macedonians were flirting with the idea of creating secret Macedonian revolutionary groups. From 1892-1894, Naum Tiufekchiev was involved in the Macedonian Literary Association,[74] along with Petar Pop Arsov, Thomas Karajovov, Hristo Pop Kocev, Dimitar Mirchev, Andrey Liapchev, Georgi Balaschev, Kosta Shahov and Evtim Sprostranov.[75] In 1892, IMRO's eventual leaders – Dame Gruev, Petar Poparsov and Pere Toshev – also briefly discussed the need for such an organization.[76]

The actual catalyst for initiating IMRO arrived in November of 1893. Gruev was walking in Solun with fellow school teacher Andon Dimitrov when they bumped into Ivan Hadzhinikolov. "The three became involved in a heated discussion about the fate of Macedonia and agreed that it was time to form a revolutionary committee, the goal of which would be to prepare the populace for revolt in

Macedonia." Hadzhinikolov insisted that three men were not enough to embark on such an important and daunting task; he suggested that they recruit at least three more men in order to "form the nucleus of the organization." One of the three selected men for the task was Hristo Tatarchev, a doctor who had been treating Gruev for eczema. The other two individuals were teachers, Poparsov and Hristo Batandziev.[77]

On December 23rd, these six visionary men formed the IMRO after a meeting in Solun. In January of 1894, at their second meeting, they named the leadership the "Macedonian Central Revolutionary Committee" and began assigning tasks: Poparsov was to write the constitution, while Tatarchev was elected President and Gruev was voted to be the Secretary.[78] These founders' involvement in IMRO were varied. For example, Dimitrov and Batandziev would not be remembered for much more than being members of the founding nucleus; Tatarchev and Poparsov were prominent before the Ilinden Uprising in 1903, but afterwards their involvement and popularity began to wane; while Gruev and Hadzhinikolov were known as the drivers of the organization well after their deaths.[79] Regardless of their level of future involvement, their initial efforts became the roaring thunder that preceded the storm. With their efforts sprouted one of the most infamous underground organizations in modern history.

The most revered of the founders, Dame Gruev, was born in 1871 in Smilevo, a village near Bitola. After completing elementary school in Smilevo, he proceeded to study in different schools around Macedonia, including Resen, Bitola and Solun. He eventually ended up at the University of Sofia in Bulgaria for his higher education (Macedonian institutions of higher education did not exist during this time). Gruev's initial ideas for IMRO came from his studies, particularly of other Balkan and European struggles and organizational schemes for autonomy. He desired to transfer this knowledge to the Macedonian peasants and began so by becoming a school teacher in his native Smilevo and then eventually relocating to Prilep.[80] This was only the beginning of Gruev's journey through Macedonia advocating for the Macedonian struggle.

In August of 1894, Gruev and the IMRO's Central Committee included a few more trustworthy and reliable men at their next major meeting, which transpired in the town of Resen. A total of about fifteen patriots attended this meeting and they began carving out IMRO's future. They discussed many topics, including how to structure their organization, the best available methods for raising funds and planning ways to market their organization to the Macedonians. They determined that teachers would have a significant role in fulfilling these missions. Further, because grammar schools in Macedonia were mostly associated with the Bulgarian Church, and thus exposed to the influence of the Bulgarian Government, they vowed that IMRO's educators would act completely independent of the Bulgarian Church so that the organization would not be swayed into becoming a tool for Bulgarian propaganda.[81]

IMRO thus initiated the work of infiltrating schools throughout Macedonia and creating local Macedonian revolutionary committees. In the summer of 1894, Gruev formed the first committee in Negotino, located in central Macedonia. Shortly afterward, he and Pere Toshev organized the first district committee in Shtip, north-central Macedonia. Gruev further toured several different areas that were favorable to these Macedonian revolutionary ideas, such as in Resen, Ohrid and Struga. The other IMRO members directed their work in these regions as well as in southern and eastern Macedonia.[82]

During his stint in Shtip in the latter half of 1894, Gruev met one of the central Macedonian revolutionary figures who would eventually embody the spirit of the Macedonian revolution: Goce Delchev.[83] Delchev was born on January 23, 1872 in Kukush, eastern Macedonia. He studied high school in Solun and was known for being a popular student with regards to his scholarship. But he was also known as an "agitator and advocate of Macedonian independence" and for attaching himself to socialist ideologies, which he carried with him his entire life.[84] For example, he once stated: "I have the soul of an anarchist, the convictions of a social democrat, and I act like a revolutionary."[85] When he atttended military school in Bulgaria, he continued to secretly read and study socialist movements. Once there, he declared that he considered "the world only as a place for the cultural rivalry of the nations." At the military school, Delchev was often in trouble for spreading his beliefs. He was eventually expelled from the school for influencing and associating with military cadets at the school who had been faulting the Minister of War with injustices against them.[86]

After the military school officials ousted Delchev, he arrived in the village of Novo Selo, just outside of Shtip, to work as a teacher.[87] When Delchev became acquainted with Gruev and IMRO in Shtip, Gruev probed him attentively about his goals and motivations for pursuing the Macedonian Cause. Delchev replied that his Macedonian brothers and sisters were still enslaved under Turkish domination. He would have drowned in shame and disappointment had he followed the path of many Macedonians who escaped Macedonia and chose to remain in Bulgaria and other free countries, living the easy life and surrendering themselves to sexual escapades and drinking. Delchev firmly believed that educated people were gifted a special responsibility to the Macedonian nation; it would be disgraceful to stand by and expect others to liberate the Macedonians.[88] Gruev welcomed Delchev to the organization eagerly and earnestly.

Delchev and Gruev remained in the vicinity of Shtip for about two years. They rapidly grew the organization by recruiting peasants into the organization instead of just relying on the townsfolk. Shtip and its surroundings therefore became the center of the Macedonian movement during this early years. While Solun was Macedonia's big city and housed IMRO's headquarters, it was much easier for Gruev and Delchev to expand the organization and promote its ideals in central Macedonia,[89] where most of the Christians were ethnic Macedonians and had suffered much hardship under Turkish misrule.

Between 1894 and 1897, IMRO was primarily focused on executing its enlightenment and recruitment agenda.[90] A Macedonian revolutionary from this time period, Hristo Siljanov, wrote in his memoirs that these first years merely had the effect of organizing groups of men who did little else than plot their revenge against the Turks. "[M]embers spent their time twiddling their thumbs and fantasizing on the possible ways of avenging the Turks for their five centuries of tyranny."[91] However, although these feelings may have been the catalyst for triggering people to join IMRO, the organization had grown in many significant ways. They formed local revolutionary committees in towns and villages and new members of IMRO swore their oath of allegiance to IMRO and its ideals on a Bible, dagger and revolver.[92] A general in the Bulgarian army spoke about these early years:

> **From 1895, the Macedonian intelligence entered fully into the revolutionary movement. In less than four years, the country was studded with secret societies, at the head of which stood a revolutionary committee managing the movement. The rural population eagerly embraced the revolution, and began to prepare itself for a rising against the abominable domination.[93]**

Thus, while the Macedonian peasants were driven by their distrust and disdain for Turkish officials, IMRO's central leadership was making significant headway in creating a massive revolutionary body.

As teachers, IMRO's leaders had access to every corner of Macedonia under the cover of bringing education to the children. For example, between 1895 and 1897, Gruev lived in Solun and worked as a Bulgarian Church school inspector, and he then joined the Bitola teaching staff in 1898 after being dismissed by the Bulgarian Church in Solun.[94] Delchev, for his part, visited the entire country as a teacher, spreading the goal of Macedonian autonomy to all attentive Macedonians; and as a result, he had much success in organizing towns and villages throughout Macedonia, such as in the areas of Serres, Solun, Bitola, Ohrid, Lerin, and Kostur.[95] Pere Toshev, who was born in Prilep in 1867 and served in the Bulgarian army against Serbia in the war of 1885, returned to Macedonia in order to spread revolutionary ideas while working as a school teacher until the turn of the century.[96] Christo Matov – who was tasked with writing literary works that shaped the form, methods and tactics of IMRO -- based himself in the Skopje region. In the late 1890s he became the head of the Bulgarian pedagogical school of Skopje, which gave him access to impressionable and inquisitive minds. He was entrusted with the power to appoint teachers and he wielded that power to place teachers supportive of IMRO's mission into prominent positions. The Skopje region would eventually enjoy great success in establishing rebel bands because of Matov's work in Skopje. By 1898, every village and town surrounding Skopje had a revolutionary committee.[97]

These and other teachers "were simply following the example afforded by yore by the 'intellectuals' in Russia; they had gone to the people." By encouraging education as the mechanism to spread their message about freedom and equality, IMRO's intellectuals were able to reach thousands of otherwise inaccessible minds. As Maurice Kahn wrote: "It is not unimportant to note that in these first steps originated the first dreams of liberty."[98]

The first IMRO Congress convened in March of 1896 in Solun. The discussions revolved primarily around tackling the obstacles and problems with the structure and methods of IMRO. The Congress resolved to adopt a constitution and a book of regulations to serve "as basic documents of the future ideological activity of the Movement." Many of the documents were prepared by Delchev and Gjorche Petrov (a teacher and writer born in 1865 in Varosh, near Prilep) in 1897.[99] IMRO's leaders were continually refining and defining their aims and methods, but they eventually determined that their organization would be based on five principles: first, to organize Macedonia into an autonomous state; second, to mold the organization into a people's movement that would be prepared for a revolution; third, to give IMRO membership solely to those individuals who resided in Macedonia, a concept defined as internalism; fourth, to struggle for a substantial improvement of economic and political conditions in Macedonia; and finally, to preserve its own independence as a fighting organization.[100]

All of these principles were viewed as inseparable from the Macedonian Cause. But the true driving force for creating IMRO was the decaying economic and social conditions under the Turks. The evil of "merciless absorption year after year of the profits of their ceaseless labor"[101] sparked tremendous disdain amongst the Macedonian population. One specific IMRO response to this unfairness was to fight against the Ottoman system of dividing the land and farm labor. A well-known motto of IMRO was, "Give the land to the farmers!"[102] Some agricultural laborers, backed by IMRO, went on strike to demand a raise in wages.[103] IMRO then "designated a minimum wage for the farm laborers." This minimum was three times higher than their previous wages.[104]

Further, the inability to secure justice within the Ottoman legal system motivated the IMRO into implementing an almost unmatchable guerrilla warfare. As one news report wrote:

> **There is no law in Macedonia but that of force, and it is quite natural that the common people in their desperation should have turned brigands and given the Turk a taste of his own medicine. The Turks cannot make head against a guerrilla warfare of this sort, and the success of these lawless brigands has inspired the mass of the people with a hope of ultimate independence through continual fighting and agitation.**[105]

The entire population knew that revolution was the ultimate aim, even though the peasants had no idea how the end result of the insurgency would look. While they wanted independence, many of the peasants thought that it would be won quickly. Thus, for the time being, the question of Macedonian independence was a matter to be dealt with in the future and the peasants main aim was revenge. One newspaper wrote: "What they do yearn for is an opportunity to avenge innumerable outrages which have been perpetuated upon them…Murders are as common in the troubled districts as theft is in London."[106] IMRO gave the peasants a vehicle with which to seek a justice the Macedonians had not known for centuries.

There were seven essential reasons why the common peasant would join IMRO's ranks, and these reasons generally revolved around vengeance: the murder of family members by Turkish authorities; the destruction of one's home or the looting of one's property; the ruining of one's business; the dishonored caused to one's family or name; the assault or offence against a wife; the rape of a blood-relative; or the abduction and ransoming of a family member.[107] These types of avengers existed in Macedonia during the entire era of Ottoman occupation. But until the revolutionary movement engrained itself into Macedonian society as a serious and relevant body – and even after the failing of the Macedonian uprising – most Macedonians had no concept of revolutionary work outside the context of personal revenges. This seems puzzling because the aim of the revolution as outlined by its leaders and the intellectuals among the group (along with those Macedonians residing outside of the Ottoman Empire who had an opportunity to experience freedom and justice) was for the liberty and autonomy of the Macedonians. To the common Macedonian, liberty meant revenge: "They were to have had no taxes to pay, and would be allowed to carry guns and shoot Turks. This was their only idea of liberty…"[108] For those who had no concept of liberty, it meant something different than for those who had already experienced it.

This, however, should not have been surprising; and furthermore, it did not contradict IMRO's aims and integrity. What led to the political and national movement for autonomy, equality and liberty was the common suffering that the Macedonians faced and the realization that they could both avenge the misdeeds cast upon them and create a better society by working in unison with their fellow Macedonians. The realization of a common suffering led to the necessity of a common struggle, and the organizational catalyst and inspiration was the IMRO.

Further, many of these avengers simply had no choice but to join IMRO bands because sheer survival depended on doing so. Many of them had committed crimes (which generally amounted to vigilante justice for the family or village because the Ottoman courts failed in executing justice) that had made them outlaws. One seventeen year-old Macedonian, who had been an apprentice to a tailor, fled to the hills after stabbing a Turkish soldier who was beating him. In another case, an elderly man and his son fled to join the IMRO after killing an Albanian land steward and injuring a Turkish police officer by throwing stones at them.[109] These men faced certain death had they not found refuge with the IMRO rebel bands. Here is another account of why one man desired to kill Turks and joined the IMRO:

> I once had a talk with a man who had drugged ten Turkish soldiers in an inn and then burned them alive. When I expressed my horror, he replied by pouring out a tale which I confess staggered me – all the recent wrongs of his village – the men carried away captive into slavery by brigands, the women forced to appear in this same inn and to dance naked for the amusement of passing soldiers...I tried to suggest that such reprisals were a mistake, since they alienate the sympathies of Europe. He replied that by murdering ten men who richly deserved it, he had obtained ten rifles for the cause of liberty. "Surely," I answered, "the good opinion of the civilized world is worth more than ten rifles?" He smiled bitterly, reflected for a moment and then, mimicking my tones, inquired laconically, "What was the good opinion of your civilized world worth to the Armenians?" I was silenced.[110]

While young men were almost expected to desire to join the IMRO, women also constituted a relevant part of the organization. Some cooked and sewed for the rebels, some transferred and hid weapons and important documents, and some even fought. Donka Budzhakoska recalls:

> **At the beginning of 1901, I joined the ranks of the Regular Macedonian Revolutionary Organization, which was working for the liberation of the Macedonian people from Turkish oppression, and to which I made an oath, crossing myself, in the presence of Kosta Shkodra, the teacher Tirchu Kare, the flag bearer, and Tome Nikle, all from Krushevo. Initially, I was made a courier, to carry correspondence and weapons.**[111]

Additionally, while the IMRO membership consisted primarily of ethnic Macedonian men and women, IMRO aimed to incorporate all Christians into their ranks, regardless of church affiliation or ethnic affiliation. Steeg, the French Consul in Solun, wrote in 1902: "Everything known of these committees leads us to believe that they will spare no effort to bring into their ranks all the Christians in the country[.]"[112] This should not be surprising because the IMRO espoused equality as an important element of any successful revolution and future Macedonian state. Matov wrote: "As one realized and knows from experience the pains of oppression, it should not therefore be imposed upon others."[113] Therefore, IMRO pursued Macedonians of all backgrounds. While they did manage to bring into their ranks many Vlachs, they had less success recruiting Greeks, Serbians and Albanian Christians, because their goals were not compatible with a free and independent Macedonia, or because they were intimidated into not joining the revolutionary movement. Still, "the insurgent movement [was] in reality a genuine Macedonian movement, prepared by Macedonians, led by Macedonians, and assisted by the passionate sympathy of the vast majority of the Slav population."[114]

Even though IMRO was a strong military force, its leaders desired their organization to resemble an alternative government rather than simply an army. IMRO rebel bands were essentially defense patrols, touring the land countering Turkish aggression and injustices; the military aspect of IMRO was viewed solely as a means for achieving independence should the political and social process fail the

Macedonians. Before the Turks began ruthlessly suppressing the Macedonians and IMRO at the start of the 20th century, IMRO avoided major battles whenever possible. "The Macedonian bands…contented themselves usually with killing intolerable Turkish officials. These they would shoot in the streets or steal off and murder them quietly."[115] One high-ranking IMRO member told a journalist about the true vision for IMRO and Macedonia:

> **Our purpose isn't to fight…The Organization represents the administrative machinery of an underground republic which has been built up as a protection against Turkish anarchy, and the regular bands are the police force of this republic. They enforce the orders of the civil courts. In each village is a local court. Then we have circuit courts travelling about the country, settling the quarrels between individuals under different jurisdictions – that is men of different villages. The local committees represent the civil local governments; behind them is the force of the bands. As the local committees are elected by the villagers, they are not likely to abuse their powers.[116]**

IMRO was divided into two basic types of membership. There were those engaged in passive or legal activities and those performing active or illegal undertakings. The passive members constituted the majority: peaceful citizens partaking in local elections of church boards and supporting the school system; influential individuals spreading propaganda and advocating the Macedonian Cause to foreigners and newspapers; and those who contributed the finances to the organization. The illegal or active members were those who had openly declared revolution against the Ottoman government. They essentially lived in the mountains organizing armed bands and accruing weapons from every possible source. An active member was someone who "declared himself voluntarily ready to take up arms and join the revolutionary *chetas*." He had to swear an oath of fidelity, loyalty and obedience to the Cause and belonged more to IMRO than to his family, blindly fulfilling orders of IMRO. This oath to IMRO and the Macedonian Cause ruled all of his future decisions:

> **I swear on my faith, conscience and honor, that I will work for the liberty of Macedonia and the Adrianople Vilayet with all**

my strength and means, and that I will never betray the secret of the revolutionary work of the IMRO. Should I do such a thing, may I be killed by this revolver or by this dagger which I kiss. Amen.[117]

These active IMRO members did not report to duty at a primary base of operations because no such base existed. Rather, there existed several committees with a detailed and organized chain of command throughout most Macedonian villages and towns. This decentralized approach was necessary in avoiding Turkish destruction, and it became more important as Bulgarian elements began to inject themselves into the Macedonian organization.

But even without a central base of operations, IMRO did have a Central Committee that made important decisions. They especially communicated with Macedonians and foreigners outside of Macedonia to push the Macedonian Cause on Europe and to keep the Macedonian situation relevant in the media:

> **The committee has no definite headquarters, and may be found at any time issuing its propaganda from Bucharest, Paris, Geneva or Sofia. It has, however, at Geneva, a representative who is the intermediary between the various chiefs. Frequently, meetings are held at Geneva, Sofia and Zurich, and Paris is used as the great distributing center for Macedonian literature dealing with the various outrages and murders which the committee sends broadcast over the whole of Europe…The power of the Macedonian Committee is immense. Thousands of peasants in Bulgaria, Servia, and even Roumania, apart from Macedonia proper, regularly month-by-month subscribe to the cause.[118]**

The Central Committee also made it a prerogative to establish courts in Macedonia. IMRO recognized that Macedonians could not seek justice from the Turkish courts and in 1900 they set up their own parallel government and courts, where "a good part of the population of Macedonia transferred all their disputes, even the most trifling." Unlike the Turkish authorities, IMRO dealt "speedy, intelligent and gratuitous" justice.[119] These courts took on different forms and functions. Sometimes they listened to peasants' grievances against the Turks and then sought justice for those crimes committed against the peasants. For example, in the summer of 1900, the regional unit of Commander Slavejko Arsov was stationed in the Prespa village of Bolno, along with IMRO bands from Bolno, Caredvor, Durmeni and Jankovec. Arsov was distributing weapons and examining the strengths and weaknesses of the fighters. A peasant from Bolno complained that a Turkish landowner had taken his animals and demanded three gold coins from them. Arsov told the Turkish landowner to return the animals or face execution. The Turk refused and was killed.[120]

However, the courts also existed to resolve disputes among the Macedonians themselves because the Turkish courts could not deliver on this front. Generally, the village priest would present one side of a dispute and the school teacher would present another. In one example, a man named Ivancho had leased some land to a peasant named Stojan. After several years, Ivancho wanted his land back. Stojan, however, would not return his land to Ivancho without some form of payment for the barn he had built on the land and the orchard he had planted. In another example, an elderly woman asked for – and was granted – a divorce because of "incompatibility of temperament," calling her husband "all right," but insisting that they could never agree on anything. In a criminal case, one man had stolen a horse from another man in a distant village. His punishment was "twenty blows from a cane." The judge also banished him to work a year in Bulgaria so he could make some good money and not succumb to his urges to resort to criminality.[121]

IMRO's members were especially respected and celebrated for their strong dedication and adherence to IMRO's principles and laws. These principles and laws served two primary functions: one was to ensure that the rebels were in the best mental, physical and emotional condition to pursue their strategic military objectives; the other was to present the peasant populace with an alternate model of governance that was opposite to the cruel, merciless and rude rule of the Turks. One of these principles revolved around the treatment of women. An author highlighted IMRO's respect for women:

> **Many of these armed revolutionaries, who, I knew, led loose lives in Bulgaria, would roam about Macedonia for years, as clean lived as the celibate monk, without his fanaticism to uphold them. This was one of the laws of the Committee I saw absolutely fulfilled…Curiously enough, even the old time**

brigands, who knew no laws but their own, were not only careful observers of women's chastity themselves, but were ever ready to avenge such wrongs.[122]

And when such chastity laws were violated, the peasants did not discriminate against men or women for violating them – both were equally punished for violations.[123] Delchev even lectured one rebel named Kice for having a sexual relationship with the wife of a gentleman who moved abroad for work because she flirted with and seduced Kice:

> **Consider, Kitse, what harm and what shame is being brought upon the Organization. This people will utterly despair if we, who say that we are working to save them from Turkish violence and rape, ourselves assault the honour of their women. You are disgracing not only yourself. You are Marko's chetnik, and the shame falls on him, too, and on the whole Organization. Let him who wants to live like other people and deprive himself of nothing go away where he likes[.]**[124]

The general observations and assessment of IMRO rebels were positive and inspiring. One American who spent much time with the rebels said that everyone he met was honest, reliable and unselfish.[125]

While many of the peasants were not fighting members of the organization, they sympathized with IMRO and trusted IMRO to protect and defend them. IMRO had won over the loyalty of most Macedonians and devised many strategies for communicating with them about danger. For example, peasants had a way to warn IMRO rebels of when the Turks or Greeks were coming. If Turkish authorities were present, they would say: "The goats have just eaten up the district." If Greeks were approaching, they would use another phrase: "The sheep are coming down the slope."[126] But if an IMRO member or a peasant betrayed the secrets of the IMRO, or refused to submit to the laws and regulations of the organization, or if one pursued policies detrimental to the organization's aims and welfare, the Committee was not hesitant to issue death penalties.[127] This became more necessary as the organization grew and subversive elements infiltrated the organization.

Of course, IMRO ensured that the members they had recruited for important tasks would be nothing less than loyal. They utilized a variety means to test for such loyalty. Some of them were simple. For example:

> **Volumes of revolutionary songs and lithographed pamphlets were entrusted to recruits, with instructions to read them, keep them hidden from the Turk, and pass them on to other patriots. Those who proved themselves trustworthy were provided with a rifle.**[128]

Because the IMRO had developed such a loyal following, it allowed them to infiltrate many aspects of Turkish society. Espionage became a critical aspect of IMRO's operations, and IMRO "seemed to know what the Government intend[ed] to do before the officers start[ed] to do it." To support their operations, they had an unmatchable "system of messengers" and regular peasants were so uninclined to betray IMRO that it was extremely difficult to extract information from them.[129]

One notoriously trusted and admired IMRO leader was Apostol Petko Vojvoda. He was one of the most accomplished and dedicated Macedonian revolutionaries in Macedonia. "If Apostol comes, then we should know all is well," Macedonians would say.[130] Apostol never said anything that he did not mean, and he always backed his words with actions, as demonstrated by the thirty-seven Turks he had personally killed by 1904.[131]

A specific example of Apostol's antics comes from the village of Melnici in the Enidzhe Vardar district. A Turk named Ali Chaush had quite brutally ruled over the Macedonians there for several years. On one occasion he attempted to convert a Christian girl to Islam and add her to his *harem*. Apostol would not tolerate this and issued a death warrant for Chaush. Two of his band members killed him and concealed his body where it would never be discovered. Apostol then sent a letter to the rest of the Turkish authorities in the district: "All you *begs* which have raised your heads and terrorize the innocent population, if you do not cease with your lawlessness, you will also disappear one day, just as the bloodthirsty Ali Chaush has disappeared."[132] In addition, Apostol demanded from these *begs* that they turn over one-third of the revenues they earned from the hard labor of the Macedonian peasants on their farms to the IMRO or else he would burn their farms.[133]

In another instance, Apostol severed the head of a spy from Barovica that the government hired to track Apostol. Apostol did not want rumors to circulate about the murder. Thus, he wrote a letter to the governor and claimed responsibility for the act:

> **Those who denounce will not be spared our knives and guns. Whether they are Muslim of Christian, we do not touch those who do not denounce, we give no harm to nice people, we kill the bad. He would supposedly deliver my head to you in return for the gold he received. Instead of him handing over my head, here I am cutting his head off in front of his family, those who see this, if it pleases them they can also continue to snitch...If the soldiers swarm in and abuse the villagers, it won't be good, if you want to see us, we are always here, if you want to meet us, we are always in the vicinity.**[134]

In his book, *Confessions of a Macedonian Bandit*, Albert Sonnichsen described Apostol as the one Christian in Macedonia for whom the Sultan Abdul Hamid had a "personal hatred." He was the "conspicuous figure of the revolution" and foreign officials would consult with him about the state of affairs in Macedonia, "believing him to be the representative of the peasant masses." Before IMRO came into existence, he was a brigand – swiping loot from the Turks and wealthy citizens – but once IMRO emerged, he veered from the path of his fellow brigands and gave up the quest for loot, exchanging it for a national revival revolution.

Sonnichsen emphasized Apostol's heroics in another description:

> **He and thirty-eight men had been trapped in a village on the river Vardar and engaged half an army corps in a twelve hours' fight. Artillery, cavalry and infantry, hurried up from Salonica by railway, had unsuccessfully attempted to dislodge him from his position. The band was finally destroyed; only two escaped by plunging into the river after dark. But Apostol was one of those two. Three hundred asker [enemy] had fallen, but the government did not mind that, for they believed Apostol finally killed. A week later the vali pasha received a letter, bearing Apostol's seal...an emissary was sent to Apostol's wife in his native village offering him a fat pension abroad if he would only stay dead.**[135]

Of course, Apostol refused. It was difficult to find a more dedicated Macedonian patriot during this time.

Throughout IMRO's early years, the Bulgarian Church's policy was to slowly inject more priests and teachers into Macedonia for its eventual subversion to Bulgaria. This was in opposition to IMRO's revolutionary work. The liberal segments of the Macedonian intelligentsia attacked those teachers and priests who were supporting the Bulgarian Church because the Church was advocating to incorporate Macedonia into Bulgaria. The Bulgarian Church leaders, for their part, distrusted IMRO's leaders and its teachers. Even teachers who were not members of IMRO frequently aligned with IMRO over the Church leadership on many issues. The Bulgarian Church leaders lashed out at those Macedonians espousing revolution, calling them atheists and scolding many for being tainted with socialism. They were worried that the peasants would be infected with IMRO's ideologies and thus hamper Bulgaria's efforts in coveting Macedonia.[136]

In 1897, the Bulgarian Church attempted to purge Bulgarian schools in Macedonia of these revolutionary and pro-Macedonian elements. They diminished IMRO's influence by removing teachers sympathetic to IMRO and priests who even hazily supported IMRO. Bulgaria found more friendly territory with the wealthier peasants and urban middle class peasants, who were fearful that IMRO agitation would damage their economic position and disrupt their business dealings. By siding with the Bulgarian Church, these wealthier Macedonians gambled that the Macedonian movement would eventually fade into irrelevancy. One of these Macedonians was a bookdealer named Kone Samardzhiev, who publicly called IMRO a "dangerous enemy." Samardzhiev toured Macedonia in the mid-1890s, giving anti-IMRO speeches and working to steer peasants away from IMRO's grasp. He persuaded people to look away from IMRO and instead turn to the Bulgarian Church and Bulgaria for their saving. For example, on one occasion in Kostur, he told his audience to strengthen the Bulgarian Church, adding that Bulgaria would free Macedonia with its 200,000 swords.[137]

However, while the Bulgarian agitation would prove to be a menace for the Macedonian revolutionary movement, the most imminent and biggest challenge for IMRO was the Ottoman system

– administrators and soldiers alike. The Ottoman authorities discovered IMRO's existence in November 14, 1897. In the village of Vinica, near Kochani, officials had been investigating the murder of a wealthy Turk, and these investigations turned into grueling tortures against the Macedonians in the areas of Kochani, Shtip, Radovish, Kriva Palanka and Maleshevo in order to uncover more information about IMRO.[138] Christ Anastasoff detailed this pivotal moment in IMRO's history:

> **A certain group of revolutionists invaded the village of Vinitza, not far from the Bulgarian border, in the Vilayet of Skopie. They captured a local Turkish Bey (land proprietor), exacted 800 Turkish liras from him, and fearing that he might avenge himself on the helpless villagers, murdered him...The search instituted by the authorities in the neighbouring villages was carried out with the usual brutality; wholesale arrests were made; torture was applied to extract confessions; and rape and robbery were committed by the soldiery. During the tortures and inquisitions which followed, the Turkish troops came suddenly upon a hidden store of dynamite and rifles, and further inquiry revealed the work which for four years the revolutionary committee had been carrying on under the eyes of the indolent authorities.[139]**

There was an earlier instance in 1896 in which the Ottomans suspected something was out of place. Muslim field guards captured a mule train being driven by Ivan 'Done Toshev' Stojanov. He was transferring rice and tobacco from Shtip to Bitola, but hidden in the bags of rice were bombs. As the guards probed the sacks, they struck metal. Stojanov fled but was captured and detained in a closet. He was then tortured with fire and hot irons, but he did not reveal anything about IMRO. The Turkish authorities believed that he was connected with a Macedonian organization based out of Bulgaria called the Supreme Macedonian-Adrianople Committee and thus focused their attention in the direction of Bulgaria instead of inside Macedonia. Donche was sentenced to 101 years in prison and is considered IMRO's first martyr.[140]

Another incident that almost gave away IMRO transpired in September 1897 when two Muslim guards were killed by IMRO members. Duncan Perry writes:

> Suspecting foul play, the authorities conducted a search of houses in Dedino and turned up a satchel of cartridges in the home of the local priest who was a MRO supporter. A few rifles were also uncovered in several neighboring houses. These discoveries triggered the arrest of 120 people, many of whom were tortured for information, and all of whom were imprisoned. Six died in jail, and six more received life sentences.

The Ottomans eventually determined that the affair was not politically motivated.[141]

Meanwhile, IMRO continued arming the peasants. One account of how the Macedonians were armed came from Nikola Neshkov Kondarkoski:

> I received an order to buy a gun for Tome Niklev, and I bought a new gun from the village of Norovo from an Albanian called Meri. The gun, for which I paid 13 Turkish lira, was a new Martini with 200 bullets. There was also an order that everybody who joined the cheta should buy a gun, so I bought a gun for the price of 11 Turkish lira and then I bought five more guns.[142]

The Macedonians acquired several types of arms and used them for many different tasks, from small scale assassinations to open warfare. In February of 1902, a Macedonian assassinated the Bulgarian Minister of Public Instruction, Kantscheff, as he was reading in his library. The assassin gained the Minister's audience by claiming "that he wanted to present a petition" to him. After killing Kantscheff, the Macedonian turned the gun onto himself and committed suicide.[143] On a larger scale, by the start of the 20th century, IMRO rebels were engaged in several actions against the Turkish army and government. IMRO had some limited successes in Macedonia against the Turks. They made appeals to the Empire, had collected thousands of rifles and weapons, captured some Turks and took out revenge on particularly obnoxious bands of Turks and soldiers.[144] While they did not outnumber or outgun the Turks, they had enough arms and enough familiarity with the landscape to engage in a fierce guerrilla warfare.

The Turks did not idly let the Macedonians run out of control causing damage to their forces. The guerrilla warfare enticed the Sultan to continually pour thousands of troops into Macedonia and develop its own spy network to infiltrate IMRO. With the manpower available to the Sultan, the Turks managed to gain enough information to secure significant inroads into the Macedonian movement. A notable incident occurred in February of 1901, when Tatarchev was arrested by Turkish officials in Solun. On him was a letter to two IMRO rebels with orders to assassinate a certain Greek traitor.[145] He and eighteen other Macedonians were tried for treason and "conspiring to establish a new form of government in Macedonia." In particular, they were charged with:

Organizing a revolutionary force against the Ottoman Government, with the object of establishing in Macedonia an autonomous government or bringing about the annexation of the country to Bulgaria, by inducing the inhabitants to join the Macedonian Committee, supplying them with arms, and stirring up their mind[.][146]

Five of the nineteen were acquitted, but the rest were sentenced harshly: three were condemned to death and seven were sentenced to life in prison. Tatarchev was sentenced to "five years' hard labour." All nineteen had maintained their innocence throughout the whole trial, claiming that the police had beaten and tortured them to agree to certain statements that were not true.[147]

Further, in the first week of April in 1901, the Turkish army discovered and cracked down on many Macedonian revolutionaries who were preparing an uprising. Hundreds of IMRO rebels were arrested in and around Bitola and Gevgelija. Over a dozen chests of dynamite were also discovered hidden underground beneath a grocery store in Gevgelija, and large quantities of small weapons were found stashed in Bitola.[148] During the tougher months, the weapons were being taken from the Macedonians almost as quickly as they were being shipped in. This strong Turkish presence was one reason why the Macedonians did not have sufficient arms or preparation for the Ilinden Uprising in 1903.

The spies employed by Turkey caused significant damage to certain aspects of IMRO operations and were spread throughout Macedonia. Some of these spies were Muslims and some were

Christians; but almost all were promised substantial wealth, important government positions or the recusal of death or criminal sentence for their compliance. Brailsford explained the story of one spy:

> A native of Northern Macedonia who had killed a Turk fled to the Southern Castoria [Kostur] district with the avengers of blood at his heels, and posing as a martyr persuaded the villagers to harbor him. Believing him to be an outlaw, they readily admitted him to their confidence and their secrets. He was a Christian by birth, but had secretly become a convert to Islam and had accepted service as a Turkish spy. In three months he had learned all he required to know, and was able to present the authorities with a list of six hundred of the Committee's partisans. Tortures and imprisonments followed on a vast scale.[149]

But Turkish spies and military crackdowns did not quell IMRO's spirit or efforts. William Le Queux wrote that, by 1902, "no nation in the Balkan Peninsula had shown such a power of organization, and such fighting qualities as Macedonians."[150] Although the Turks were increasing their intrusion into IMRO and the Macedonian people suffered many difficulties in sticking to their principles and missions, the Macedonians were bent on accomplishing their aim – at any cost – of shaking off Ottoman rule. This is because IMRO's membership included a combination of people, including patriots, "self-seekers, adventurers, and people with a grievance,"[151] meaning that there was a continual source for IMRO to pull from amongst the peasant population. Moreover, the IMRO network was so big that, in the early months of 1902, Greek sources were reporting that only 130 villages in Macedonia were not aligned with IMRO. Further, the Greeks outlined that the most likely areas where a general insurrection would occur would be the more remote places in Macedonia, such as Tikvesh, Kavadarci, Ekshisu, Zagorica, Prilep, and Pozartaiou.[152]

Thus, as the Macedonians settled into the new century, IMRO kept up their fight against all those elements stoking divide in Macedonia in addition to countering the unjust and corrupt Turkish officials. Toward the end of March, 1902, IMRO members and peasants connected to them murdered a "Serbophile Greek" named

Patrioti. Patrioti was a Greek by origin but employed by the Serbians as a school inspector in Dojran and its surroundings. He had "enjoyed a degree of influence which made him obnoxious" to the Macedonian organization. Thus, on the evening of March 30th, he was surrounded by eight Macedonians in the marketplace of Dojran, "who gagged and pinioned him, stabbed him nine times in the back, and then nearly severed his head from his body." Thirty Macedonians were detained and three were imprisoned.[153] Macedonians warned their fellow Bulgarian, Greek and Serbian Christians that their efforts were to be subverted and IMRO was not to be trifled with.

The intolerable Turkish field guards were also increasingly targeted as a means of protest and resistance to the unfair treatment and intolerable extraction of the peasants' money. Here is an account by J. Micko Josevski of Zhvan:

In 1902 in our village Zhvan we had a poljak, a Turk, by name Mesole Bajram, from the Turkish village of Sunhodol in the Bitola region. This field guard became a source of great terror and violence...people could not endure all that he did in the village, and so they sought through the Revolutionary Committee for the poljak to be executed. I was appointed, along with my brother Stojan, by the Committee, to carry out the killing. On 18 March 1902, when the poljak was due to eat lunch at our house, I and my brother Stojan killed him with a hatchet...After the killing, I and my brother Stojan became komitas and my father went to Bulgaria.[154]

As mentioned, targeted killings increased and so did the intensity of battles and skirmishes. For example, in May 1902, Turkish authorities arrived in Tursie to search for arms and rebels. The local leader Ghele was discovered and Ghele was wounded in a fight. He managed to escape, but he lost his brief-case containing secret documents. In these papers were lists of people who possessed rifles and the number of the rifles. Thus, the authorities sent more troops and police to confiscate arms. Meanwhile, IMRO chiefs and some of their bands arrived there, including the bands of Pando Klashev, Vasil Charkalrov and Marko Lerinski. The Turks descended on a house occupied by the rebels in Tursie. Klashev later recalled:

The Turks did not know that we were inside. But they knew from the list they had that in that house there were some rifles. Simultaneously, we opened fire from the three houses. The Turks sent for reinforcements from Lerin, and meanwhile we sent for aid from the nearby villages. Our cheta had already called to arms fifty men from the village of Tourie and these hasted to our assistance. But before our assistance arrived we decided to open our way thru the siege and escape. This momentous action was to be taken because the Turks were already contemplating setting fire to the houses where we and the other chetniks were quartered. Already, twelve Turks had been killed. Soon one by one we managed to get out thru a window, entering the adjacent house; then, thru the nearby ditch we succeeded in getting out of the village. While were running up this hill on the northern side of the town, we noticed the numerous reinforcements of troops on the opposite hill arriving from Lerin.[155]

In the summer of 1902, one of the most heroic and deadly Macedonian rebellions took place near Bitola. Here, over five dozen rebels "armed with machine guns and dynamite bombs attacked 2,000 Turkish troops, the fight lasting 15 hours." The IMRO members fought until every one of them was either dead or wounded. The Turkish soldiers killed the wounded rebels, in revenge for the 148 Turkish soldiers killed and the 216 troops injured.[156]

Heroics were common despite the odds facing the Macedonians. In Novo Selo, near Shtip, in December of 1899, a wounded rebel named Sando was holed up in a house. He had been betrayed and the house was surrounded by soldiers and police officers. He engaged in a battle with one hundred of them for three hours:

> The cool, accurate fire of the lone defender had already accounted for some ten Turks, when a fire pump was brought...to spray the house with kerosene, but Sando managed to escape from the flames into a neighboring house. Later he died from his wounds.[157]

Thus, it is clear that IMRO was revolutionary in its resistance to Turkish tyranny. But as mentioned previously, it was more than that: it had courts, a postal service, police, taxation policies, and several other elements that made it not just a bunch of armed men wandering in the hills. While engaging the enemy when possible was important to demonstrate that the revolutionary movement had teeth, it was by no means the only aspect to IMRO. As Sonnichsen noted:

> **When an organization begins to number two million members, including whole cities and provinces en masse, it ceases to be a club or a committee. By now it must be evident that…it had become, in fact, a provisional system of government established by the Macedonian peasantry to replace Turkish anarchy. Though imperfect in details by the very force of the obstacles opposing it, it was still a well-articulated republic in form, swelling to burst through the artificial surface of an obsolete system.[158]**

It was the leaders of IMRO who made this possible, and no greater leader of the Macedonian movement can be any other than Goce Delchev. He was the spirit of the organization, and his intelligence and emotion combined to not only inspire and motivate Macedonian peasants, but also to bring together the leaders to focus on the positive ways to develop the Macedonian nation and execute the Macedonian agenda. He understood that that "revolution of the mind, heart and souls of an enslaved people" was his greatest task.[159]

Further, Delchev was very sensitive to, and repulsed by, Macedonians not getting along and acting brotherly, especially when they disagreed. He saw no point to yelling and bickering with one another because that course could only lead to division. He instead preferred heart-to-heart discussions that brought people together. MacDermott gives one description of this:

> **Once Gotse was present at a quarrel between Dame Gruev and Pere Toshev which had reached a point at which the two men were sitting in icy silence, each avoiding the other's gaze, and fuming with nervous rage. Gotse watched them in agony, with tears running down his face into his thick moustaches, and then, in all seriousness, he handed his revolver to each in turn, begging them to shoot him if they were going to devour each other, because he could not bear it. When neither would take the weapon or break the dreadful silence, Gotse threatened to**

shoot himself, and, putting the revolver to his head, he might well have done so had not Mihail Chakov leapt at him and caught his hand, so that the bullet flew into the ceiling. Everyone screamed, and Gotse collapsed onto the floor, unhurt but obviously overcome by emotional stress. A moment later there was a tearful reconciliation as Dame and Pere joined Gotse on the dirty floor of the hotel bedroom, hugging both him and each other.[160]

Because Delchev was a man of the people, and because everything he did was for the Macedonian people, these heart-to-heart discussions and his relentless effort to unite the Macedonian people under the Macedonian Cause was directed at every peasant. Delchev did not want to see one Macedonian lost to the Cause; and when others gave up on someone, Delchev would not relent. Here is one case:

There was, for example, the case of a shoemaker, called Spiro Kilimanov, who got wind of the underground activity in the town and begged with tears in his eyes to be allowed to join the organization. Dame categorically refused to accept him, because the man was a notorious drunkard, but Gotse, while agreeing that drunkards were an inadmissible security risk, decided to take him in hand and reform him.

Every evening when Spiro was about to close his shop, Gotse would pass by and either talk to him or take him for a stroll, so that he would not be tempted to drop into a tavern. Afterwards, Gotse would see him home and urge his family not to let him go out or drink at home. After about ten days, Spiro began to visit Gotse on his own accord and would then go straight home. After a month the change in him appeared so permanent that even Dame relented, and he was accepted into the Organization. Spiro never reverted to his old habits, and became a valuable and thoroughly reliable revolutionary.[161]

Delchev loved his Macedonians and believed in them. But there was another group of Macedonians that he had to contend with that made him miserable. These Macedonians were based out of Bulgaria; and while many had the same goals and aspirations as the IMRO

Macedonians, many others were under the influence of the Bulgarian government and executed questionable methods. This group of Macedonians deepened IMRO's problems and compromised many of their efforts. At times, their agenda was completely contrary to Macedonia's independence ambitions and put a halt to any Macedonian progress. Delchev was flung into dealing with them for some years as an IMRO ambassador, but they infuriated and depressed him so much that he alone could not tolerate their decisiveness and pro-Bulgarian bent. The grunt work in confronting these Macedonians, thus, was dealt with by two other Macedonian revolutionaries, Jane Sandanski and Gjorche Petrov: two giants of what would eventually be considered the left-wing faction of IMRO.

III.

The Intrusion of SMAC

In 1895, Prince Ferdinand of Bulgaria helped establish the Supreme Macedonian-Adrianople Committee (SMAC) in Sofia – also known as the External Organization – which publicly espoused freeing Macedonia through warfare. This group was a separate entity from the IMRO, but occasionally and periodically the two groups formed alliances and worked together on issues.[162] Most of its members were Macedonians living in Bulgaria. The formation of SMAC, in many ways, was intended as a rival organization to IMRO. Prince Ferdinand viewed Macedonian autonomy as a prelude to unification with Bulgaria and SMAC was his way of achieving this.[163]

There had always been a divide between the official views of Bulgaria and the aims of IMRO. The Bulgarian government viewed IMRO as a potential tool for executing its foreign policy, while the young IMRO agitators were enamored with ideas of independence and cosmopolitan idealism. IMRO was not a product of Bulgarian ambition or a direct result of Bulgarian government policy. Bulgaria was essentially forced by the Macedonians, especially through propaganda of leading Macedonians in Bulgaria and the excitement of the press, to do something about the condition of the people in neighboring Macedonia. SMAC gained the confidence of the Bulgarian prince and served chiefly as the representative of the revolutionary movement to foreign powers; but IMRO's real leaders inside Macedonia always suspected SMAC's Central Committee of being too eager to cave into Prince Ferdinand's ambitions.[164]

This is not to say that all – or for that matter, the majority – of SMAC members shared the same intentions and views as the Prince's Bulgarian agenda. Rather, Prince Ferdinand recognized that there was a large population of Macedonian refugees and immigrants in Bulgaria that were passionately dedicated to ensuring Macedonia's freedom, and he sought to capitalize on that passion by offering financial and material support. Formed in December of 1894, many of the founders were familiar faces to the Macedonian Cause –

Naum Tiufekchiev, Dimitar Rizov, Andrey Lyapchev, Tome Karaiovov, Nikola Naumov and Trajko Kitanchev.[165]

Ivan Hadzhinikolov was the first senior IMRO member to initiate contact with the SMAC leaders based in Sofia. In March 1895, he traveled to Bulgaria to meet with Kitanchev to learn about the plans and goals of the new organization. Hadzhinikolov stressed that IMRO was open to working with SMAC, but that IMRO must retain its full independence from the External Organization. Kitanchev agreed and iterated that SMAC would not act without informing IMRO and further would obtain their consent regarding important matters.[166] This allowed IMRO to work with SMAC on some issues. For example, through his connections in Prince's Ferdinand's palace, Naum Tiufekchiev secured 4,000 decommissioned military rifles, 300 bombs and caseloads of ammunition and transmitted them to IMRO.[167]

After Kitanchev's death from an illness in August of 1895, however, the subsequent SMAC leaders did not adhere to Kitanchev's promise.[168] At its second congress in December of 1895, Bulgaria's Macedonian committee dissolved and formed a new body (to which the SMAC name was first attributed). Its first president was Bulgarian-born General Danail Nikolaev, with Karaiovov and Rizov serving alongside him as central committee members.[169] Even with Kitanchev dead and new leaders installed, most SMAC members still only wanted autonomy for Macedonia and opposed sending armed bands into Macedonia to provoke the Turks. Nevertheless, they collected funds for the future possibility of engaging in such work. Gradually, SMAC's leaders began concentrating the power and decision-making of SMAC within its leaders and heeded little attention to the wishes of their membership and the local and regional SMAC groups throughout Bulgaria.

These early developments and disagreements foreshadowed their future relationships. Many Macedonians protested. Evtim Sprostranov, for example, disengaged from revolutionary activity because of the divisions that were being caused in the Macedonian community.[170] Naum Tiufekchiev decried the results of this second SMAC congress and demanded representation from IMRO and the Macedonian association based out of Constantinople (modern-day Istanbul). This latter group was founded in 1895 by mostly Macedonians whose resided in the Turkish capital. Because they were not included, Tiufekchiev and some others seceded and created a new committee in Bulgaria called the Macedonian Committee. To the Bulgarian government and SMAC leaders, Tiufekchiev and his followers were espousing an extremist view focused on terror, fighting and independence. To control this splinter organization, the SMAC leaders promised to appease them by preparing a plan for future military actions and to find the resources for strategic defense and offense inside Macedonia.[171]

A crucial and central figure to SMAC's early years was Boris Sarafov. Sarafov's family had long struggled against both the Turkish and Greek subversion of Macedonia. His grandfather and his uncle, Kosta Sarafov, struggled to create a church for Macedonia's Slavic speakers that was independent from the Greek Church, and they thus supported the Bulgarian Church's efforts in spreading throughout Macedonia. Moreover, both his father and grandfather were imprisoned in Solun for spreading a national Macedonian education independent and outside of the sanction of Greek Church. One author described the effect this had on Boris:

> **He saw them in chains dragged thru the streets of Salonica in the presence of a malignant multitude; he saw them when they were brutally thrown in to the bottom of the ship which immediately left the harbor of Salonica and sailed for the land of the sufferings, where they were to undergo a living death. This episode shook [his] soul, and it was this particular event that shaped his future activities.**[172]

Sarafov eventually enrolled into the Bulgarian military school in 1890 and became a Bulgarian army officer by 1893. While serving in the army, he met many future Macedonian rebel leaders. In Sofia, he came into contact with Trajko Kitanchev. By 1895, both Kitanchev and Sarafov began organizing and dispatching armed bands into Macedonia, particularly into the towns of Razlog and Melnik.[173] Sarafov made a mark for himself when, in July of 1895, he headed over five dozen fighters into Macedonia from Bulgaria and took over the town of Melnik, seizing the post and telegraph office and capturing 15 Turkish police officers. They then fought off a contingent of 100 Turkish soldiers, killing or capturing at least 50 of them. After burning Melnik's government buildings, Sarafov "delivered a fiery speech" to the Macedonian villagers and proclaimed the beginning of a new Macedonian revolution to fight off the Turkish yoke. After a day of festivities, larger convoys of Turks arrived and attacked Sarafov's band. They were forced to escape from Melnik.[174]

While Sarafov was establishing himself as a useful Macedonian in Bulgaria's eyes, the SMAC leadership was trying to work with the IMRO. In February 1896, SMAC's leader General Nikolaev met with Delchev. Delchev iterated to Nikolaev that IMRO's independence was of utmost importance for achieving Macedonia's aims. Nikolaev stated that SMAC would materially support the IMRO but only on the condition that IMRO would recognize the SMAC leadership as the commanding force of IMRO, with authority over the entire Macedonian movement. Nikolaev added that the IMRO would be useful in spreading propaganda, but that allowing peasants to fight was ridiculous. Delchev lost his temper:

Our struggle is for our life or death. We do not need others deciding if we live or die or when. The people will decide when the uprising is to begin…And know this, we do not seek protectors.[175]

Nikolaev was taken aback and called the idea of peasants liberating Macedonia childish, iterating that with peasants nothing positive could be accomplished. Delchev spat at him and stormed out of the room.[176] Delchev's statement to Nikolaev rested squarely in his belief that Macedonia's liberation could only come from internal revolt. He said: "Whoever thinks that Macedonia can be otherwise freed is deceiving both himself and others."[177]

The only central figure associated with SMAC to offer any support to IMRO in this time was Tiufekchiev, the leader of the splinter SMAC group. When Andre Lyapchev, a Macedonian-born SMAC member, sent a handwritten letter of eight pages to IMRO's central committee demanding that IMRO subordinate itself to the SMAC because it had designated itself the chief and high leadership of the liberation movement, IMRO responded by saying it did not recognize those elected at the SMAC congress and that the idea of supreme control was a perversion of an earlier understanding between Hadzhinikolov and Kitanchev. They also warned that if SMAC did not stay out of Macedonia and out of IMRO's affairs, those who refused who not meet mercy by IMRO. Tiufekchiev, however, welcomed this attitude and approach by IMRO, and despite SMAC's resistance to IMRO's desires, he willingly and enthusiastically agreed to continue supplying IMRO with arms.[178]

Despite the welcomed Tiufekchiev support, Delchev was deeply bothered by SMAC's antics and positions. He wrote about his fears of SMAC in a letter to a friend:

> **That committee made such an impression upon me, and had such a powerful chilling effect upon me, that I'm not worrying about whether they'll help, but, rather, I'm fearful lest they inflict some major damage on the cause.**[179]

In November 1896, SMAC held its third congress. Nikolaev was reelected president, and four others elected to the central committee of SMAC were Lyapchev, Karaiovov, Ljubomir Miletich, and Hristo Stanishev, a moderate from Kukush. Their agenda was first, to figure out how to raise money or secure a loan; and second, how to mount a propaganda campaign in Macedonia to win supporters.[180] Around the same time, IMRO decided to stop future dealings with the Bulgarian government as SMAC's tactics became more clear. In Skopje, a Bulgarian government agent, Dimitur Risov, decided to give IMRO 6,000 *leva* in cash and 20,000 *leva* in arms on the condition that none of the weapons were to be sent to Adrianople, another province in Turkey seeking autonomy. IMRO refused this condition, arguing that such a condition amounted to meddling in their internal affairs. The Bulgarian government then decided not to hand over the cash and instead gave them rifles without ammunition, telling the IMRO that they had to pay for them, even though the government knew IMRO had no cash. This confirmed for IMRO that the Bulgarian government was more interested in controlling it than aiding it.[181]

Delchev explained IMRO's reasoning for refusing the Bulgarian government's conditions:

> **If once you take money from the government under current political conditions, that implies engagement and ties…The Bulgarian government harbors the desire to rule Macedonia. As soon as it begins to provide money, it will know how to use the situation which its help will create and will not be content with a platonic relationship, only with tangible benefits. Moreover,**

other Balkan and European countries already maintain that the Organization is inspired by Sofia ruling circles... All these considerations force us to look for other means, other sources, always independent of Bulgaria.[182]

Delchev also believed that Macedonia and its movement belonged only to the Macedonians. He said that "whoever hankers after, and works for unification with Bulgaria and Greece may consider himself a good Bulgar or Greek, but not a good Macedonian."[183]

Still, between 1897 and 1901, Delchev was IMRO's representative to Bulgaria, and he was touring big towns and small villages gathering the support of the Macedonian refugees and emigrants living there. He needed more help, though. In addition to his efforts being a lot to handle for one man, he did not like confrontation, and he was always running into confrontation with Bulgarian government agents and SMAC obstacles. He therefore requested Gjorche Petrov, who was a strong, resilient and dedicated Macedonian. Gruev at first opposed this request because Petrov was invaluable to the work inside Macedonia, but Petrov was such an agitator of the Bulgarian Church that he was also becoming an obstacle within Macedonia. Therefore, he sent Petrov to join Delchev in Sofia.[184]

Petrov was Delchev's opposite in their work in the sense that he liked confrontation. He even employed SMAC's tactics, telling Bulgarians and Macedonians in Bulgaria that SMAC was really an auxiliary and extension of IMRO in Bulgaria.[185] Petrov, who had been involved in Macedonian revolutionary activity since the 1880s, which included a 700-plus page book he wrote called "Materials and Research on Macedonia", was more similar to Delchev ideologically than most others and was Macedonia's most consistent revolutionary. In 1896, he took part in the IMRO Congress and was on the Central Committee in Solun. He fiercely opposed external interference into IMRO's operations. And he had similar views as Delchev about the moral revolution of the individual:

> **The fight is to be celebrated! In it you change. You will not remain what you are: you grow in a moment, become great, your spirit becomes proud, your will firm, your comprehension clearer and you become alert and unhesitating...You ask yourself: Is this me? You grieve for him who does not**

participate in the fight, he will never have a notion of greatness and humanity, of his mission on earth.[186]

By 1898, SMAC was on the verge of becoming irrelevant. IMRO seized the opportunity to finally covet the SMAC into IMRO's corner. Petrov received IMRO's approval to revive it by erecting a pro-IMRO member at its head. Unfortunately, most candidates he approached in Bulgaria refused, which left Petrov only with the moderate but charismatic Sarafov who had slowly been proving his worth to the Macedonian Cause. Sarafov had spent some time touring Macedonia with Delchev and Gruev and had learned much about the needs of the Macedonian revolution. Sarafov won the election amongst the SMAC members, which made Delchev and Petrov happy. They both thought they had one of themselves in the organization. This was the beginning of a temporary harmonious relationship between SMAC and IMRO.[187]

Yet, it was not long before IMRO started running into trouble with Sarafov. For example, in 1899, Delchev helped Sarafov establish a military training school in Sofia for Macedonians dedicated to IMRO's ideals. The training was to be supported by SMAC but controlled by IMRO. As Mercia MacDermott explains, Delchev and Sarafov clashed on this matter:

> [Delchev] wanted to find some house where the young men could live more economically, under hostel conditions, but Sarafov began to pay them princely salaries, totally out of keeping with the Spartan traditions of the Organization. This led to the moral corruption of some of them...Eventually, Sarafov set up his own 'barracks', where, dazzled by over-generous pay and Sarafov's picturesque charm, many young men succumbed to Supremist [SMAC] influence.
>
> Not all, by any means, fell victim to temptation: Hristo Chernopeev and Mihail Popeto were so disgusted by the Supreme Committee's offer to give them money to buy fine clothes and other luxuries, that they stormed out of their first meeting with the officers, took their guns and went straight to Macedonia, where they became voivodei of Marko's mould...Gotse had been so upset and nauseated by Sarafov's conduct that he had left Sofia, without even saying goodbye to

him, and had fled back to Macedonia in order to soothe his nerves.[188]

The relationship between IMRO and Sarafov would swing between amicable and contentious as the years progressed. Some days Sarafov was their strongest Macedonian ally in Bulgaria; other days he was the largest headache.

While IMRO was becoming distracted by SMAC interference, the Bulgarian authorities, in addition to slithering their way in the Macedonian struggle within their own borders, explored other ways to subvert the Macedonian Cause. In March 1897, a Bulgarian named Ivan Garvanov co-founded a society in Solun called the Brotherhood of Mercy.[189] Garvanov, who was "a big man, with a cross in one eye, a red face, and a bald head,"[190] helped mold the Brotherhood of Mercy into an instrument of the Bulgarian Church aiming to prevent ethnic Macedonians from attending Serbian schools, "which were without charge for the poor." The Brotherhood of Mercy used its resources to lure teachers away from Serbian-backed schools to teach at the Bulgarian-backed schools. Another Bulgarian-sponsored organization in Solun that closely overlapped the Brotherhood of Mercy was the Revolutionary Brotherhood, which was a more active organization and had the goal of swaying IMRO from its "misguided path". In 1898, these two organizations, the Brotherhood of Mercy and the Revolutionary Brotherhood, merged to form a more cohesive and effective anti-Macedonian force.[191]

This non-Macedonian organization based in Macedonia advocated using violence to win its way with IMRO. They often criticized IMRO for recruiting membership from within schools, but then turned around and followed suit. There is only one recorded instance where the IMRO and the Brotherhood agreed on an issue – when a Serbian agent in Solun murdered Hristo Ganev, a Macedonian school teacher. They worked together to kill the Serbian perpetrator, and Tatarchev even treated Garvanov for a wound he received in the incident. But that harmonious cooperation was a fluke and the two organizations' disagreements escalated throughout the years.[192]

The Brotherhood established small branches in Prilep, Veles, Tikvesh and Kavadarci. Still, only a handful of peasants joined their ranks, as most opted to align with IMRO. The Brotherhood had no more than a few dozen members, but they had Bulgarian financial and political backing, which kept them afloat and relevant. Garvanov visited Sofia in 1899 and he held a brief meeting with Gjorche Petrov while there. Garvanov demanded that the Brotherhood be allowed to take over the leadership of IMRO. Petrov, taken aback, "flatly refused." By the dawn of the new century, the Brotherhood and IMRO were so disenchanted with one another that the Brotherhood made plans (which ultimately failed) to kill off some of IMRO's leaders, including Gruev, Matov, Hadzhinikolov and Toshev. Little did the Brotherhood know that IMRO was plotting the same type of acts against the Brotherhood. For example, the IMRO leadership had plotted to kill one of the Brotherhood members, Atanas Naumov, in Solun, but the deed never transpired. Garvanov later even claimed that Gjorche Petrov had planned two attempts to assassinate him while he was in Bulgaria, once in Sofia and once in Stara Zagora, his birthplace.[193]

The Brotherhood created an armed band in the summer of 1900 to contend for power in Macedonia. Yet, this initial band consisted only of five people, and they were quickly defeated when an IMRO assassin killed the band's leader while he was rolling a cigarette. Boris Sarafov, who was in charge of SMAC during these early revolutionary years, sent an agent to Solun in 1900 to settle the differences between the Brotherhood and IMRO. The Brotherhood agreed to disband and join the IMRO. This played well into the Brotherhood's intentions, which were to subvert the IMRO – the union gave them an opening to subvert the IMRO from within. Garvanov was given the post as the head of IMRO's Solun regional committee. Petrov, Delchev and Toshev, however, considered this merger as a disaster for IMRO and that these enemies were going to take over its agenda and use IMRO as a tool to implement Bulgarian chauvinistic pretensions in Macedonia. On the other hand, Hadzhinikolov and Matov thought the merger would cause an end to the "internecine struggle" between the two factions. But for Delchev and Petrov, this merger was the first fatal error for IMRO. The second was rushing the Ilinden Uprising.[194]

In 1900, a Bulgarian general named Tsonchev was working covertly to put SMAC under his control and thus under the control of Bulgarian military officers. With his influence, SMAC wrote a letter to IMRO saying that SMAC should be allowed to have two members on IMRO's governing body because Delchev and Petrov had been involved with SMAC as IMRO ambassadors. The letter also demanded that no correspondence could pass between Solun's IMRO headquarters and their representatives in Sofia (generally meaning Delchev and Petrov) without SMAC's knowledge.[195]

IMRO did not agree to these demands, so Tsonchev and his followers plotted to assassinate Petrov and Delchev. Delchev was not ignorant of SMAC's designs and bluntly told Sarafov that if he, Tsonchev, or any officers pressed hard, they would meet the bayonets of IMRO. Tsonchev and Sarafov eventually had a falling out, and Tsonchev even began plotting Sarafov's assassination.[196] At one point, Sarafov wanted to assassinate Tsonchev but Delchev urged him not to, iterating that IMRO should not stoop to killing its own and wanted to wage the struggle legally in Macedonia through newspapers. Sarafov replied to Delchev: "I can't stay here and watch Tsonchev's people mocking us and terrorizing us, while I have to fight solely through the newspapers like an old woman."[197]

All of this ill will deepened Delchev's disdain for the Bulgarian government and SMAC, which had been simmering for years. He once told an IMRO recruit:

We Macedonians have many enemies, and must combat them all, wherever they come from. In the first place the vrhovisti [SMAC] are our enemies. They are loyal servants of King Ferdinand, and even though they are Macedonians, do not work for Macedonia, but for him.[198]

But by the turn of the century, IMRO had to also start seriously contending with a more familiar foe: the Ottoman authorities. The Turkish leaders were increasingly becoming aware of IMRO and SMAC's plotting. In the summer of 1900, the crackdown on Macedonian revolutionary activity in the Empire escalated. For example, Aleksandar Nikov, the secretary of the Central Committee of IMRO, and Milan Mihajlov, a former SMAC partner of Sarafov, were arrested in Solun. Nikov eventually escaped but Mihajlov was tortured into revealing the names of several IMRO members. Soon, the leaders of the movement were targeted: Matov, Tatarchev, Gruev and Toshev were taken into custody immediately. Hadzhinikolov, who was the last IMRO Central Committee member at large, feared he would be arrested so he forwarded all sensitive and secretive information about IMRO to Garvanov to hold on to. Hadzhinikolov was right in his suspicions that he would be arrested, but was wrong to trust the information with Garvanov, who shared IMRO's documents with the SMAC's leaders. Most jailed Macedonian leaders received stiff sentences: while Tatarchev received only a five-year prison term, Toshev, Matov and Gruev got life terms.[199]

Delchev and Petrov were in Bulgaria during the mass arrests in Solun, but they now realized that, with IMRO's Central Committee disbanded, Garvanov had an opening to take over IMRO. Delchev and Petrov sent a letter to all regional IMRO committees explaining that the Central Committee members had been arrested and that, for a while, regional captains should carry on as best they could in a decentralized manner. They also warned leaders about being persuaded into a premature revolt and that SMAC would militarize them at the expense of peasant participation. This letter made an impact, and SMAC was temporarily prevented from making significant inroads into the hearts and minds of regional, district and local committees. Garvanov was blocked from fulfilling his objective, so in 1901 he visited SMAC's leaders, General Tsonchev and Mihailovski (the president of SMAC in 1901); and in a lengthy meeting he promised to give IMRO to SMAC as long as IMRO maintained some autonomy. While this was going on, IMRO's Bitola division heeded Delchev's and Petrov's advice and held a congress. Its fifteen leaders decided to activate armed bands in order to protect against both the Turkish authorities and SMAC.[200]

This time was a critical juncture for both IMRO and SMAC, and old and new Macedonian advocates were choosing their sides and sealing their fates. Mihail Stavrev, one of Stambolov's assassins, slipped into Sofia in 1901 for the election of the new SMAC president. He went to Simeon Radev's hotel room and warned him: "Do not hinder Macedonia's freedom!" Radev responded: "How dare you appear before my eyes, you, whose name has embarrassed Macedonia?" Stavrev did not embarrass Macedonia, but his life was on a downward spiral. He was arrested in late November, 1901 at a Sofia tavern while drinking brandy. The authorities found four revolvers on him. He was then tried for Stambolov's murder, and the main evidence was the wound in his neck. Stavrev claimed to have been injured as a rebel. But the court did not buy his story and he was sentenced to death. In a stroke of good fortune, through the

Court of Appeals, President Todor Nikolov reduced his penalty to 15 years in prison. Stavrev was eventually paroled and his tracks were lost forever after he slipped into Macedonia.[201]

Radev, the man Stavrev was trying to intimidate, would go on to have a more influential role in Macedonian affairs. Radev came from wealthy roots in Resen – one of his grandfathers became rich from trading fruits and vegetables during the Crimean War in the 1850s, and his other grandfather worked for a prince in Istanbul. Radev studied in schools in Resen, Bitola and Ohrid, and in 1895, Delchev administered to him the IMRO oath.[202] He moved to Geneva in 1900 and began editing newspapers and became a contributor to some. At this time, he also began cooperating with SMAC.[203] He favored Boris Sarafov over Tsonchev,[204] but often found himself in opposition to IMRO's left-wing.

Around the same time, Sarafov, who had been considered the link between the two organizations keeping the alliance afloat, was running into his own troubles. In 1901, he was imprisoned by Bulgarian authorities for the assassination of an editor in Romania who had criticized Sarafov's methods of raising money (which is detailed in the next chapter).[205] This editor, Stefan Mihaileanu, was a Macedonian-born Vlach. He was against the Macedonian revolutionary movement and had published several articles that spotlighted IMRO's structure and operations, as well as exposing names of important individuals. Sarafov was charged with orchestrating the murder in Bucharest. This entire affair severely strained the relationship between Bulgaria and Romania, almost causing these two countries to enter into a war. Thus, to smoothen things over with Romania, the Bulgarian authorities made an effort to seek justice against Sarafov.[206]

Jane Sandanski and his comrade Nikola Maleshevski visited Sarafov in prison when they came to Sofia for the SMAC Congress. Sandanski, who was born in Vlahi in 1872, was a committed follower of Delchev and ally of Petrov. He had watched his village burn when he was six years old during the Kresna Uprising of 1878 and eventually became a Macedonian refugee in Bulgaria. In the mid-1890s, he joined SMAC bands in penetrating Macedonia to fight Turks, but soon realized he was being deceived by pro-Bulgarian elements. He wrote:

I then gave my word not to move anywhere anymore, not to be anybody's tool until I had thoroughly probed into the actual situation of the liberation movement, and examined whether there really was an organization in Macedonia itself.

When Sandanski met Delchev in 1899, he "immediately realized that Delchev was indeed a man who was quite familiar with the details of the Organization and everything that it was against." The next year, he cemented his opposition to SMAC.[207]

Sarafov, now feeling betrayed by the Bulgarian government and other SMAC leaders, "began to warm towards the members of the Internal Organization" such as Sandanski and leaked SMAC's secrets and deception:

He told them what he and Tsonchev had decided at the officers' meetings held behind the Internal Organization's back. He warned [Sandanski] and [Maleshevski] that Tsonchev was 'the Prince's man', an allegation he had also made on more than one occasion to [Petrov], and urged them to support him at the Congress in the hope of being re-elected in spite of everything. The Organization, however, decided to take a neutral line in the quarrel between the officers. [208]

Sarafov was confident that he had so much popular support and connections in Bulgaria that he would be found not-guilty at his trial and would thus be capable of leading SMAC and steering it toward IMRO. He emphasized this point at his trial by calling for the separation of the Macedonian Cause from government interference:

When asked whether he had any remarks to make before the jury retired to consider their verdict...he made an impassioned declaration denouncing the infamy of Turkish rule, and concluding with an appeal to all patriots to disassociate the Macedonian question from all Government and Court influence, and to devout themselves with renewed ardour to the accomplishment of their sacred task.[209]

As a matter of fact, by now Sarafov was advocating for the complete independence of the Macedonian movement. He explained to foreign newspapers the line of reasoning that Delchev, Petrov and Sandanski had been pursuing:

> In 1895 we young men were sent to Macedonia to prepare an insurrection, or, at all events, to try and start an outbreak of some kind, if only to show Europe that Prince Ferdinand constituted a powerful factor in the Balkan Peninsula and that his deposition would be a greater danger for the peace of the continent. It was only after these disturbances that the Powers, one after the other, recognized Prince Ferdinand as chief of the new Bulgarian dynasty. This first phase of the Macedonian movement, owing to the fact that it was subordinated to different party interests, acquired no hold on the bulk of the population in Macedonia.
>
> We young people have therefore been endeavoring for some years past to separate the Macedonian cause from Bulgarian domestic politics. If the rulers of the Principality now declare that they cannot tolerate us as a State within the State, it shows that we have at least succeeded in emancipating ourselves from the pernicious influence of the Bulgarian government. It is only because we are no longer disposed to sacrifice ourselves for this or that party, and regard the liberation of Macedonia as a question of honor for the entire people, that the Bulgarian Government is persecuting us.
>
> It is a grievous error to suppose that we seek to acquire Macedonia on behalf of Bulgaria. We Macedonians consider ourselves to be an entirely separate national element, and we are not in the least disposed to allow our country to be seized by Bulgaria, Servia, or Greece. We will, in fact, oppose any such incorporation with all our might. Macedonia must belong to the Macedonians. The misunderstanding has arisen through our residing in Bulgaria. The circumstance of our having prepared a Macedonian insurrection while living in this country led to the conclusion that we were aiming at a union between the two Slav provinces. That is, however, perfectly absurd. If we were to be expelled from Bulgaria and were to settle in Switzerland nobody would suppose that we intended to liberate Macedonia on behalf of Switzerland.

But, wherever we may be, we wish to keep our movement distinct from the national aspirations of the independent Balkan States. We shall energetically resist any attempt on the part of those States to secure Macedonia for themselves. We have been reproached with wanting to disturb the peace of Europe. That leaves us indifferent. What do we unfortunate Slavs care for the peace of Europe! Russia has frequently promised us that she will soon take our cause in hand. Only a short time ago a Russian statesman told me that we should be patient, as whenever Russia was no longer occupied in East Asia she would come forward in favour of the autonomy of Macedonia. My own conviction is, however, that Russian diplomacy will first begin to think of us when it decides to realize its own ideal of the conquest of Constantinople. Its object will then be not the emancipation of Macedonia, but its subjugation.

Consequently, my friends and myself are resolved to separate entirely the movement we are prompting from Russia's Balkan policy. Without in any way wishing to identify our efforts with the policy of Vienna, I am nevertheless of opinion that Austro-Hungarian aspirations are infinitely less dangerous for the autonomy of Macedonia than are those of Russia. The conquest of Macedonia by Austria-Hungary is impossible, owing to the composition of that Monarchy and to the resistance which such a plan would find on the part of all the Balkan peoples…

I must, at the same time, clearly state that we neither ask for, nor would accept, any official support of our movement from Austria-Hungary. We will have nothing to do either with official Bulgaria or with official Servia, nor yet with official Austria-Hungary. We are revolutionists, and count only upon one-half of the peoples of Europe. In order to put an end to the misunderstandings among the Slav States of the Balkans concerning the movement in which we are engaged, two of our friends will shortly go to Servia and then proceed further in order to deliver lectures. Macedonia must no longer be a source of dissension among the Balkan countries. Emancipation must form the basis upon which the federation of those countries can be founded.[210]

Sarafov was eventually acquitted for the murder. Yet the relationship between IMRO and SMAC continued to deteriorate. IMRO abandoned relying on SMAC for funds and were left figuring out how to finance their revolution. Tsonchev became the new president of SMAC. Tsonchev was Bulgaria's best man for the position because, unlike Sarafov, he was "amenable to Government control."[211] He was personally intimate with the prince of Bulgaria, and instead of advocating for a free and independent Macedonia, he wanted a Macedonian union with Bulgaria. Sarafov and his supporters did not appreciate this and seceded from the SMAC to create their own external Macedonian organization.[212]

Meanwhile, with Tsonchev at its head, SMAC reinitiated their assault on the Macedonian revolution and continued trying to mould the Macedonian Cause into the Bulgarian Cause:

Tsontcheff proceeded to rid by force when necessary the revolutionary movement of its autonomist elements. Thus, by the fall of 1901, those within the External Organization and IMRO who refused to see annexation as the only solution to the Macedonian question were having to fight a two-front war, one against the Turks and one against Tsontcheff.[213]

For example, while most IMRO leaders were imprisoned, SMAC used its influence to subvert IMRO and used IMRO's official organs to publish articles espousing SMAC's views, and all donations went to Tsonchev and SMAC leaders instead of to the IMRO treasure chest.[214] Most Macedonians had thus "repudiated" Tsonchev and SMAC by this point. According to one IMRO leader, Chernopeev, the Macedonians operating in the interior could not recognize "a Bulgarian general appointed by Prince Ferdinand" as the Macedonians' representative. Furthermore, the Macedonians were infuriated that Tsonchev took it upon himself to govern the entire Macedonian organization.[215]

So many leading Macedonians, like Chernopeev and Sandanski, resisted him. But because Tsonchev was financed by Bulgarian money and the Turks were cracking down on all the Macedonian fighters, exiling them to Asia Minor, Tsonchev took this opportunity to send armed bands into Macedonia, where they engaged in battles with Sandanski's and Chernopeev's bands. The Macedonians in Macedonia were cut from the funding, and the Macedonians in

Bulgaria did not know what was going on, least of all that their donations to the Macedonian Cause were being used to support armed attacks against their fellow Macedonians.[216] Chernopeev later wrote about this: "It was a desperate situation. It looked as if we and the whole organization would be swept out of existence and Prince Ferdinand's hirelings would possess themselves of the field to do with it as they liked."[217]

On August 2, 1902, SMAC held its 10th Congress and both Mihailovski and Tsonchev were reelected to their positions. Delchev was "invited to present a report" on IMRO issues, but he refused. He stated that SMAC "had not represented honestly the actions of the IMRO" in the past and that SMAC was in fact "more trouble than the Turkish authorities." Without any IMRO representation and the SMAC Congress, Mihailovski and Tsonchev figured they could successfully argue for an armed infiltration of Macedonia. Stanishev, a former moderate president of SMAC, vehemently opposed any such suggestion. With several followers, he seceded and created a rival 10th congress, declaring the other one illegal. However, about two-thirds of the delegates present sided with Tsonchev and Mihailovski, leaving Stanishev with a minority.[218]

Thus, SMAC gave the green light to bring violence to Macedonia and agitate for a fight, both with the Turkish authorities and IMRO. One of SMAC's leaders during this time was Atanas Jankov, who was born in Kostur, Macedonia and had become a Colonel in the Bulgarian army. In 1902, he initiated revolutionary activity in the Kostur region with the backing of SMAC and many Macedonians in Sofia; but the local Macedonians and IMRO wanted nothing to do with his revolution.[219] For example, he contacted two IMRO leaders from the Smrdesh region, Vasil Chakalarov and Pando Kliashev. Jankov tried to convince them to start a rebellion. Those two believed IMRO was not ready for a rebellion and had received no orders from their superiors to do so. Thus, Chakalarov and Kliashev sought counsel in Bitola from the regional committee. Still, Jankov promised the two that Russia and Bulgaria would assist them and started agitating the population after setting an uprising date for September 20th. This upset Chakalarov and Kliashev, who feared the reprisals of a premature rebellion, and they attacked Colonel Jankov's band and defeated them. Jankov fled to Greece and into Bulgaria and most of his men switched to IMRO's side.[220]

Sarafov soon called for a "cessation of the insurrectionary movement" because he thought that conditions would not favor a Macedonian victory. Meanwhile, a newspaper reported "that the two opposing Macedonian committees [were] neutralizing each other and that the movement [would] soon die."[221] IMRO and SMAC were clearly shown to be at odds publicly and not just privately anymore. Even though SMAC was mostly composed of Macedonians, the people in Macedonia knew that it served primarily Bulgaria's interests and not the needs of the Macedonian peasants.[222]

Still, SMAC would not quit. In 1902, SMAC tried once again to initiate an uprising in Macedonia, but IMRO challenged them not to. On September 23, 1902, Tsonchev's army crossed over from Bulgaria into Gorna Djumaja with Bulgarian troops and only 350 local Macedonians joining them to fight against the Turkish troops.[223] They were up against Turkish force of 17,000 troops but nevertheless started attacking Ottoman garrisons and the Muslim population in Gorna Djumaja and surrounding villages. Two IMRO members, Hadzhinikolov and Sava Mihailov, believed that the whole purpose of this pointless attack by SMAC was to force Ottomans to increase their terror on the peasant population. It might have also been a bid by Tsonchev to take over IMRO. As a matter of fact, IMRO bands did not side with SMAC during this fight; Delchev's band even fought against SMAC bands during this period.[224] Delchev stated: "While my shoulder carries a gun, Macedonia is beyond the reach of the Bulgarian officer."[225]

SMAC fled into Bulgaria and IMRO and the Macedonian population had to deal with the aftermath, including the destruction of 28 villages, the rape of 100 women, and an unknown number of murdered peasants.[226] However, the consequences of this SMAC intrusion were limited and localized because IMRO had managed to prevent SMAC from making inroads except in the border regions.[227]

In the fall of 1902, Gjorche Petrov met Matov and Tatarchev (who had recently been released from jail) when they came to Sofia. Petrov had been struggling against Tsonchev and his only reliance was on Stanishev's Macedonians; however, Petrov thought they were not tough enough and were too yielding when it came to dealing with Tsonchev. "I maintained the position of exclusivism – we must always stand here as a pure nucleus and not amalgamate."[228]

Tatarchev and Matov eventually became two new delegates representing IMRO to SMAC – the positions for which Delchev and Petrov had been removed. They appealed to Garvanov and to SMAC to reconcile differences and to issue a new big uprising together. This is what Garvanov had desired.[229] Finally, the Bulgarian government found itself being set up to be in an ideal position to get what they wanted in Macedonia through SMAC and now IMRO. The leftists and independence-oriented Macedonians were weakened, and the moderates and Bulgaria sympathizers had crept their way into power.

IV.

Financing the Revolution

Despite IMRO's conflicts with SMAC, Macedonian revolutionary activity against the Turks was well under way. Villages were organizing committees; armed bands were confronting Turkish authorities; and Macedonian teachers were spreading national and revolutionary ideas amongst the population. Still, as with most revolutions, the Macedonians could not successfully revolt without money. For a while, IMRO had been partly dependent on SMAC to raise funds from Macedonians living in Bulgaria. But because of their falling out and the continual fracturing of the Macedonian organizations, IMRO's leaders were often left to their own devices to muster the necessary funds. While Turkish authorities and Bulgaria-backed SMAC were the two largest obstacles to IMRO's agenda, perhaps the most frustrating reality was the lack of funds.

Because most Macedonian peasants were extraordinarily poor, IMRO's leaders could not depend solely on the masses to finance their movement. Therefore, IMRO dabbled in a variety of schemes to fuel their movement. From taxation to kidnapping, the Macedonians let no opportunity slip through their fingers. There were many disagreements between SMAC and IMRO – and even amongst IMRO leaders themselves – on how to collect the funds and further how to manage the funds. However, most Macedonians believed that the funds were being directed to the cause of capturing their freedom and independence.

The most controversial mode of raising funds was through taxation. Forced taxation in some villages especially brought about some dislike of the IMRO, as the local peasants felt they were now being double taxed, both by the Turkish authorities and now by the IMRO. Nevertheless, before the Ilinden Uprising began in August of 1903, the Macedonian organizations had in place a network of secret conscript officers that made each man pay an ammunition tax according to his ability to pay. Many peasants gave what they could voluntarily and those who had nothing to give were exempted from giving. But those who refused to pay because of loyalty or obligation to the Sultan were shot down or marked for assassination.[230]

However, significant confusion would arise within Macedonia and Bulgaria about the taxation. SMAC – and especially Sarafov – were particularly notorious for forcefully extracting money from Macedonians and claiming the money was being sent directly to the IMRO. IMRO's leaders, on the other hand, were more sympathetic and understanding of the peasant's dire economic conditions and generally refrained from forceful methods. Still, Sarafov's and other SMAC members' method of fundraising impacted the entire movement's image. Here is how one author explained Sarafov's taxation system:

> **An agent of the committee presents a bank receipt to a wealthy merchant, and bargains with him regarding the amount he should contribute to the revolutionary cause. If no agreement is arrived at, the local committee arbitrarily fixes the sum. A receipt for this amount is then presented to the merchant and the money peremptorily demanded. If the victim is still reluctant to pay, a revolver or something equivalent is held at his head, and in nine times out of ten the desired amount is then forthcoming. In the 10th case, when the victim is obdurate, he is summarily 'executed' for his lack of zeal in the Macedonian cause.**
>
> **In this way the Macedonian committee has established a reign of terror, and has instigated a large number of atrocious murders, for which the primary responsibility rests on Sarafoff as the organizer of the whole movement. In this respect, Sarafoff has allowed his fanaticism to transform him into a bloodthirsty desperado, whose enthusiasm for a good cause has become a pretext for a system of blackmailing, robbery and murder on an unprecedented scale.**[231]

Plenty more specific examples of Sarafov's reckless system are abound. For example, after a Greek millionaire named Patriotis refused to support the Macedonian Cause, Sarafov's compatriots killed him. Similarly, "[t]he revolutionaries…murdered a Greek bishop named Poropulos at Melenko, Macedonia because he refused to subscribe to the Macedonian committee."[232] A wealthy Armenian in Bulgaria was asked to donate, but when he rudely refused, he was severely beaten in public by another Armenian who was sympathetic to the Macedonian Cause.[233] No wealthy or influential person residing in Macedonia or Bulgaria was safe from Sarafov's reach. If they had money, he went after them.

One of Sarafov's men, Chokalov, was particularly ready to use his gun on anyone who did not donate to the Macedonian Cause. It is widely known that he attempted to kill a Romanian in Sofia, but failed; and that he shot a Greek who refused to donate money to the revolutionary cause.[234] Other prominent Macedonians associated with SMAC would specifically call out wealthier individuals in a public letter, and put how much they were required to contribute to the Macedonian Cause next to their names. Haim Calme, an Austrian banker, was summoned to pay 5,000 *francs*; Nassim Israel, a Greek subject, 3,000 *francs*; and Bon Marche, a Turkish shop owner, 2,000 *francs*. Some of the more prominent SMAC Macedonians who would order such donations were Malchev, an engineer; Gata Zuev, a contractor; Aleko Jordanov, a merchant; and Dalmetre Konstantinov, a broker.[235]

In some parts of Bulgaria, the Macedonians were even forbidding the Bulgarian peasants to pay their taxes to the Bulgarian government and instead redirecting that money to the Macedonian revolution war chest. Using much of this money acquired, they would "corrupt underpaid officials" in Macedonia to learn the secrets and plans of the Turkish authorities.[236]

Occasionally, SMAC Macedonians encountered legal troubles for their fundraising methods. In the spring of 1901 in Sofia, there was a public trial for Atanas Murijev from Prilep, a SMAC member living in Sofia. He was accused of extorting money from a Vlach, Alexis Tsovarov, who was also born in Macedonia (in Malovishte) and considered himself a Romanian (despite having never been to Romania). Tsovarov claimed that, in 1899, Murijev had been demanding 500 *francs* from him, but that he replied he could only donate 100 *francs* to the Macedonian Cause. After being threatened with a dagger, Tsovarov gave the money to Murijev. Murijev approached Tsovarov again the following year utilizing the same exact methods to extort money, and witnesses at the trial recounted similar stories about how they had offered to donate less than what was requested, but felt forced to pay after they were threatened with harm by Murijev and others. Several witnesses were called on both sides, and eventually Murijev was acquitted due to a lack of proof of extortion.[237] The Macedonians in Bulgaria earnestly welcomed this ruling.

While Sarafov and the SMAC may have been popular among the Macedonians in Bulgaria, these tactics did not win them much popularity within Macedonia itself. Mary Durham, who visited the Prespa region after the Uprising began, spoke of the people's ill will toward Sarafov:

> **Sarafov was very unpopular. The local leader, Arsov, many of them still believed in. But as a whole they dreaded the committee almost as much as they did the Turks...Each village had been visited by secret agents, and the people lured by promises or forced by threats to join the movement. Each family had to pay heavy toll in cash or kind.**[238]

However, Sarafov was also known as the representative of the Macedonian revolution to Europe. With his tours around Europe, the war chest of IMRO and SMAC grew substantially, and many modern weapons were introduced. Yet, most of his contributions came from the Macedonian immigrants in Bulgaria.[239] He even attempted to form a Macedonian revolutionary committee in Belgrade in 1902 in order to acquire more funds, but he met little success there.[240]

Sarafov first made his international rounds in 1900, visiting senior members of the Russian royal court. He then met with senior Austrian officials, and soon began raising money to fund a Macedonian newspaper. Sarafov was a frequent visitor at Vienna casinos and lounges, acquainting himself with wealthy and powerful people from Europe. When in Paris, he met with prominent politicians and discussed the Macedonian Cause. In Budapest, he began negotiating with representatives of the Serbian court and assured them that the IMRO was the true Macedonian organization and that SMAC – led by Tsonchev at the time – was not. He asked them to have confidence in him and to stay away from SMAC and Tsonchev.[241]

Other Macedonians were using less forceful – and more emotional and intellectual – means to acquire funds for the Macedonian movement. Dr. S. J. Shoomoff, a Macedonian involved with SMAC, and also a graduate of the University of Chicago and the University of Pennsylvania, appealed to funders in New York City during the time of the Uprising:

> **We have waited for twenty-five years since the treaty of Berlin for the inauguration of reforms and for the establishment of home rule, that were promised by it. Instead, we have been the slaves of the Turk – disfranchised in every court, our women taken ruthlessly from our homes, our goods and our lives placed absolutely at the mercy of those who are merciful only when they kill.**[242]

Further, Macedonians outside of the Balkans in Europe and North America were giving as much as they could to see that the Macedonian revolution was a success. A Bostonian Macedonian who sold candy from a street-cart "contributed his entire two or three months' savings" to the Macedonian Cause.[243] Other Macedonians were continually pumping their hard-earned dollars into Macedonia – whether it was to supply Macedonians with arms, food, clothing or other necessities for maintaining the revolution for as long as possible.

But from the onset, it was evident that the Macedonian movement could not be kept afloat simply by forced taxation and voluntary donations. Brigand work – primarily theft and kidnapping for ransom – were employed regularly throughout the first decade of IMRO's existence. Yet, these revolutionaries were clearly amateurs when it came to much of this, and it was evident early on. Take the case of Naum Zaltarev, a young postal clerk in Kyustendil, Bulgaria. He "stole a considerable amount from the Bulgarian postal department in January 1897, eluded the authorities, then fled to Macedonia." The considerable amount he stole was worth $5,600 in US dollars at the time. He handed over $5,000 to Vasil Glavinov, a highly trusted IMRO operative, who was to then convey the funds to Delchev. After failing to reach Delchev, Glavinov decided to bury the money on a riverbank. The river flooded the surrounding area and the money was never to be seen again, supposedly washed away with the rest of the river bank. As this was a huge amount of money for the organization in such early stages of their development, Delchev was furious. Suspicions even arose suggesting that Glavinov really took the money for himself.[244]

Delchev was generally against thievery and kidnapping. He believed, however, that to participate in it was a personal sacrifice to move the Cause forward. He tried both a few times, and was not very successful. In Veles, in the late 1890s, he planned and executed the kidnapping of a Muslim lord's son in Strumica area. But the son escaped:[245]

[Delchev's] band hid for two days by the Strumitsa-Vasilevo road, waiting for their victim. On the afternoon of the second day, they managed to grab him as he passed. Approximately four days later, the father received a note demanding the delivery of 6,000 *lira* ($24,000) and an end of Turkish patrols in the areas in return for his son. The patrols stopped, and the father sent 1,500 *lira* with his regards and a request that the smaller sum be accepted because the year was bad...Delchev returned the money but agreed to negotiate.

On the third Sunday after the kidnapping, the two sides agreed on 3,000 *lira*. That same night, Delchev, racked by the stomach pains which plagued him throughout his life, lay oblivious in one corner of the band's hut, while the rest of the group, except for the guard and the boy, slept. Nazlim bey was so loosely bound that he managed to untie himself and seize Delchev's revolver. He asked the guard to take him outside for a minute, and as they left the hut he shot the guard and disappeared into the woods. Nazlim bey met the people bringing the ransom to the band, and he returned home with it.[246]

Unfortunately, this was not the only escape from Delchev's band. Sometime after that, they had kidnapped a Greek moneylender name Dimitrakis and demanded 2,000 *lira* from his brother for his release. While negotiations were continuing, Delchev took half of his band with him to intercept government money that was coming to Serres form Nevrokop. While Delchev and his men were failing to secure that government money, because it was guarded by a squadron of 65 soldiers, Dimitrakis escaped from his captors when the guard fell asleep. He then messaged his brother not to transfer the money.[247] Delchev's band – and IMRO in general – were not experienced brigands and were not meant for the criminal life. They failed miserably, especially in IMRO's first few years.

Yet, they had to support their revolution; and when IMRO and SMAC hostilities escalated in 1901, brigandry was IMRO's only worthwhile pursuit. The kidnapping and ransom that most captivated international attention was that of Ellen M. Stone, an American missionary working both in Bulgaria and Macedonia. The ringleaders of the capture were Sandanski and Chernopeev. Most of the captors with them were school teachers released from their positions for turning into radical Macedonians. These Macedonians captured Stone because an IMRO member had told them that doing so would furnish them with money, as Turkey would pay the ransom to avoid an international spectacle. After all, the world's attention was on Turkey and how it was failing to make changes to its governing policies. Thus, two days before they captured her, Sandanski and his men roamed around Bansko, dressed as peasants, stalking Stone, watching her every move, thinking about how to capture her. The Bansko residents pleaded with Sandanski not to kidnap her in Bansko in case the Turkish authorities exacted reprisals on them. So Sandanski's men dressed up as Bashibazouks (Turkish and Muslim irregular soldiers) outside of Bansko and patiently waited.[248]

On that sweltering summer day of her capture in 1901, Stone was traveling from Bansko to Djumaja with a party of ten, a trip that was set to take several hours. That's when Sandanski's band of Macedonians proceeded with their plans:

> **As they were resting in the mountains, a party of thirty to forty armed men suddenly surrounded them and ordered the party to proceed up the mountain side. After going a short distance the prisoners were halted and all stripped of their watches, money and other valuables. Then all, with the exception of Miss Stone and Mrs. Tsilka, were set free.[249]**

One of those released explained how he was robbed of his entire tuition money for the theological institute he was a student at.[250] Chernopeev later claimed there was only twenty of them who captured the ladies.[251]

However, the Macedonians were so "famished" that they stole the captives' lunches and ate all the pork, which signaled to the ladies that the captors really were not Bashibazouks, as Muslims did not eat pork. Still, they had killed an Albanian in front of the captives, and those who were released had immediately reported it to the newspapers, which reported that the men did it to scare the women. In reality, the Albanian that they had killed was a land steward that squeezed money out of the peasants and had also raped two Macedonian girls. The villagers said IMRO was of no use to them if they did not avenge such justice.[252] Sandanski and Chernopeev were there to move forward the Macedonian revolution, and part of the revolution entailed delivering justice once and for all to Macedonia.

One analyst summed up why capturing an American was sound strategy on the part of IMRO:

The capture of an American was regarded as good strategy, because the United States is a rich and powerful country. If discord could be created between the United States and Turkey, it might lead on to hostilities, and whatever dismembered or disintegrated Turkey would mean the unification and advancement of Macedonia...There are numerous advantages, from the standpoint of the captors, for why they should detain Miss Stone for a long time...they were saved from dodging the police, from pursuit by soldiers, from having their accomplices arrested. They were safer from conscious or unconscious betrayal. The ransom money was secure, and one brigand could not steal it from another. There was less liability of quarreling among themselves, of one getting drunk and while intoxicated betraying the others. Delay would not endanger all possible ransom money, nor conditions of amnesty: it afforded time in which to make insinuations against the fellow missionaries of the captive, charging them with indifference, inaction, love of money rather than of their captive associate. Foreign correspondents could be induced to become the unwitting agents of the brigands, by publishing baseless rumors, criticizing officials and missionaries more or less at random.[253]

For the international community, the fact that an American woman had been kidnapped by brigands and rebels was all the rave. The people were fascinated by the story and obsessed over daily updates on the matter. Stone was certainly the star of the story. For her part, Stone wrote some letters while in captivity during the negotiations process. On September 20, 1901, she wrote a letter to W.W. Peet, the Treasurer of the American Missions. This letter captured a glimpse of her captive life for the public to experience. Here is an excerpt:

> [O]n the 3d of September I was captured by a great number of armed men (some forty) as I travelled from Bansko to Djumaia, with about twelve teachers, students and others. They took with me for my companion Mrs. Catheirne Tsilka. The reason for which they have captured us is for a ransom. The price which they demand for us is twenty-five thousand Turkish liras (and this is without the Knowledge of the Turkish and Bulgarian governments) in a term of eighteen (18) days from now. In my first letter I had mentioned that the condition in which Mrs. Tsilka is decided the limit, as she is to give birth to a child in three months. But now as the circumstances have been changed, and we know that we are pursued by a Turkish army, this short term has been fixed. I beg Dr. Haskell himself to go to Constantinople to exert himself for the payment of the ransom in Samakov, where the men will receive it only on presenting an order from me.
>
> The men who captured us at first showed courtesy and conducted very well toward us. But now, since Turkish soldiers and 'Bashi-Bazouks' have begun to pursue us, and the ransom is delayed, our condition is altogether changed. Therefore, I beg you to hasten the sending of the sum (i.e. of the ransom decided), and that as much as possible you will insist before the Turkish government that it stop the pursuit of us by the soldiers and 'Bashi-Bazouks,' otherwise we shall be killed by the people in whose hands we are."[254]

Early into her captivity, it was determined that the Stone's capture was purely political. While many of the initial reports suggested that hardened criminals had captured the women, some writers and commentators eventually realized that this kidnapping was about Macedonia's freedom. For example, one Boston newspaper wrote:

> The [Macedonian] committee avows the doctrine that the end justifies the means, and hence it is immaterial whether a woman be the captive, how long she is held or how large the ransom demanded or what governments become involved or how many

innocent people suffer, provided only that Macedonia becomes free or is headed toward freedom and independence.[255]

Thus, in one sense, IMRO's actions did bring the tragic situation of Macedonia in the Ottoman Empire to the forefront of the media's attention. But much of that attention was negative and there were many critics of IMRO's tactics. Regardless of how people felt about IMRO and the Macedonian movement, there were many appeals throughout the United States and Europe to raise money for Stone's release. One professor at a woman's college in Massachusetts, Wellesley College, wrote a letter to the media hoping to inspire her fellow teachers:

> **Will not every institution of learning make a subscription list (so that the money be returned in case it should not be needed, as was stated in some paper of Oct. 12)? France was poor when she paid Dugueselin's ransom, and the people never got tired working and spinning until the money was raised. Who of us could not give at least $1 for Miss Stone's ransom?**[256]

Such fundraising efforts by organizations and newspapers worked to the advantage of Sandanski and the captors. The newspapers would report how much money had been raised and IMRO operatives in the United States would relay this information back to Sandanski's group. Therefore, Sandanski could not be fooled into accepting a lower ransom.[257]

Initially, United States President Theodore Roosevelt supported leaving Stone to her own devices and not interfering in her release. In a letter to Alvey Adee, the First Assistant Secretary of State, he wrote:

> **Every missionary, every trader in wild lands should know and is inexcusable for not knowing that the American government had no power to pay the ransom of anyone who is captured by brigands or savages.**[258]

But for political purposes – and perhaps out of chivalry – he could not abandon Stone. Although he thought that women had no business in being missionaries in "wild countries" and that men who were captured and ransomed do not expect the government to intercede, he emphasized that "it was impossible to adopt this standard about women."[259]

But the early months failed to satisfy Sandanski's appetite for revolutionary funds. Stone's third and last letter, dated from late October, 1901, was directed to Dr. H.C. Haskell. She feared that her life would be taken as the ransom had not yet been paid:

> **I have awaited every day an answer to my letter to you, but up to the present I have no word at all so as to know, at least, what my friends have done...Today is now the last day set for the ransom, and the men in whose hands we have been already five weeks wish to fulfill their threat to destroy us; but they have shown mercy to us in that they have added ten days more from today to our time limit and allow me to write this last letter...I need not say that I shall await its answer with impatience, for if at the end of this set time there is no answer, or, on the other hand if the answer is unsatisfactory, we are lost. Remember us in your prayers, all of you, as we remember our loved ones.**[260]

By November, the US Consul General, Dickinson, had commissioned two Macedonian brigands "to try and get in touch with the missionary's captors." Sandanski's band was bothered by Mr. Dickinson's offer of one-fourth of what Sandanski had demanded. One of the Macedonian agents sent to negotiate with Stone's captors said that Sandanski's band did "not want to agree to terms that would disgrace them with their brethren."[261] Sandanski was playing hardball. The international community knew little of how desperately IMRO was in need of cash.

The local Turkish authorities, for their part, were initially impediments to securing Stone's release. They were convinced that she and other missionaries were accomplices to the plot, and wanted to prove their theory by all means. The authorities would round up Macedonians and interrogate them by beating them into confessing some sort of knowledge. However, no one knew anything and many Macedonians in the area went into hiding to avoid the beatings. The Ottoman authorities also demanded that a handful of Macedonians who sympathized with the missionaries' work to produce Stone and Tsilka. Even two of the guides that had been accompanying Stone the day she was captured were suspected, and one was beaten into confessing that he recognized the face of one of the brigands.[262]

The winter months came suddenly and harshly and Tsilka's baby was born in these turbulent conditions. But it was not until late January that the public pressure to secure Stone's release begin to overwhelm the Americans. Throughout December and January, the missionaries working to secure Stone's release were accused of numerous mistakes and of generally being incapable of securing Stone's freedom.[263] But by the middle of January, the money had finally been secured. The demanded ransom was sent with the dragoman of the American Consulate in Sofia to Jenidasulaf, on the Macedonian frontier with Bulgaria. While the ransom party was staying at a house in a Turkish village one night, the house was set on fire. Everyone managed to escape alive – and they saved the ransom, too – but fear overwhelmed the ransom party, and they were convinced that the longer they held onto the money, the more likely they would meet an ugly fate. Many believed that the reason for the attack on them was because the local Turks objected to the payment of the Macedonian rebels on Turkish soil.[264]

The two men carrying the $66,000 in gold to Sandanski had actually experienced a lot of trouble due to the Turkish government. For nearly all of January, they were followed around Macedonia by a sizeable detachment of Turkish troops. "The Turkish authorities, while pretending to cooperate, were determined to prevent the payment of the ransom" and instead wanted to use the opportunity root out Sandanski's band. After the two escorts secretly contacted Sandanski and his band through a third party, they negotiated Stone's release and eventually paid the money in February. To evade the eyes of the Turks, they took the money out of the guarded cottage chunks at a time and replaced it with its equal weight in lead.[265]

Sandanski's band did not indicate where they would release Stone (to avoid pursuit by authorities) and Stone arrived suddenly in Strumica on the morning of February 23rd. A telegram was sent by the American vice-consul in Solun to Mr. Dickinson, the American general consul at Constantinople, indicating Stone's release. At the time, they didn't want to divulge where and how the ransom money was paid. The American Board of Commissions also received two telegrams about Stone's release. One simply read "safe", while the other addressed to Secretary Barton read: "Miss Stone and Madame Tsilka and child released in good physical condition and good spirits." The first one was signed by Edward Haskell, the missionary of the board stationed in Solun, and then was taken by Reverend Judson Smith to Stone's home in Chelsea, Massachusetts.[266]

After several months in captivity, Stone was glad to be free. But Sandanski, Chernopeev and their Macedonians were just as glad to have been rid of Stone and Tsilka, as well as to have the money out of their hands so they could focus on the next task at hand (the funds were handed over to Delchev, who hid them in Sofia for use for the Cause.)[267] "God," said Chernopeev in an interview. "Who would have thought it was going to last five months…have you ever found yourself in a position of strong opposition to a middle-aged woman with a determined will, all her own?"[268] But Chernopeev was more seriously bothered by European and American politicians and journalists for the way they characterized the kidnapping and the complete ignorance of the Macedonian struggle:

> **I am indifferent for myself – but, the others – most of them died for their ideas – never had so much as a *lira* in their ragged pockets. But they were only brigands. God! What greasy hypocrites they are! The smug diplomats and editors and the clergy, with their hanging jowls and rotund bellies. Yes, brigands, we are. They allow our women and small babies to be outraged and slaughtered, and when we ask them for help, only to stop it, in the name of Christ, they give us soft, lying words. And then when we give one of their women a few months' worry and discomfort, which we more than share with her, only to give us the means to save a million women from death, or worse, we are brigands…For that we are brigands, outlaws, criminals. No, damn such a civilization. It isn't real.**[269]

The American in charge of the negotiations for Stone's release, Spencer Eddy, based in Istanbul, reaffirmed the political (and non-criminal) nature of the kidnapping on arrival New York at the time of Stone's release. Eddy stated that Sandanski's band targeted Stone because the Macedonians believed Americans had the most money. When asked if the rebel band ransomed Stone for self-gain, he responded with sympathy for the Macedonian Cause:

> **No, they did not, and that is where the people in America do not understand this case. It is entirely a political matter, and all the people in Macedonia are in sympathy with the kidnapping, for**

they believe it is a step toward freeing Macedonia from Turkish rule, the same as Bulgaria had been, and the money they demanded, $100,000, was intended for the Macedonian cause. If we had been dealing with professional brigands who wanted money pure and simple, instead of the political ones, Miss Stone would have been released long ago. It is very likely that this capture was deliberated upon for a long time, and the victims selected were considered best to serve the cause, when compared with those of other nationalities.

The Macedonians are rather friendly toward the missionaries than otherwise. They desired to attract the attention of the world to their cause and incidentally to get some much needed money. I have every reason to believe they have given Miss Stone and her companion in captivity they very best of treatment. When Mrs. Tsilka's baby was born she received the kindest of care, from all we can learn…Turkey will have a problem on her hands if she attempts to punish the ringleaders, for the Macedonians have risen up as one man in their demand to be free from Turkey, and this kidnapping of the two American missionaries may be called chapter one in their plan for liberty."[270]

Ultimately, IMRO added a lot of money to their war chest, even though the world's powerful government refused to interject themselves against Ottoman domination of Macedonia. Still, even with the failure of getting the United States to directly intervene in the Stone case, the Macedonians would not give up on trying to hold the world's attention. Delchev was not supportive of the abduction of Stone initially, but he was excited about the amount of money IMRO received and believed momentum was on their side.[271] As mentioned before, Delchev was not fond of such work, but he understood its significance. He said: "There can be no boundaries to such sacrifices even though they might destroy your name and honor…If we consider the opinion of the people, we can have peace of mind…many are man's measure of morality and immorality."[272]

Therefore, Stone's capture would not be the last one coming from Macedonia to make international headlines. In the summer of 1905, Macedonians captured an Englishman named Wills, who worked for the Turkish tobacco revenue department. He was captured in the southeastern part of Macedonia and the captors were tired of not having received money for his release. So in October, they sent a package to the British consulate in Bitola that contained a human ear and a letter demanding $5,000, or else Wills would be killed.[273] The ear was not Wills' ear,[274] but the gesture showed how serious the Macedonians were about obtaining money for their revolution.

There were other plans and attempts to kidnap and ransom by Macedonians, especially those concocted by Sarafov. In early October of 1903, Sarafov's band abandoned a plan they had to capture the Chicago millionaire Charles Crane on his trip to Bulgaria. It was Tatarchev, the then leader of the IMRO, that convinced Sarafov not to because he thought it would cost them the support and sympathy of the international community. For Sarafov, this ransom would have been huge: not only was Crane wealthy, but he had very close relations with several influential Americans, such as President Roosevelt and ex-President Cleveland. Sarafov wanted to capture him on his visit to the Rila Monastery on the border with Macedonia, where the bands were very active. Crane laughed this off when the Bulgarian General Petroff warned him about it. He did not realize how close he was to being kidnapped and ransomed.[275]

There were many more plans that originated in Sarafov's mind, and some were far-fetched. In 1896, he suggested that IMRO should kidnap him in Solun. He would use a forged Russian passport and then Russia would pay the ransom. IMRO was not willing to execute such a task. Sarafov then suggested kidnapping King Alexander Obrenovic from Serbia, during his visit to Mt. Athos in 1897.[276] Sarafov was also ready to sell rights to Macedonia's natural resources to secure money. When in London on a tour of European capitals, "he attempted to raise a loan of two or three million pounds, and, when asked for some firm guarantee, he offered the right to exploit Lake Ohrid after Macedonia had been freed!"[277] Sarafov's mind was plagued with many ideas, but the more realistic Macedonians were not ready to board the same ship as him.

Non-Macedonians were also striving to support the Macedonian Cause. One notable example is Eugene Lazarovich, along with his wife Eleanor. Eugene claimed lineage from medieval Serbian royalty (the Nemania-Heblianovich ruling house, which served from 807 AD to early 1700s), and Eleanor was originally a Calhoun from America. Her father was Judge Calhoun, a major politician in California. Her grandfather was Senator John C. Calhoun from South Carolina, who threatened to pull South Carolina out of the union.

In 1903, Eugene and Eleanor toured Europe together managing fundraising efforts for the Macedonian revolution. They had aimed to raise $10,000,000 to give as a loan to Macedonia that would be repaid when Macedonia secured self-government. Eugene said:

> **Our object is to recruit with this money an international army of 60,000 to be displaced at the disposal of the powers as Macedonian police, to preserve order after peace is restored... A rich American, whose name I am unable yet to state, has promised $500,000 provisionally...There are 18,000 insurgents now in the field. The object for which we are working is to drive the Turkish soldiers to desperation by guerrilla tactics and cause them to rebel against the Sultan...We have every reason to be satisfied with the progress of the insurrection, and we can continue our present campaign indefinitely.**[278]

Eleanor also tried to gather support from American public. Both were barred from entering Serbia because the ruling Serbian king knew Eugene could possibly contend for the throne of Serbia as Eugene became a chief of the family line. However, he was a socialist and a revolutionary and had no ambitions to be king. In 1887, at the age of 24, while living in Austria, Eugene had the idea to compel the Sultan to stop tyrannizing the Macedonians. Many Macedonians had fled to Austria to escape death. He organized many of these refugees and formed several small insurrectionary committees. Because of his commission in the army, he could not locally organize in Macedonia. He therefore sent for Stephanos Makedon, who was living in Athens as a refugee, to build up the committees in Bucharest, Sofia, Athens and Belgrade. Eugene directed from Vienna and eventually had to leave his position in the Austrian army because of his revolutionary activity. He went to Paris and London, buying arms and ammunition, and poured them into Macedonia. Between 1893 and 1903, he spent $500,000 of his own money to help gain Macedonia's freedom to realize his true ambition of creating a union of South Slavic states.[279] In these regards, he shared similar ideals and aspirations as IMRO's left wing members, such as Sandanski, Delchev, Petrov and Toshev.

Yet, none of this would come to fruition if the Macedonians could not throw off the Turkish yoke. The years were ticking away and Macedonia was becoming more chaotic as the Ottoman Empire drowned in poverty, corruption and religious and ethnic tensions. The year 1903 would thus prove to be the most pivotal year during the revolution – the most inspiring and the most devastating.

V.

1903: The Year of the Uprising

Many Macedonians remember 1903 as the year of the Ilinden Uprising: August 2nd, the day thousands of Macedonians rose up and reclaimed towns and villages across Macedonian territory. However, 1903 was pivotal in many more respects: the revolutionary movement lost one of its greatest leaders; anarchists wreaked havoc in Macedonia's most cosmopolitan and international city; and there was extreme conflict regarding the timing and manner of the revolution, which was a critical turning point in the fracturing of the Macedonian movement into left and right branches. There are some years that are markers for a nation's struggle, and 1903, coming a decade after the creation of IMRO, was one of the most significant.

The months leading up to 1903 showed a strong push by SMAC leaders and certain elements in the Macedonian movement to initiate an uprising. The IMRO moderates were also becoming increasingly swayed by the arguments for a revolution, and it was becoming evident that there would be an enormous Macedonian uprising soon. In the first week of January 1903, IMRO held a Congress in Solun to make such an action official. There were 17 delegates present, most of who were of secondary importance and were only occasional participants of the Macedonian movement. Garvanov employed several distortions and lies to attempt to convince the present delegates for a spring uprising.[280] Of IMRO's original founders, he first swayed Tatarchev and Matov.

The opposition to a 1903 uprising at the January Congress essentially consisted of Delchev and Petrov attempting to convince the leadership that an uprising was not inevitable for 1903 and that, more importantly, it was not yet desirable. Prior to the Congress, however, Garvanov had sent a letter to the delegates about his desire for an immediate uprising, and Matov and Tatarchev were among the few that knew that the upcoming Congress would decide the date of the revolution. At a meeting in Sofia, Matov and Tatarchev had prepared convincing speeches for the uprising and many of the delegates initially agreed with them. Delchev was then given the platform; but he was so disturbed and wrought with emotions over the idea of an early uprising that he could barely convince anyone. Petrov later wrote that Delchev "became heated, broke into a sweat and began to bluster…His nerves were too weak to withstand mental torture, and his eyes – too soft to impose his will upon a meeting of comrades who did not agree with him."[281]

Petrov, however, made up for Delchev's weakness. He gave a six hour impassioned speech against an uprising in 1903 and won over the majority and together they wrote a letter to IMRO's Central Committee (still headed by Garvanov) in Solun against an uprising. Garvanov did not bother to take Delchev's and Petrov's followers' views into consideration. There was only one individually present at the January Congress in Solun who put up any debate, and his name was Lazar Dimitrov. He later wrote about the incident:

I was against, first, because our area – Serres – was not prepared for a rising, and I knew that the others were not prepared either…Apart from this, I already knew the opinion of Sandansky, Delchev and others who were against. It was Garvanov, first and foremost, who took issue with me.[282]

Why were Delchev, Petrov, Sandanski and their left-wing followers against an uprising? Like Dimitrov, they argued that the peasants were not sufficiently armed or trained and that many regions were still severely deficient of basic preparation. Many of the people had insufficient time to prepare – not just for battle, but for all other aspects that come with such a revolution, including medical acquiring medical supplies, storing and delivering food, and handling logistics and communications. They believed that the Macedonians needed more time and perhaps even more political capital.[283] However, other leaders, such as Garvanov, Matov and Tatarchev, maintained that the Macedonian movement had already lost significant ground to the Turks. The Turks were frequently uncovering IMRO weapons caches and plans, as well as arresting, imprisoning or killing IMRO members. They feared that the complete destruction of IMRO would soon transpire and ten years of preparation would have been wasted.[284]

Meanwhile, another group of Macedonians – young anarchists, mostly from Veles – had been planning the demise of the Ottoman Empire on their own, using their own anarchist and terrorist tactics.

They at first referred to themselves as the Troublemakers (inspired by Russian heroes), but later adopted the term 'Boatmen' – by which they could identify themselves with those who abandoned the daily routine and limits of legal order and instead sail towards freedom and the wild seas beyond the law. They bought explosives in Constantinople and smuggled them as cases of sardines into Solun. They rented a grocer's shop opposite the Ottoman Bank, dug a trench, and packed it with those explosives.[285]

The story originates several years prior, when Svetoslav Merdhanov traveled from Geneva, Switzerland (there was a small network of anarchist Macedonians living there) to Solun in 1898. He was there for the express purpose for conceiving of terroristic acts on a large scale. He was representing a group of Macedonian students in Geneva that had contacts with Russian social revolutionists. When in Solun, he met with the Boatmen, whose leader was Jordan Pop Jordanov. The Boatmen had concrete ideas on what they wanted to accomplish and how, but they needed money. To achieve this goal they thought of many plans. Stoyan Christowe wrote:

> **Two of them agreed to have themselves kidnapped so that a ransom might be collected from their own fathers. Gotse Deltcheff, who sympathized with them, though the Central Committee of IMRO disapproved of their projects, offered to help them, but he could give then no money from the IMRO treasury. However, he cooperated in the kidnapping hoax and collected one thousand dollars from the father of one of the boys."**[286]

However, despite Delchev's and other left-wing Macedonian support, the Boatmen often ran into much opposition. In January of 1903, in a meeting of IMRO revolutionaries at a chemistry lab in a high school, the older revolutionaries denounced the plotters for their stupid childish games. Further, rumors of the plot had been circling by April 1903, and a Greek secret agent with the local Turkish police, Panayiot Effendi, was heavy on their trail. Additionally, when the manager of Hotel Colombo, which was next to the Ottoman Bank, reported that his drains were blocked, the plotters feared discovery and were forced to accelerate their plans. Around the same time, they also decided to magnify their plans by blowing up the French ship Guadalguivir simultaneously.[287]

In the early morning hours of April 28, 1903, one of these Boatmen, Pavel Shatev, describing himself as a merchant, and possessing the requisite paperwork for travelling in Turkey, bought a second-class passage for Constantinople aboard the Guadalquivir. He boarded the ship with his heavy luggage (12 kilograms of dynamite) a few hours before the ship was set to sail. He inspected the boat, pretending that he was simply curious and amazed by such a creature, and learned that the strategically best rooms for his plans were assigned only to passengers with first-class tickets. To get one of these rooms, he paid the difference in fare and transferred his dynamite into a cabin closer the engine room. A few minutes before the ship was scheduled to set sail, Shatev "hailed a small boat and went ashore, ostensibly to speak to a friend on the quay, leaving all his baggage behind." The ship set sail without him.[288]

The boat had hardly sailed for a few minutes before an incredible explosion "wrecked the engine-room, cut the steering gear off from the wheel-house, and set the vessel afire." There were some severe injuries, but no one was killed. Another vessel rushed to rescue the crew and passengers and tug the ship back into the dock.[289]

That night, another bomb exploded on the railroad tracks as a train arrived at the main station. However, because the anarchists were rookies when it came to explosives, the bombs only inflicted minor damage. The next morning Shatev fled from Solun and the police were notified, as he was the only passenger to not show up to reclaim any of his valuables or a refund. He was immediately arrested at the train station in Skopje that afternoon. Back in Solun a few hours later, around 8:00 pm, another Boatmen blew up the main pipeline leading from the gas station, and all lights in the city went dark.[290]

This was the start of an all-day affair of bomb attacks and gun fights with Turkish police. Just as the city lights went out for the evening, a carriage arrived in front of the main café street along the water-front, while other carriages arrived in other parts of town. Each carriage was loaded with two or more Boatmen and their arsenal. Some of them "jumped out and threaded their way to the midst of the wondering crowds, before hurling their deadly missiles." They targeted areas where their bombs would inflict the most disaster and create the most chaos, especially aiming for the larger groups of the "foreign element and the most prominent citizens."[291] Bombs were thrown at the generating station and at the Alhambra café, where a waiter was killed. The bar on the ground floor of Hotel d'Angleterre was attacked, and another Boatmen set fire to the Bosniak Han. Outside the Ottoman Bank, two members pulled up in a carriage, jumped out and scattered bombs and grenades, killing a guard and a solider and wounding two others. In the grocer's store across from the bank, Jordan Jordanov took his cue from the dark cityscape and set off the fuse in the tunnel leading under the building. A thunderous explosion ripped through the city and only the outer walls of the bank were left standing, while several people were buried underneath the rubble.[292]

About half an hour after the bank fiasco, while a little party of Americans (American missionaries and their families) watched the burning bank from their sanctuary, bombs began exploding around their house. The Boatmen were not targeting the Americans' property, but rather the German school next to it. The Boatmen "had waited until the troops from the fort were drawn off to other parts of the city before beginning their job." Frederick Moore explains:

> **They threw their bombs from the balcony down at a corner of the building, where they exploded. The detonations were deafening, but the whole damage to the school was less than that which a single bomb would have wrought if put into one of the rooms. But the fort opposite had not been left entirely deserted, and a few minutes after the first report it opened fire from the battlemented walls. The Turks were soon reinforced by two detachments of troops which came up from opposite directions. One force, in the darkness, mistook the other for insurgents and fired into them. For more than two hours the fight continued, during which probably forty bombs exploded and hundreds of rifle cracks rent the air.**
>
> **One of the missionary's wife said she had seen one of the Macedonians light their fuses in the room, then dash out on the terrace and throw the bombs into the street below. Several times the Turks attempted to rush the place, but the street was narrow and stoutly walled, and whenever they came up the [Macedonians] dropped bombs into them and drove them back. … [T]he insurgents staggered out and only dropped their bombs. As they lit the fuses the Americans saw one of them**

bleeding from a wound in the face, and the other from the chest. Finally the defence ceased, and the Turks charged the little fortress successfully. They battered in the door and dragged out the garrison, both undoubtedly beyond earthly suffering.[293]

The anarchists succeeded in making the Ottoman authorities look helpless and not in control, which helped draw international attention back onto Macedonia. Foreign consuls cabled their governments to ship in their navies, fearing that the Ottoman authorities would indiscriminately massacre Macedonians. Their fears were justified. Soldiers conducted house-to-house searches, killing several suspects in courtyards and streets (both guilty and innocent). A curfew was imposed on the population and troops patrolled the streets. The authorities feared that these attacks were the signal for a general uprising, so they invaded the Macedonian section of town and arrested dozens of men. The following day, the local *pasha* ventured through all neighborhoods promising his protection to all innocent people and warning the local Muslims not to take the law into their own hands.[294]

But the young Macedonians were not finished with their task. That night, one of the anarchists had planned to blow up a mosque during Friday prayers but was arrested before he got to it.[295] The next day, another Macedonian intended to blow up the telegraph office and arrived dressed in modern European garb. He was loitering about the place, which made the authorities very suspicious:

> **When he collected his courage and started to enter, one of the sentries at the door challenged him. The young man, holding a paper in his hand and feigning indignation, is said to have exclaimed, 'Let me pass! I want to send off this telegram.' The guard answered, 'I must search you before you go in.' Here the young Macedonian thrust his hand into his pocket for a bomb, but before he could withdraw it, the stalwart guard, who was twice the size of the young man, grabbed him by the throat, threw him on his back, and sent two balls into him. A letter was found on the boy's body stating that he had successfully carried out one piece of dynamiting and hoped to accomplish this.**[296]

Within a few days, the Macedonian perpetrators were either killed off or arrested, and 800 others (most who were not affiliated with the Boatmen) had been arrested. Many of them were sentenced to death and the remaining leaders were transferred to the Fezzan jails in the Sahara Desert in Libya (part of the Ottoman Empire at the time). Most of them who had survived the battle in Solun died there. The only two to have survived, Shatev and Bogdanov, returned to Macedonian in the general amnesty of 1908 after the Young Turk Revolution. Bogdanov died a few years later, but Shatev lived to old age until 1952, and he even served as the Minister of Justice for the free republic of Macedonia as part of Yugoslavia.[297]

Furthermore, a result of the Turkish response to these attacks, over 100 Macedonians were killed by Turks. But activities by rebels and counter-moves by the Turks were only in their infancy. One Macedonian disguised himself as a Muslim priest and attempted to "throw a dynamite bomb in the city telegraph office." But the Turks prevented this and immediately captured and then executed the man. In Skopje, "large stores of hidden dynamite" were uncovered by authorities.[298] Similar discoveries were made throughout Macedonia.

The authorities in Bulgaria even began cracking down on people suspected of being involved with, or connected to, the Solun terrorist attack. The Bulgarian government iterated they had "no sympathy or connections with such actions" of the Macedonian terrorists and arrested over 100 Macedonian revolutionaries, peasants and two ex-captains in the Bulgarian army "who were found loitering on the Bulgarian side of the Macedonian frontier."[299]

One news correspondent claimed that the Turkish authorities knew about the plot in advance "and that they were either grossly negligent or deliberately inactive."[300] Perhaps they wanted these Macedonians to conduct the attacks to show the recklessness of the Macedonian Cause; or perhaps they thought that the young Macedonians could not pull off any serious assault on the country. Either way, Frederick Moore in his trip to Macedonia in 1903 met no less than three people in Solun who said they knew the Macedonians were planning outrages on specific dates, and that the bank was specifically going to be targeted.[301]

The Boatmen emphasized (before the attacks, and by the surviving members after the attacks) that their terror campaign was conducted "as a threat and in punishment for the non-interference of the civilized nations in behalf of the Christians of Macedonia." The Imperial Ottoman Bank, for example, was mostly owned and operated and constructed by the French and Italians, and the ship they blew up was also French.[302] The terrorists knew going into the terror campaign that they would likely die. They also knew that they would not overthrow the Ottoman Empire with this one act. However, they believed that their actions would give hope and encouragement to other Macedonians, while signifying to the world their desperation.

Meanwhile, encounters between Turkish authorities and IMRO bands increased during the spring, and these battles escalated after the Solun bombings. The Turkish authorities had by now even issued a hefty reward for Delchev's capture, dead or alive, as they viewed him as the central figure of the Macedonian push for independence.[303]

Delchev was widely known as one of the leading figures of the revolution. He always spoke and wrote about the need for Macedonian independence. The Turks were aware of his writings and speeches. However, in addition to supporting Macedonia's freedom from Turkey, he was against the usurpation of the Macedonian Cause by Macedonia's neighbors. He wrote: "The liberation of Macedonia is possible only by an internal insurrection. Whoever thinks otherwise for the freedom of Macedonia, he fools himself and fools the others." He was vehemently against annexation to Bulgaria as well as opposed to all movements that did not profess the unity and independence of Macedonia. He even said that "the purpose of the organization is not to make Bulgarians or Greeks, but to work for their freedom from the Turks and then let anybody become whatever he pleases."[304]

Further, as mentioned earlier, Delchev was opposed to an uprising occurring in 1903. He believed the Macedonians were not ready. But he remained loyal to IMRO and the decision to revolt. He continued traveling throughout Macedonia, preparing the peasants for the revolution and teaching them about national freedom and socialist ideals. Yet, he encountered his tragic destiny in April of that year:

While roaming thru the southern part of Macedonia, preparatory to the anticipated general insurrection...he arrived, April 10, 1903, in the village of Banitza, in the district of Serres. Simultaneously two other chetas (bands) arrived, one under the leadership of the voyvoda [captain] Georghi Brodiliata and the other under the voyvoda Dimitre Goushanoff. Altogether there were twenty men. They settled in two houses for the evening. The next day, before daybreak, the village was surrounded by Turkish soldiers, more than a thousand of them.[305]

Delchev decided to withdraw instead of remaining in the houses for refuge because, once the Turks discovered them, he knew they would burn the village. As he led his IMRO compatriots from their shelter to the outskirts of the village, a small group of children – scared for their lives – ran toward them from the edge of the village. Delchev asked them if any Turkish soldiers were hiding just outside the village, but the children were too scared to answer – any slip of the tongue could mean death for them, because a thousand Turkish soldiers were laying behind a wall that separated the outskirt of town from the farm fields. The Turks rushed from behind the wall as the children fled, sending volleys of bullets at the IMRO band. Delchev saw them immediately and rang out shots. The other rebels instinctively fell to the ground, but not Delchev – he stood his ground and reloaded his weapon. As he was reloading, a bullet ripped through his skull and he slumped over.[306]

Gushanov and many others were eventually killed, and only eight Macedonians survived, including Dimo Hadzhidimov and Chakov. Hadzhidimov later said of the incident:

For fifteen hours, because of our bullets, the Turks dared not approach our dead. For fifteen hours, we looked upon the dead Gotse, lying as though bent over the grave of Macedonia. For fifteen hours, our hearts bled[.][307]

Delchev, the great Macedonian revolutionary, was dead. But the revolution did not stop. Even though Macedonia was grieving, the IMRO leaders decided to push through with their agenda of a summer uprising. The IMRO held a Congress in Smilevo in May that was attended by 32 delegates. Over one-hundred IMRO rebels were stationed in the vicinity within a five kilometer radius, guarding the

Congress from the suspicions of the Turks. Gruev was the chairman of the Congress and the secretaries were Popchristov and Cvetkov. The general consensus was that they should leave some time for the population to supply itself with food and for the armed bands to acquire more arms and ammunition. But they knew the approximate date for an insurrection.[308]

There were two main reasons why IMRO decided to stage an uprising so soon, even though they did not have enough people, support, arms and funds. First, the new Inspector General of Macedonia was Hussein Hilmi Pasha, and he was set on completely eradicating IMRO before they became too powerful. The IMRO delegates were convinced that Ilinden Uprising must transpire as a self-defense maneuver. Second, many of the moderates firmly believed that such an uprising would open up Europe's eyes to the injustices of the Ottoman Empire and that the international community would act on behalf of the Macedonians.[309]

Dame Gruev had been locked up for years, but after being released, he managed to make it to his home town for the Congress. He had been arrested in August of 1900 during the widespread crackdown on IMRO by Turkish authorities. He was confined in a Bitola jail until May of 1902, and while there he continued to write secret papers for the Cause and stayed in touch with various local revolutionary committees in the Bitola area. In 1902, he was exiled to Podrum-Kale, a prison in Asia Minor. He remained there until Easter of 1903, when after a general amnesty, he was released. Gruev was originally opposed to the decision the Committee had made to begin a general uprising because he believed the Macedonians were not prepared, but he figured it was too late to oppose it, so he went along with it.[310]

Thus, a General Staff for the Uprising was elected. The delegates elected Gruev, Sarafov, and Lozanchev to lead the Uprising. The three substitutes chosen were Petar Atsev, Lazar Pop Trajkov, and Georgi Popchristov. The General Staff adopted rules and regulations for the conduct and discipline of the insurgents. Furthermore, Macedonia was divided into battle districts, with central areas in Bitola, Prilep, Kostur, Ohrid, Kichevo, Solun, Serres, Kukush, Gevgelija, Voden, Struma, Skopje, Veles, Radovish, Shtip, Tikvesh and Kochani.[311]

With the Uprising planned, the organization continued preparing for the Uprising on August 2nd, although the date had been kept secret from the masses. In the meantime, familiar Macedonians were still agitating and provoking. In June, a news correspondent reported that Boris Sarafov threatened to release the plague on Turkey if Turkey did not implement the required reforms in Macedonia. The correspondent wrote:

> [T]he Macedonian revolutionary leaders threaten to use Indian plague *bacilli* to cause an outbreak of that disease if their demands are not met... [A] supply of bubonic *bacilli* sufficient to spread death and panic in Constantinople, Salonica and many other places has been in readiness for a long time...the plague germs once set free would multiply by millions...The Plague would demoralize the Turkish army and disperse it. As for the Macedonians they may save themselves as their fathers always did when a plague visited their lands...In the mountains the Macedonians can subsist for a long time on their flocks of sheep and goats, and can even grow corn without venturing into the plague stricken plains.[312]

The Macedonians did not go through with this dangerous scheme concocted by Sarafov and instead focused on the Uprising at hand. However, it shows that there was no consideration too dangerous or too radical if it meant the possible liberation of Macedonia.

The Uprising was not going to be easy, though, because the Turks were well aware that Macedonia was going to erupt into flames. By June of 1903, the Turkish Empire had 200,000 troops stationed in Macedonia, almost four times the amount that it had at the beginning of the year.[313] Thus, throughout the early summer weeks, the Macedonian rebel bands were constantly clashing with Turkish troops and police. On the evening of July 20, the IMRO band led by Ivan Trajkov Gule clashed with Turkish troops in the village of Krushie. At first, there were only 50 Turkish soldiers; then the number swelled to over 350. Gule's band retreated. The Turks then killed many villagers and burned the village. The IMRO band from the neighboring village of Loreka came to help Gule's band, but the Turks were not fooled and eventually destroyed the Loreka.[314]

On the same date, in Dolna Prespa, Nikola Kokarev of Tsaredvor and B. Iliev from Smilevo led a battle against another battalion of

Turkish troops. Over 200 insurgents demolished a contingent of 100 Turkish troops. This frightened many of the peasant Turks from the area's villages, and they fled to towns and cities by the time the Uprising began.[315] The larger towns and cities were safer during rebellions during that time in Macedonia.

Finally, a week later on July 28th, the IMRO leadership circulated a letter amongst its members (and, subsequently, the peasant populace) encouraging all Macedonians to join IMRO in its planned uprising against the Ottoman forces. Their plea was impassioned but succinct:

> **Finally, the much expected day for the altercation with our age-long enemy has arrived. The blood of our innocently perished brothers from Turkish tyranny cries for retribution. The honor of our mothers and sisters demands rehabilitation. Enough of so much torments, enough of so much ignominy. A thousand times, death is preferable to a shameful and beastly life. The specified day, in which the people throughout Macedonia and Adrianople province must rise, openly with arms in their hands against their enemy, is August 2, 1903.**
>
> **Brothers, follow your chiefs on that day and rally around the banner of liberty, and be obstinate in the struggle. Only in a stubborn and lengthy struggle lies our salvation. Let God bless our just cause and the day of the uprising. Down with Turkey. Down with tyranny. Death to the enemy. Long live the people. Long live liberty.**[316]

The IMRO leaders had framed Ilinden as one of good versus evil:

> We are taking up arms against tyranny and barbarism; we are acting in the name of liberty and humanity; our work is above all prejudices of nationality or race. We ought therefore to treat all as brothers who suffer in the somber Empire of the Sultan…We regard the Turkish government as our sole enemy, and all who declare themselves against us, whether as open foes or spies, and all too who attack old men, women and defenseless children instead of attacking us.[317]

Writing letters had been a critical method used by IMRO to spread their message. Writing, possessing and transporting letters was never an easy or risk-free task. For example, Lazar Svetiev, a courier, was transporting a letter from Bitola to the countryside that had ordered Macedonians to set fire to the haystacks to signal the start of the uprising. He explained his ordeal:

> **The courier Sekule Kantar, from the village of Mogila, Bitola region, was standing at my side and I had to give him a letter, but at the time Bitola was under military blockade. At the market the Turkish officer was looking directly at us and we had to wait for him to go away in order to pass the letter. When the officer had left I gave the letter to Sekule and he left through the burned shop beside us, but the Turkish officer came back and shouted after Sekule: "Wait, old man!" But Sekule replied, "Ah let me meet you at the other side." At that instant Sekule threw the letter in a gutter filled with water and stepped on it and then continued to meet the officer. The officer took Sekule to the police garrison, and there they undressed him completely in order to find the letter, but couldn't find anything and so Sekule was released.**[318]

IMRO also released a statement shortly after the uprising explaining why they were taking arms against the Ottoman Empire and what they wanted to see happen:

> **We have had recourse to this extreme measure after exhausting all pacific means to secure the intervention of Europe to enforce the provisions of the Berlin Treaty. At the present moment, this intervention is the only means of remedying the evil and stopping bloodshed. The sporadic efforts of the powers to secure reforms having failed, they resulted in merely in a recrudescence of Turkish fanaticism and government oppression. It is evident that reform measures, to be efficacious, must include the appointment of a Christian governor general of Macedonia, someone who has never held the office under the Porte, and who must be independent under the Turkish government in the exercises of his functions, and further appointment by the powers of a joint permanent administrative board, with full powers to deal with any disturbance.**[319]

Statements and letters aside, the Uprising was under way and the Macedonians had many successes in the first few weeks. In Voden, shortly after the resurrection started, they stole 2,500 pounds of sterling for the revolution. Near Ohrid, IMRO robbed the Turks of 80 wagons of meat.[320] On the night of the initiation of the Uprising, in Kostur, the telegraph lines were cut. The next day, plans to liberate Kostur from the Turks were called off, as the Macedonians were highly outnumbered. Instead, 150 insurgents engaged a Turkish post in Visheni in a 3 hour battle. The Turks fled in a panic to Kostur, leaving behind guns, ammunition, food and other supplies.[321]

Of the 500 Macedonians who had been mobilized in the Lerin region, 100 of them were from Ekshisu. On that evening, 200 IMRO rebels led by Georgi Popchristov set off an explosion at the Ekshisu railway station, destroying equipment and supplies belonging to the Turks. Mihail Chekov, who took part in it, wrote about it in his memoirs. Many of the people who showed up to rebel were older people that could not really fight well, such as Priest Ivan Markuzov. They took their weapons from them and sent them home. The capitan who headed the local bands was Tego Hadjiev. Boris Sarafov assigned Georgi Chakurov from Bansko to be the explosives expert. Chekov wrote:

> **First, we informed the station-master and the staff of our attack, so they could leave the premises, as they were our supporters. I was assigned to oversee Georgi Chakurov who was charged with destroying the small bridge by the station and the railway switches. The raid on the station was assigned to Georgi Pop-Christov and Tego Hadjiev. Georgi attacked the station from the south side and was successful. The station was guarded by some Turkish soldiers who opened fire. Four of those soldiers were killed and a few were wounded. On our side, Tego Hadjiev and my cousin Chekov were wounded. Tego was taken into Ekshi-Sou where his wounds were bandaged. When Ilia Chekov saw that his wound was fatal he took his own life.[322]**

Much of central and southwestern Macedonia was quickly engulfed in war. Three Turkish battalions attacked 1,000 Macedonian insurgents near Bitola and after a six-hour fight, the Turks retreated with 210 killed and wounded.[323] On August 5th,

Lazar Pop-Trajkov's detachment surrounded the village of Zhernevi, a once-Christian village converted to Islam. The villagers were fanatical Moslems that oppressed and maltreated surrounding Christian villages, and would not surrender their arms or remain neutral in the uprising. The villagers opened fire on Pop-Trajkov's detachment, killing two and wounding four. Pop-Trajkov and his men burned down the village.[324] On August 9th, Turkish soldiers with artillery from Kostur destroyed the village of Dumbeni. On August 10th, Macedonian rebels snuck up on the Turks stationed in the hills outside of Dumbeni, dislodging them from a battle that killed 20 Turk soldiers. The Macedonians also captured two soldiers. The Turks were chased all the way back to Kostur. Also on August 10th, a Turkish expedition burned down the village of Vrbenik for retaliation of the attack on Bilischa.[325]

The IMRO military victories caused the Turkish army to flee their posts in Kosinets, Zagorichani, Nestram, Rula, and Gabresh, among others. But the Turkish garrison remained in Psodery, above Armensko, guarding the strategic Bigla Pass. Between 600 and 700 Macedonians from the Lerin and Kostur IMRO units engaged 2000 troops with artillery and cavalry here, but were unsuccessful in taking it over. However, the Turkish soldiers lost 40 men while the Macedonians lost six.[326]

The most revered element of the Uprising occurred in Krushevo. Krushevo was a town of merchants and craftsmen, north of Bitola and west of Prilep. On August 2nd, during the feast of Saint Ilija, 800 insurgents took their positions surrounding the town. Before the first shot was fired at midnight when August 2nd turned into August 3rd, a detachment destroyed the telegraph station. By dawn, only the Turkish barracks was still in control of the Turkish army. Pitu Guli's band arrived in the afternoon and soon burned down the barracks. They also held off 300 Turkish soldiers on the outskirts that were headed to Krushevo. The population rejoiced – a flag waved over the town with "Freedom or Death" inscribed on it, and a republic was proclaimed with a civil administration. Nikola Karev, a native of Krushevo, was elected the President and Vangel Dinu was elected as the Prime Minister. Additionally, a 60-member Council was elected and that council elected an executive committee consisting of six people. Because Krushevo was an ethnically mixed town – and because IMRO strived to be an all-encompassing national liberation movement – the Council and Committee were divided equally between ethnic Macedonians, Vlachs and Albanians (all members of varying Orthodox Churches of the time).[327]

Even though Karev was the leader of Krushevo, he had not been convinced that the time was ripe for a revolution. He also followed Delchev's line of thinking, incapable of separating Macedonian nationalism with socialist ideology. He constantly condemned foreign – particularly Bulgarian – intervention in the Macedonian Cause, and devoted himself to waking up the Macedonian masses. He sincerely believed that, in August 1903, the masses were not ready: all Macedonian districts lacked sufficient arms and other districts were still recruiting and preparing. But, like all Macedonian patriots, he submitted to the will of the majority and retired to continue preparing his Krushevo natives for the uprising.[328]

Karev was now president of a republic, and after the Krushevo executive committee was formed, he sent the following letter to the surrounding Turkish villages of Plasnita, Norovo and Aldantsi – as well as to other villages throughout Macedonia – and was written in the local Macedonian dialect:

> **Since we have lived peacefully as your brothers in this part of the world from the time of our ancestors, we see you as our own and wish it to remain so. We have raised no gun against you. That would be to our shame. We do not raise our guns against peaceful working people, who feed the future. We did not come to slaughter, butcher, steal or plunder. We have had enough of terror in our poor and bleeding Macedonia. We do not intend to baptize your mothers, daughters, wives or sisters, or force them to become Christians. We are revolutionaries who have sworn to die for justice and liberty. We are fighting tyranny and slavery; we are fighting against our Turkish feudal masters, against usurpers of our honours and against those who exploit our work. Do not be afraid if us. We wish no harm to anybody.**
>
> **We want you as our brothers since you are slaves just as we are: slaves of effendis and pashas, slaves of rich people, slaves of despots and tyrants, who forced us to take the action we took yesterday. We are taking steps towards justice, liberty and human life and we invite you to join our fight. Come brother, Muslims, come and fight our centuries-old enemies. Come, and**

join forces under the flag of autonomous Macedonia. Macedonia is our mother and she calls for our help. Come and help break our slaver's chain and free ourselves of suffering. Come to us, brothers, that we may unite our souls and hearts, and save our children, so we may live and work in peace.

Dear Neighbors! As Turks, Albanians and Moslems we know that you think that this is your kingdom and that you are not slaves. You will soon realize and understand that it is not so and you are sinning. We will fight for you as well as ourselves. Freedom or Death is imprinted on our foreheads and on our bloodstained flag. There is no turning back. May our struggle be blessed! Long live the fighters for freedom and justice, and long live all honorable sons of Macedonia![329]

Soon, the freshly elected government in Krushevo established a hospital, bakeries, munitions workshop, a revolutionary court, and a commission for the collection of taxes. There was even plans for postal service and stamps.[330]

But the Turks were reorganizing and reinforcing their displaced and disoriented soldiers. On August 12th, the Turks arrived with 18,000 soldiers, cavalry and artillery (in addition to hordes of Bashibazouks following behind), much of which came in from Prilep. IMRO's leaders urged the rebels to flee in order to avoid civilian casualties, but several hundred rebels stood their ground to defend their newly freed territory from the Sultan.[331] When the Turks engulfed Krushevo, the IMRO bands were stationed strategically throughout town: Georgi Naumov's band was on the steep cliffs above the Bitola-Prilep road, Ivan Naumov's was on the Busheva Cheshma slope by Deni Kamen and Sheshtar above the road to Kichevo; Atanas Karev's band was stationed at Koev Trun standing guard over the road to Kochisha; Andrey Kristov's band was at the Sveti Spas Monastery; Pitu Guli was at Mechkin Kamen; the village capitan occupied the road to the Pomak (Macedonian Muslim) village of Norovo.[332] Most of these IMRO fighters and their bands were eliminated battling the thousands of Turkish soldiers, with many revolutionaries taking their own lives in order to not be taken prisoners. Krushevo was pillaged and burned: 100 civilians were killed, 150 women and girls were raped, and 350 houses and stores were destroyed.[333]

While Krushevo was engaged with the Turks on their assault to subjugate the town, IMRO officials released a statement discussing their successes and losses. They claimed to still have had 8,000 insurgents located in the Bitola district who were supplied with guns purchased in Greece. They also said that 600 troops defeated several Turkish detachments in the vicinity of Kichevo but failed to capture that town. They also laid out other victories, such as how they destroyed the Turkish town of Drugove because those villagers had aided the Turkish army near Kichevo in repelling IMRO bands.[334]

Throughout August and September, there were hundreds of fierce battles between IMRO and the Turkish authorities. In late August, an IMRO band "defeated a small detachment of Turks who were guarding the railway bridge between Kuprili and Zeliniko[.]" IMRO's plan was to blow up the bridge as soon as a train carrying Turkish soldiers passed over it. But the train conductor "stopped the train before it reached the bridge" because he was suspicious of the absence of troops entrusted to guard the bridge, thus averting IMRO's plans. Still, a rebel managed to throw a bomb at the train and killed four soldiers.[335]

By early September, the Turks had discovered that IMRO was receiving "its arms and ammunition by means of ships which landed their cargos on the coast in the vicinity of Iniada."[336] This discovery was part of a general interruption of supply routes to the rebels, but they still engaged in heated battles and secured minor victories against the Turkish army through September. In Baroitza, 120 Macedonian rebels killed 30 Turkish soldiers in a shootout without suffering any losses. In Solun, 50 wounded Turkish soldiers poured into that city after a defeat at Vitchu.[337] Nearly 10 percent of a Turkish force of 7,000 was killed in a battle near Kochani. At Kresna Pass, over 300 Turkish troops were killed or injured, including five officers.[338]

However, the tides soon changed as the Ottoman Empire pumped more troops and artillery into Macedonia and as the Macedonians started running out of the means to hold off the Turks. Although the Turkish troops were poorly paid and generally possessed low morale during the wars, there were hundreds of thousands of them facing off against the Macedonians. Further, since 1889, Germany had been supplying the Sultan with arms, training and money for the Turkish military.[339] Some analysts consider Germany to have been most at fault – outside of Turkey – for the conditions imposed on Macedonians during the last few decades of Ottoman rule in Macedonia "because its government sustain[ed] and protect[ed] the Sultan in his atrocious policy of administration."[340] Regardless, the Ottoman Empire had a bottomless pit of weapons and men to pluck from, while no country in the Balkans or Europe decided to lift a finger to support the Macedonians. After all, an independent and free Macedonia was in no one's interests, except for the Macedonians.

But even though the Uprising began to face a series of devastating defeats by the end of September, the revolutionaries were working to garner support from wherever they could. G. M. Tsilka, whose wife was captured by IMRO nearly two years earlier, rallied Macedonian members of the Illinois militia at a meeting of Macedonians in Chicago to help their brethren in Macedonia by taking up arms against the Turks. "When the meeting adjourned those present dropped their contributions into the folds of the Macedonian flag as it lay half furled at the door."[341] All of this was in vain, however. By November, the Macedonian movement was essentially halted. By 1904, all progress achieved before the Uprising had been reversed, affirming the attitudes of the left-wing Macedonians like Delchev, Sandanski, Toshev, Petrov and Misirkov that IMRO who believed Macedonia was not ready for an Uprising. The moderates and pro-Bulgarian Macedonians believed that such an Uprising would have provoked the international community into acting and that inaction would render the past ten years of preparation as wasted. But they were wrong.

Now, the prospects for success were further off than before. The Turkish authorities hammered down on them, and neighboring bands from the Balkans increased their presence and chaos in order to force the population into becoming Serbs, Bulgarians or Greeks to make those respective nations' chances of successfully occupying Macedonia at some future point more plausible. There were still some die-hard Macedonian rebels that were trying to resurrect their insurrection. Some vowed to "enlist and organize armed bands of Americans" to help fight the Turks.[342] Others sporadically attacked Turkish troops. However, the Ottoman authorities had unleashed havoc on the populace – burning villages, slaughtering innocent peasants, raping women, and looting homes – whenever they defeated rebels, or whenever the rebels evaded them.

This destruction was too much for the Macedonians to handle. The Macedonians in south-west and central Macedonia faced the worst onslaught and reprisals by the Turkish authorities. This was due to the fact that, out of the three vilayets in Ottoman Macedonia, only the Bitola vilayet was called to conduct a major uprising because it was sufficiently far away from the borders of Bulgaria, Serbia, and Turkey. This is the main reason why other areas in Macedonia did not rise up against the Turks to the same extent as southwest Macedonia: the General Staff had decided against it. Of the 239 skirmishes that happened from Ilinden through the middle of September, the six week period of sustained revolutionary activity in August and September, 150 occurred in the vilayet of Bitola.[343]

The revolutionaries were praised as heroes and the way they conducted themselves throughout the Uprising. Here's one author describing a dramatic event:

> **The members of IMRO were wildly heroic. The Company of Prilep had exhausted its ammunition. The rebels poisoned themselves – a bottle of strychnine was found in the hand of the last who had drunk from the bottle neck. Spurred on by the call of the past ten years the youth of Macedonia followed their fathers to the sacrifice. There was no escape for them, they went to their death. One would stab himself in a frenzy, another blow his brains out for love of the cause.**[344]

Mary Durham also noted the bravery of Macedonians on her visit to Macedonia in 1903. She noticed that many of the Macedonians were fighting not only for the freedom of their nation, but in the name of ancient Macedonia and Alexander the Great. Such is the example of a man she visited in the hospital: "Poor Georgie! He spoke a Slav dialect, and was possibly a mixture of all the races that have ever ruled the peninsula, and all he had gained was a Mauser ball through his right hand in the name of Alexander the Great." Durham noted, however, that this feeling of belonging to the Macedonian land and identity was strong. She noted: "A song was sung during the late Macedonian insurrection in which an eagle, who is soaring over the land, asks what is the cause of so much excitement, and is told that the sons of Alexander are rising."[345]

There was a small handful of Macedonian revolutionaries that crossed the line from bravery into immorality, committing excesses during the Uprising, valuing the ends over the means. For example, on two occasions railroads were blown up with women and children on them, and several non-military boats were blown up.[346] Even Tatarchev acknowledged the immorality of some atrocities and inhuman acts being conducted by IMRO members and sympathizers during the Uprising. But he stated that most of the Muslims who had been targeted were the Bashibazouks:

> **It is morally wrong to assassinate the Bashi Bazouks. But if a horde of human devils were to set about burning the towns and villages of an Anglo-Saxon people, torturing their inhabitants, violating their women and young children, would your Anglo-Saxons be able to curb their passions and carry out the ethical laws which are now so glibly quoted? There is a wild beast in every human breast, and it has been aroused in ours. The insanity of despair knows no law; Europe has encouraged Turkey to drive us thus insane, and is now shocked at the result.**
>
> **But its fruits may be more terrible still. Our people, goaded to madness at the sight of their sisters, wives, and children bestially tortured to death, have indeed done indefensible deeds, but then they are not masters of themselves. Would the Anglo-Saxons be more self-restrained in our place? It is in accordance with morality for Christendom to connive at, nay, encourage, the Turks to leave the armed insurgents unharmed while doing to death every man, woman, and child in the province, and burning all the villages on the way? The Christian powers are acting thus calmly, deliberately, in cold blood. They have no provocation and feel no remorse. We have been driven mad, and if the system of extirpation be persisted in, there is no enormity from which maddened human nature will recoil.[347]**

Still, the IMRO did commit killings that were not conscionable and were against the proper conduct of war. For example, it was reported that IMRO bands slaughtered much of the remaining Turkish Muslim population in Kenati, near Monastir.[348] In a village near Kostur, they buried alive a Greek priest with only his head kept above ground. In other villages they tortured and then killed some

Greek school teachers.[349] For the most part, however, IMRO acted with dignity, courage and respect for life and property. There were very few cases of looting, pillaging, raping or murder.

IMRO's uprising was also praised for being all inclusive of all ethnic and religious groups. Even Serbian Orthodox priests from Macedonia joined IMRO on the Ilinden Uprising. One was Toma Nikoloff of Kichevo. His motive for joining IMRO was not dissimilar to most people's motives: Turkish atrocities and injustices. A girl from his local church had been kidnapped by Turks and her parents begged him to intercede in bringing her back home. When he did, the abductor and the girl appeared in court, but she was dressed in Turkish garb and declared herself a Muslim out of fear. He complained to higher officials but was denounced and arrested by Turkish authorities. First, they imprisoned him in Kichevo for eight months, and then transferred him to a prison in Bitola for five months. Facing a second arrest for treason and other bogus charges, he escaped to the mountains and joined IMRO.[350]

As emphasized, not all Macedonians supported the Uprising, even though they participated in it. Sandanski's, Petrov's and Delchev's opposition has been made quite clear. But there were several others. Krste Misirkov – considered one of the fathers of the standard Macedonian language – called the Uprising a "complete fiasco" and that the little gains made by the rebels could not justify the number of homeless and dead. "What has been gained might have been gained without a drop of blood being shed."[351] However, Misirkov did acknowledge that one of the "more worthwhile results" of the Uprising was that it "prevented Macedonia from being partitioned,"[352] at least temporarily.

Still, the failure of the Macedonian uprising had the consequence of further deepening the divisions amongst the Macedonians. Despite their disagreements, they had managed to unite around the common aim of freedom and independence in a unified assault on the Sultan. But in defeat, the Macedonians fractured and turned against each other, sealing the fate of the Macedonian movement for the next three decades.

VI.

Macedonia Between Left and Right

After the failure of the Ilinden Uprising, the rift between IMRO and SMAC widened. Much of IMRO's leadership had been consumed by SMAC loyalists and IMRO was being torn into two groups: the "left wing" and the "right wing." The left-wing was comprised of the socialists and social-anarchists who strived for an independent Macedonia, with the potential to join a Balkan confederation on equal standing with other Balkan states. They were also more hesitant to rush into war than the right-wing. The right-wing, on the other hand, wanted Macedonia to be incorporated into Bulgaria as a province, or they supported an autonomous Macedonia but looked to Bulgaria for support. This rivalry between the two factions quickly evolved into a bloodbath, which further complicated a Macedonian scene that was already under siege by the Turkish army and bashibazouks, as well as Bulgarian, Greek and Serbian armed bands.

Not every Macedonian, of course, fit neatly into these two categories. There were opportunists who forwent ideology and believed in using any means to achieve freedom; there were those whose ideologies were not formed; there were those who believed more in working with the system rather than against the system; and there were those who straddled the middle ground.

But throughout Europe there was a socialist-versus-bourgeois movement that had been raging for decades. Serbia, Bulgaria, Macedonia, Turkey, Greece, Romania, Croatia, Russia – all of these nations were having these internal battles (Macedonia, to a lesser extent, as the Macedonians were essentially peasants fighting the ruling Turks). These agendas and ideologies knew no borders. For example, the Russian socialists and anarchists cooperated with Macedonians to share tactics on defeating the ruling class. A Russian revolutionary organization, the Combat Technical Group, sent an agent in 1905 to learn bomb-making techniques from Naum Tiufekchiev, who was considered "a talented innovator in combat technology." For many years, these Russian Bolshevists would collaborate with Tiufekchiev and his squad of socio-anarchist Macedonians on such matters. Several of Tiufekchiev's Macedonians often traveled to Russia after this contact to establish laboratories and shops for manufacturing explosive devices. The experience that Tiufekchiev brought in terrorism against Turkish authorities was highly prized amongst the Russian revolutionaries.[353]

Although the Macedonians were primarily concerned with freedom of their nation, after the revolution was crushed, the different Macedonian factions were blaming each other for the failures of the Ilinden Uprising. Just as importantly, they disagreed on how to proceed now that their movement had suffered serious setbacks. Macedonians began killing Macedonians, and Serbian, Greek and Bulgarian bands threw themselves into the mix, attacking Macedonians and each other.[354]

Sandanski placed the blame squarely on the right-wing Macedonians, calling them traitors of the Macedonian Cause:

We are being accused of cruelty, ferocity and ruthlessness. Yes, we are cruel, we are fierce and ruthless, but only towards spies, towards the enemies of the Cause of Liberation. There is no mercy and forgiveness for such people: for them there is only one punishment, only one reward—"Death". Death to the spies, death to the traitors, death to all who stand in the way of the Cause![355]

Sandanski was furious at the right's wavering allegiances, and for the next ten years he and his loyal followers kept up the Cause for a free and independent Macedonia despite a strong Bulgarian-backed resistance. In his later years, he knew that his fierce opposition to right-wing Macedonians and Bulgaria would cost him his life. He had been a target of the SMAC Macedonians – and now their right-wing derivatives – ever since he joined the revolutionary movement as an ally of Delchev and Petrov. He expressed his acceptance of looming death to his friends:

I am a marked man. Sometime or other they will kill me. There's no point in taking care. Even if I did take care, one day, when I'm drinking coffee, some guttersnipe will come, primed with the idea that I am to blame—let us say—for Macedonia not

being free, or for something else, and, without my even suspecting him, he'll shoot me from behind.[356]

But a lot was to happen before the Macedonian revolution would fraction to the point where its most revered leaders would be taken so cruelly from it. The year was now 1904 and the Macedonians had much work to do. Take Gruev, for example, who, after the failure of Ilinden Uprising, toured Macedonia's villages disarming the insurgents. He reasoned that IMRO needed to enter a rebuilding stage and should stock up for a future rebellion.[357] Removing guns from the populace would ensure both that the weapons were secured from Turkish raids and that local populaces would not engage in small rebellions that would be destined to fail and only cause greater Turkish reprisals, once again pushing back revolutionary efforts. Like Sandanski, Gruev was disheartened by traitors to the cause. He once told his comrades that the Macedonians' strength did not lie in its armed capabilities, but rather "in the loyalty of the people."[358]

After the revolution, the Macedonian masses put their faith and hope in Sandanski and Gruev, especially now that Delchev had been removed from the movement. Sandanski and Gruev were idolized for good reason – these men were not only heroic rebels, but idealists whose vision for a future society corresponded with that of the masses. Dr. E.J. Dillon wrote the following about Gruev:

Like Pompey of old, he has only to stamp on the ground to summon bodies of armed men to appear and follow him. His flow of eloquence is said to be as irresistible as were the magic sounds of the pipe of the Hamelin rat-catcher. He can lead his peasants to the jaws of death, and they march on blithely singing war songs. In this way he has persuaded thousands of very hard-headed men to leave their houses, their crops, and their families, and to risk their lives in a supreme and desperate effort to shake off the yoke of the Turk.

The 'Macedonian Garibaldi' is the nickname which this demagogue has received, and he certainly has not usurped it. He possesses the invaluable gift of making his hearers see things as he himself views them, and of communicating to them the fire that burns within him. His eloquence is thrilling, his enthusiasm infectious, his appeal irresistible. He is a

sympathetic, fiery-eyed, brown-skinned man of about thirty-three years, whose short career has been characterized by daring ventures and remarkable escapes. He knows his country and his people better than any of his fellow-compatriots, and is adored by the masses, who look up to him as to their savior.[359]

Sandanski, too, had won a favorable impression of the masses for his own traits and qualities. For example, unlike the mode of the times, he never smoked and seldom consumed alcohol. He was always "frugal in his habits" and "thrift to the point of fanaticism."[360] Mercia MacDermott writes:

> Of all the numberless converts that Gotsé [Goce Delchev] brought to the Cause, none was so undeviating in his allegiance, none so faithful unto death, as Yané [Jane Sandanski]. There was in Yané's character a powerful mixture of integrity, vision and sheer obstinacy, which, once he had set his mind to the plough, forbade him to turn back, no matter how interminable the task, or how arduous the conditions. And, because he could never be content with half-measures, or lull his conscience into accepting a fraction for the whole, it was with an act of searing renunciation that he now re-dedicated his life to the service of the Cause...
>
> Yané never married. Once, when he was already a voivoda, a woman relative happened to notice him at a window of the Harizanovs' house in Dupnitsa, intently watching a passing wedding procession from behind the lace curtains. She was both surprised and disconcerted to see that there were tears running down his cheeks, and she later told her daughter that Yané must surely have been feeling oppressed by the hard way of life that he had chosen.[361]

Sandanski believed in sacrificing his life for the Macedonian Cause, because the Macedonian Cause had become his life. The Macedonian masses respected and admired his sacrifices for their nation.

Even though Gruev and Sandanski found themselves as two of the larger-than-life champions of the left-wing faction of the Macedonian Cause following Ilinden – two of many notable Macedonians who sacrificed the normalcies and pleasures of life for their land, their countrymen and their ideals – most left-wing and moderate IMRO members were revered for how they conducted themselves throughout their stints as rebels. One author explained:

> They are a race by themselves – these Macedonia chetniks. All young, hardy, and intelligent...Since the days of the crusades, of Coeur de Lion and Canderbeg, no more romantic type has evolved itself in the tangled meshes of the world's history. Their lives are dedicated to their country. They do not know the meaning of the word fear; in a sense this is literal, for I have spent several hours trying to impress upon one of them a definition of the word...Among each other, they are wonderfully gentle...But it is in time of battle they show up to best advantage. There seems to be an unwritten code among them, that no man is to consider his own life, when the life of a comrade is in peril. And what magnificent fighters they are! It is a sight such as makes life worth living, to see one of them holding off three askares [enemies] from a wounded comrade. The Turks fear them with a fear that is often comic...
>
> In their outward appearance, it is true, the chetniks are more like the brigands of the stage, than modern soldiers. They wear their hair long, in flowing locks, of which they are very proud and take great care. They keep their weapons in perfect order, and like to carry as many revolvers and knives as they can find room for in their belts – not for effect, let it be understood, but because the more revolvers a man has, the more shots he has at his disposal in a melee...
>
> In many ways, too, they are nothing but schoolboys, reckless, volatile, quick-tempered, and whimsical...Most of them are handsome beggars, and they know it; their muscles are hardened and their frames trained down to the last ounce of flesh. But they care nothing for women. Such as their married seldom see their families after they have dedicated their lives to Macedonia. Their wives and children are looked after by relatives, willing to help along the holy purpose of fighting the Turk. The pleasure of the flesh have small hold on a chetnik. I have never seen one drunk and they do not even use tobacco inordinately.[362]

However, the right-wing was not as adorned by the local communities in Macedonia during this period. This right wing was being led by the pro-Bulgarian element, such as Garvanov and Tsonchev; long-time IMRO leaders, Tatarchev and Matov; and the unpredictable but charming Sarafov, who seemed to have been constantly changing his allegiances. Hristo Uzunov, who had been an IMRO leader in western Macedonia, despised Sarafov and voiced the general Macedonian view about him at that time in a letter he wrote while death was waiting for him. Uzunov and his men had been surrounded by an impenetrable number of Turkish soldiers on April 11, 1905, and Uzunov made sure to call for Sarafov's death in his final remarks:

> **My final advice to all comrades is this: let all those who serve the Cause be devoted to it, because devotion and purity of heart alone raised the Internal Organization, and they will also save it from the abnormality into which it has now been driven by our unscrupulous comrades. See to it that you annihilate as soon as possible those hitherto leading forces in the Organization who have inflicted damage upon the Cause, like Sarafov, and don't punish only simple workers.**[363]

In a village, outside of Kichevo, Uzunov killed himself after his comrades died and the Turkish soldiers encircled him.[364] His letter, however, survived to make its impact on his fellow Macedonian followers.

Uzunov's views were an echo of Gruev's beliefs about Sarafov. Gruev's secretary told a news correspondent:

> **There are Bulgarian politicians who are no more our friends than are the Greeks. Under the names of well-known chiefs, they try to send bands into Macedonia to agitate for the annexation idea. What more natural than that we should order them out when they appear? And if they, feeling secure in being of our own flesh and blood, defy us, what can we do but drive them out? There is only room here for one organization, and that is the people's organization. Neither Tsoncheff nor Sarafoff have been elected by the people; and if they try to come over here to assume arbitrary power by force of arms, we,**

representing the people, must meet them with the same force they present against us.[365]

While the IMRO always had an uneasy relationship with Sarafov and the SMAC – who often found themselves on opposing sides, too – the mood of the left-wing Macedonians drastically shifted after the Ilinden failure. At an IMRO meeting in early 1904 in Sofia, IMRO clearly drew their lines. Tatarchev, Matov, Sandanski, Sarafov and Hadzhidimov were all present. The right-wing was headed by Tatarchev and Matov, who wanted to maintain the existing leadership of the organization (with Tsonchev and Garvanov in high positions). The left-wing was headed by the revolutionaries from the Serres district (such as Sandanski) and by several other distinguished revolutionaries. The left-wing demanded changes in the initial structure of the organization and would not cede until IMRO was decentralized and given a more democratic overhaul. Instead of a three-man committee making all the decisions, they wanted to distribute decision-making powers to local committees and individuals. They primarily wanted protection from repeating past mistakes that Garvanov and Sarafov created, and they wanted better implementation of revolutionary tasks.[366]

At that meeting, much of the left-wing's platform prevailed. There was a general recognition that reconstruction and consolidation of IMRO could only happen if each revolutionary district held congresses in democratic arenas for electing leadership. The first one took place in Prilep, in May of 1904, for the District of Bitola, and stark differences once again emerged. This time Gruev shifted to a more moderate stance to bring the two sides together by advocating for less decentralization, while Petrov and Toshev were adamant about keeping IMRO decentralized and democratic. These differences played out across Macedonia until the IMRO met again at a Congress at Rila monastery in October of 1905, where tensions boiled over. Tatarchev and Matov were not allowed at the meeting, but their views and voices were represented by Sarafov and his associates. The left-wing was represented by Toshev, Sandanski, Dimov, and Petrov. The Congress requested that Tsonchev disband SMAC, and Sarafov was severely deplored for accepting money from the Serbian government in return for allowing Serbian troops to enter into Macedonia. Sarafov was "sentenced to death on probation."[367]

Evtim Sprostranov, a vehement adherent of Dame Gruev, was elected to the Central Committee.[368]

Petrov continued his relentless ideological assault on pro-Bulgarian elements throughout this period. In his work, "On the Aims, Means and Tasks of the Macedonian Liberation Movement", he wrote:

> **We should be wary of any direct or indirect attempts by any government to become involved in our affairs as much because of the danger of a bad interpretation from outside as from the point of view of our ideology. We should be deliberately careful and wary in our relations with official Bulgaria because it is a thorn in the side of everyone interested in our problems and struggle and, above all other, she could become for us a wolf which has entered our fold.**[369]

After the Rila Congress, however, the right-wing reorganized and oriented itself to being even more pro-Bulgarian while labeling the left-wing as anti-Bulgarian. Moreover, the left-wing was ridiculed for being internationalist, Marxist, socialistic and anarchistic in their outlook and ideology. With the support of the Bulgarian government, the right-wing Macedonians waged a new battle against the left-wing. They seceded from IMRO and took the well-recognized and revered IMRO name with them. Moreover, they began plotting to assassinate the left-wing leaders, and Sandanski was at the top of the list.[370]

This right-wing sentiment had been simmering since the mid-1890s, when SMAC aimed to eliminate those Macedonians who sought independence and opposed annexation to Bulgaria. Tsonchev constantly and tirelessly worked to annex Macedonia to Bulgaria, and stated that this could be the only solution to the Macedonian question. To do this, since 1901, after Sarafov fell from grace with Bulgaria and SMAC, he waged a war also ridding SMAC and IMRO of its pro-independence and autonomist Macedonians. After Ilinden, his targets were the most dedicated independence seekers and leftists: Sandanski and Chernopeev. As on author described:

> **Two IMRO members who refused to abandon the cause of Macedonian independence were Yani Sandanski, a former school teacher, a socialist, and a veteran revolutionary, and**

Hristo Tchernopeef, a rugged chetnik chieftain. Both were...fanatical autonomists...'Tsontcheff's rank impudence was backed by Ferdinand's gold,' Tchernopeef later wrote, 'and with the pretense of revolution he began sending big, armed bands across the frontier to oust us out of our rayons [fortified camps].'[371]

When the right-wing could not root out Sandanski, they went after his allies. For example, in late March of 1906, right-wing leaders, Stojko and Risto, led a group of about a dozen men dressed in Bulgarian army uniforms into the village of Libolka, near Serres. They specifically targeted the house of Angel Mencho, who had once harbored Sandanski. Angel was not home, so they burned his house along with the surrounding homes. They forced Angel's wife and two daughters – aged eight and three – to lie down on the floors of one of the houses already burning. "A French gendarmerie officer who afterwards visited the village found among the ruins some human teeth and bits of calcined bones."[372]

Divides were not just created based on ideology and goals, but also on methods. While annexation to Bulgaria was advocated by some right-wing Macedonian leaders, the heart of the question for many IMRO members was not whether Macedonia should be independent, but on how IMRO should proceed. There were a variety of views. One right-wing member, speaking from Sofia in 1906, urged tactics that would cause wide scale massacres so Europe would intervene:

> If there are any Greeks or Bulgarians who check us, they must be removed in the interests of Macedonian independence. The time for argument is gone. We shall run no risk from traitors...I know Europe is getting sick of the Macedonian muddle. But Europe has got to be stirred. The only thing to stir it to interfere and take Macedonia from Turkey will be a great massacre of Christians. This is the way by which Macedonia will get its liberation.[373]

Still, while small, the pro-Bulgarian element on the right was strong and influential. Much of this division, of course, stems from when Garvanov was an influential leader of SMAC. He had promised Tsonchev that if he was head of IMRO's Central

Committee, he would oust the autonomist Macedonians and those who did not want IMRO involved with SMAC. When he became a member of the Central Committee, he ousted Delchev and Petrov as delegates. This fueled Delchev and Petrov – and subsequently Sandanski and Chernopeev – to be left-wing leaders against the Bulgarian intrusion into the IMRO.[374]

Boris Sarafov's strategy was especially worrying to the left-wing. Sarafov never showed a strong attachment to the pro-Bulgarian element – he was a rogue element who sided with whoever offered him and his cause the most benefits. His sometimes extreme positions stoked fear that his methods would cause just as much devastation to the Macedonians as it would to the Turks. For example

> **[Sarafov] established a policy in two parts for fighting the Turk. The first principle was that a guerrilla war must be waged tirelessly, in which all Macedonia should be finally forced to join. But a guerrilla war against the Turks would never reach anywhere of itself. Therefore, the second principle followed — that the Balkans must be embroiled and mutilated in such a shocking way that the powers would be forced to attend to the Turk. This is the principle which is desperate and relentless, and which wounds Macedonia as deeply as it wounds the Turk. It has been named "Sarafoffism" in Europe. Its only excuse is fierce enthusiasm for liberty, but it is for liberty bought at a price as heavy to the Christian as to the Moslem.[375]**

"Sarafovism" had been raging since he became involved in the Macedonian movement in 1895. He had toured Austria, Hungary, Switzerland, France, England, and Russia, among other places, pleading on behalf of Macedonia, even when he was not acting as an official IMRO representative. For a while, his main gigue was to hold interviews with newspapers and raise money. He often boasted about his relevance to the Macedonian Cause. He would tell newspapers about his sway in Geneva, saying: "I complained to an Englishman about our conditions in Macedonia and he twice gave me 8000 Turkish liras, requesting me not to reveal his name."

But this was Sarafov – his personality attracted media attention and he brought in money for the Cause. Further, he was always full of ideas. In 1897 he visited the U.S. consul in St Petersburg and "offered his services with five hundred Macedonians to assist the American army against Spain." Sarafov explained:

> **The Spanish-American war was then in progress. I wished to manifest our sympathy with the Cubans. I intended with five or six hundred men, to join the American army so that we might be able, in return for our services, to acquire means to arm ourselves…The American Consul at St. Petersburg told me that they had no pressing need for men. He listened to my offers with kindness.**[376]

In the winter after Ilinden, Sarafov was so upset with the Christian Orthodox countries, especially Russia, for not offering the Macedonians assistance in their fight against the Turks, that he suggested that the Macedonians should become part of either the Catholic church or the Protestant church. Of course, Macedonians had attached themselves to the Orthodox Church(es), not so much for religious and spiritual reasons, but as a significant marker of their identity and way of life that distinguished them from the Turks.[377] To many Macedonians, Sarafov and his methods were too abrasive and controversial. His lavish and larger-than-life European lifestyle also removed him from the comprehension and sympathies of the peasants, who were poor and desperate. Delchev, Sandanski, Petrov and Gruev were leaders that the masses could rally behind, because they were like peasants and of the peasants. Sarafov did not help his reputation with his greedy nature: he was continually accused of stealing and misappropriating IMRO funds for his personal gain.

Of course, these were not the only Macedonians working the revolutionary and political scene in Macedonia. It is impossible to comprehensively detail the individuals, organizations and movements influencing the situation at the time. But some were more notable than others, not just for what they did at the moment, but for how they would insert themselves into the cause in the future. For example, in 1904, Protogerov – a future IMRO leader who would often find himself on different sides of the IMRO division – founded a club in Solun known as The Red Brothers:

> **The aims of its members were limited – to assassinate the King of Bulgaria and the King of Serbia. For the assassination of Kings money is necessary, and the club raised its funds from**

interested countries. When funds were required it would invent two fictitious emissaries bound for murder abroad. These emissaries having been denounced, they would hold them and the governments concerned would show their gratitude accordingly. [378]

These plans never blossomed, but another Macedonian group's plans almost succeeded in shaking the entire European political scene. In the summer of 1905, several Macedonian insurgents attempted to kill the Sultan in Istanbul:

> **The infernal machine which killed so many men and horses and destroyed so many vehicles was exploded by a clockwork apparatus, set to act at the moment when the Sultan was due to descend from the steps of the mosque on Friday. The machine was placed in a cab, which was drawn up in the line of vehicles as near as possible to the carriage of the Sultan, who had a narrow escape, one of his aids-de-camp and the tutor of his sons being killed on the spot.**[379]

Killing the Sultan would have been a major boost to the morale of the Macedonian populace and would have potentially resulted in the demise of the Turkish state. Many left-wing Turks were also pushing for a revolution and would have likely seized on this moment to grab power. However, favorable conditions for the Young Turks – as these left-wing Turks were known – was not quite cemented.

Meanwhile, back in Macedonia, rebel bands were still organizing and constantly engaging Turks, Bulgars, Serbs and Greeks. While the majority of rebel fighters were young men, some women had gained notoriety for their bravery and dedication to the cause as rebels. For instance, take the story of Marija Kainjardi. A couple years after the failed Ilinden Uprising, her sweetheart, Anton Armensko, was leaving from Sofia to be second-in-command of a band of rebels in his native Macedonia. On the night that he had left, he asked Marija, "are you not just a little sorry I am going away?" "No," replied Marija. "For I shall be with you."

Anton laughed this off, said goodbye and went on his way into Macedonia, recruiting several young fighters. When he presented the troops to his band's leader, the leader asked him to vouch for all the soldiers. As Anton reexamined his recruits, especially looking to see if any were Albanian spies, he noticed that one was quite boyish looking. As he looked into his eyes, he realized it was Marija. Although her presence surprised him, he did not tell his commanding officer and instead vouched for all of the recruits. After three days of marching, he found an opportunity to talk with Marija.

> 'Why shouldn't I be a soldier?' she asked him. 'I am alone. My father and my two brothers were soldiers and they were killed by Turks. My mother was killed. Don't you see why I hate the Turks? Haven't I a good cause? And besides,' she said. 'I wanted to be with you.'

From then on, the two lovers fought side-by-side in Macedonia against the Turkish forces. Her secret had been exposed when she was shot near the chest and her other comrades realized that she was not a man; but they did not mind, as she built a reputation of being an extremely valuable member of their band. Soon after, Anton was injured when their detachment lost a battle with the Turks. Marija tended to him as he lay dying on the field. But the Turkish soldiers soon came and started massacring the wounded soldiers. They let Marija live when the Turkish commander realized she was a lady. But Marija had little will left to live – her family had already been exterminated, and she had just lost the love of her life.

The Turks took her captive after killing all the other prisoners, except for one other – who also happened to be a woman fighter dressed in men's clothing, and who also was forced to watch her sweetheart murdered by the Turks. The Turks desired to ship them to Istanbul for the slave market. However, Marija and the other girl escaped by killing the lackadaisical guards and fled into the mountains. Instead of going back into Bulgaria for safety, the two young ladies stayed in the mountains of Macedonia for three months, exacting their revenge on Turkish soldiers. They worked together and with no one else. Marija killed no less than a dozen Turkish soldiers in those three months, and finally made her way into Sofia. Among her possessions upon arriving into Bulgaria was arsenic, which she had acquired to use had she been recaptured by the Turks.[380]

Another Macedonian rebel woman was Kristina Atanova. In 1905, at the age of 26, she enlisted as a Macedonian rebel. She had formerly been a school teacher, but a band of irregular Turkish troops massacred many of her students. This barbarity ignited a fury in her; she gave up teaching and "pledged her life for her country," evolving "into an expert guerrilla fighter." One correspondent wrote of Atanova:

> **Miss Atanova is known to all the revolutionists as the 'Mascot of Macedonia,' for whenever she is with a band she brings luck. Miss Atanova is a crack shot, and has killed five Turks in small skirmishes, besides having participated in several battles.**[381]

But even with a plethora of fearless and dedicated revolutionaries, the post-Ilinden fight was tough and slow. With an increasing ferocity by Greek armed bands – and Turkish soldiers heavy on their tails – the Macedonians were bound to suffer irreparable losses. One of these was the loss of Gruev in December of 1906 in a village outside of Maleshevko.[382] He and his men were given up to the Turkish authorities by a traitor:

> **His little escort of eight men was lying for the night in the hut of a Greek shepherd...It was bitter cold, or they would have slept out of doors, as is the usual custom of the insurgents. They trusted the Greek because he had received kindnesses from them, in the past, and had always pleaded friendship, unlike most of his countrymen...The Greek gave the chetniks goat's milk and sireny, the white cheese of the country, and when they were settled to sleep, he slipped out to watch his flock, he said. But he travelled as rapidly as he could through the thick snow, to the nearest Turkish outpost, and at dawn the askares broke from the forest edge, upon the hut in which lay Grueff and his men.**

> **The fight was short and sharp. Outnumbered as they were, the chentiks smashed a hole in the Turkish ranks with well-aimed volley from their Mannlichers...A last, when only four were left, a bullet struck Grueff in the thigh. The wound bled freely, but he could walk, and his comrades begged to be permitted to stay with him. He refused. He knew that the askares would have no trouble following the trail left by his bloody bandages, and he gave his men strict orders to leave him, and make their way to the place where the congress was to meet. 'Ask their blessing**

for me,' he said. 'Leave me as many cartridges as you can spare and go.' They went – weeping.[383]

Gruev's death was a huge blow to IMRO's goals, especially to the left-wing Macedonians and autonomists. Gruev's camp had wanted to suspend revolutionary activity because the population was exhausted and the political scene in Europe was unfavorable. The right-wing Macedonians wanted to continue revolution until exasperation. The annual IMRO Congress in January of 1907 was supposed to be where the left-wing Macedonians finally ousted the right-wing Macedonians and pro-Bulgarians from the internal revolutionary movement, but Gruev's death hampered this. Matters quickly spiraled out of control to the point where the left-wing Macedonians boycotted the Congress and IMRO was completely taken over by the right-wing.[384]

Furthermore, and unfortunately, traitors to the Cause only became more common. Several Macedonians could not withstand the constant pressure and perseverance of the Turkish authorities. In June of 1907, Georgi Katibov, who was considered quite the notorious IMRO rebel, and Anton Panteli turned themselves into authorities in Vrandi. They confessed many names and activities to the authorities, including Dimitri Trendafil, the village teacher in Vrandi, and Jovan Gilo Mihal – both were local IMRO chiefs. Villagers corroborated Katibov's and Panteli's story, accusing the IMRO chiefs of storing arms and ammunition and sheltering IMRO rebels.[385]

Panteli and Katibov were released and were accompanied home to Vrandi by a contingent of Turkish soldiers on July 5th. As Panteli was having dinner with his family the next day, "several men, initially unidentified, entered his house and opened fire, killing him." His killers were identified as Tashko, a miller, who pulled the trigger, Jovan Savati and Vasil, a shopkeeper and shepherd from Vrandi. Savati recruited Tashko and Vasil, but Tashko was the main culprit:

> **Tashko was seen acting suspiciously on the day that Anton and Georgi arrived in the village. Even though he should have been at work, either at the mill or in his field, he idled around the village all day, briefly went into Anton's house, and came out. He then searched for Georgi and ran into him walking back**

home from the marketplace. He said, "I am coming too," and joined Georgi on his walk. When they reached his home, Georgi said goodbye, but instead of leaving, Tashko stood by and waited in a bizarre manner, "twisting his moustache," until Georgi finally went inside and closed the door. As he was going in, Tashko said "oh well, we'll see each other tomorrow, right?"

Tashko reportedly went over to Yovan Savati's store right after this incident. Savati then closed down his shop early and disappeared. Tashko was later spotted in the village walking about aimlessly. After sunset, he walked to Anton's house, pushed open the unlocked door, and went up and joined the family at the table and had some raki. As they were still eating, he got up and "against established customes," noted the report, left the family at the table. He went downstairs, but nobody heard the door open and close. The attack took place while the family was still at the dinner table.[386]

Katibov survived an attempt on his life, although his friend was killed. Still, Katibov climbed the Turkish social ladder and was made a police officer as a reward for informing the Turkish authorities.[387] However, Mihal and Trendafil – the two chiefs Katibov betrayed – faced the ultimate penalty – death. After their arrests, a trial took place and the date of the execution was to be on October 31st, 1907 at 6:30 am. Two Roma (then known as gypsies) erected the gallows, and the prisoners had to climb onto a stool that was on a table. Major Foulon gave the details:

After passing around their neck a rope coated with soap and oil they toppled the table and the stool, as a result of this fall from about a meter, death should be almost instantaneous, in any case, no convulsions were observed on either of the corpses. After a display of three hours, during which a large group of people – where the Christian element was scarcely represented – went around the gallows, the corpses were placed in caskets. The mutasarrif himself came to the place and lectured the crowd, essentially telling them that from that moment on, the imperial government which until then had shown much leniency toward the troublemakers was firmly resolved to let the people who had been convicted of crimes such as be executed.[388]

The cycle of eradicating traitors was gaining momentum and the most consequential death executed by the left-wing happened in 1907 and was committed by Sandanski's lieutenant, Todor Panica.[389] Panica had spent some time befriending Sarafov and Garvanov and one day invited them over to his house for dinner.[390] After finishing their meal, Panica shot both men in the head, Garvanov dying immediately and Sarafov succumbing to his injuries about a half-hour later. Rumors surfaced that Sandanski ordered Panica to kill Sarafov in exchange for compensation by the Turkish authorities because Sarafov was planning a new campaign against the Turkish government.[391] But Sandanski's faction claimed that Sarafov was gunned down for misappropriating $100,000 from the IMRO war chest. Sarafov's allies countered this by exclaiming the funds were "honestly expended in preparing the spring uprising and that friends and foes alike knew exactly how it was used."[392] One American author wrote in 1908: "It had been absolutely proved that he [Sarafov] embezzled $100,000 of the organization funds, a large sum in the Balkans, but the band of cut-throats that owned his sway, was so devoted that none dare move against him. He was too valuable to the Prince's government for it to assist efforts to bring him to justice."[393]

Sandanski began to deal with traitors in a merciless manner. As MacDermott describes:

Yane lived and worked in a hard and ruthless environment, full of enemies of all kinds, and therefore he himself was hard and ruthless, notwithstanding his undying devotion to the compassionate and all-forgiving Gotse. Yane never forgave a traitor and was utterly uncompromising in his attitude towards enemies. He himself admitted that he could never rest until blood had been avenged with blood... He never punished without incontrovertible proof of guilt...but, where such guilt was proven, he would never temper the law with mercy.[394]

It was not long after Sarafov's death that the Young Turk movement reached its zenith. Sandanski was a significant part of this Turkish Uprising originating in Macedonia that was focused against the Ottoman leadership. The Young Turks promised equality for all ethnic and religious groups, as well as a socialist platform that Sandanski and the left-wing Macedonians could stand behind. Further, with the flood of Greek, Bulgarian and Serbian bands into Macedonia, the left-wing Macedonians saw union with the socialist Turks as the best way to protect Macedonia's integrity as an autonomous unit. Many left-wing Macedonians aligned with the Young Turks. For example, Naum Tiufekchiev returned to Macedonia specifically to work with Sandanski and Young Turk leaders, such as Niyazi Bey and Enver Bey.

However, the right-wing Macedonians – and several moderate Macedonians – were outraged by Sandanski's alliance with socialist Turks. Many of the Young Turks' leaders had significant positions in the Ottoman government, and the right-wing Macedonians viewed them just as much as Macedonia's enemy as the Sultan himself. They did not trust the Young Turk movement; and more importantly, they considered Sandanski's alliance with them an act of treason and betrayal.

During the Young Turk revolution, one of IMRO's three Committee leaders was Christo Matov. Under his command, IMRO was officially disintegrated in 1908 at the March Congress of Kyustendil.[395] Evtim Sprostranov, for his part, pushed to heal the divide between the left and right and to focus the Macedonians' agenda on fighting propaganda emanating from neighboring countries, but his unification call was to no avail.[396] Sandanski had been ejected from the IMRO and Matov had become opposed to Sandanski, aiming to finally rid him from the Macedonian movement. When Macedonians were granted political rights in the autumn, public political campaigning became a new freedom for the Macedonians. Matov saw an opportunity to cut into Sandanski's remaining left-wing stronghold. Sandanski warned the Young Turks to not let Matov campaign in the Serres district, as that was his camp's last bastion of control. The Young Turks failed to influence Matov to not to campaign there. Therefore, Sandanski's "men shot down five of the Matoffists, killing three of them."[397]

The left-wing Macedonians, however, began making other inroads. Several prominent Macedonian men formed the 'Popular Federal Party'. These men included Dimiter Vlahov, Todor Panica and Hadji Dimov. They advocated for the use of the Macedonian dialects to be used in Ottoman schools.[398] They also hoped to use more peaceful methods to bring about cultural and political freedom for the Macedonians. But there was to be no peace between the rivaling Macedonian parties. At midnight on a late August Saturday in 1909, a shot rang out in Solun and a bullet pierced the chest of Sandanski. Sarafov loyalists had aimed to avenge Sarafov's murder two years prior. Fortunately, Sandanski survived.[399]

Several Macedonians had opposed Sandanski before Sarafov's murder, but several more opposed him afterwards. Only a select few, however, were willing to go through with murdering him. One of the main opponents of Sandanski was Simeon Radev. He was opposed to Sandanski both for ideological reasons and because of the murder of Sarafov, with whom Radev had been closely associated. Panica almost eliminated Radev as he did Sarafov, but a Young Turk leader, Enver Pasha, intervened.

Meanwhile, while the IMRO divides and factional rivalry were continuing to play out, bands of Macedonians began attacking the new Young Turk government because, not only had it failed to deliver on reforms, but the new Turkish leaders began a national campaign of Ottomanization, attempting to make all ethnic groups part of one Ottoman identity. Not only did many right-wing Macedonians now see Sandanski as a traitor – or at least a fool – for having trusted the Turks, they were intent on starting another war with the Turks. In the village of Konare, Macedonians bombed the seat of government; in the stations of Zelenich near Skopje and Kilindir near Kukush, stations and police posts were bombed; in Dojran, a train was attacked with dynamite; in Veles, the freight depot was destroyed; and plenty of bombing outrages against Turkish authorities occurred in Radovich, Bitola, Ohrid, Kavardarci, Prilep, Krushevo, Kitchevo, Solun, Dojran, Shtip, and Kochani.[400]

These Macedonian bombings accumulated and the Turks began reacting out of proportion. Two bombings in particular provoked widespread massacres by the Turks, a reaction for which the right-wing had been waiting:

On December 11, 1911, a bomb exploded in a mosque at Shtip...wounding several people. The Muslim population attacked...killing 25, wounding 169. On August 1, 1912, bombs were also set off in the bazar of Kotchana, an important trading

center...in the resulting general massacre 150 persons were killed and more than 250 wounded.[401]

Meanwhile, in addition to being a target for Sarafov's murder, Sandanski was now being targeted by right-wing Macedonians for his ties to the Young Turks. In February of 1910, one of Sandanski's captains, Jovan Jovanovich, was murdered by a group of these Macedonians. Jovanovich was a Montenegrin who had become loyal to Sandanski and Panica, and had also been the inspector for the Christian schools in Macedonia. He fought in the Young Turk movement against the Sultan and was rewarded with the position of school inspector in Bitola under the Turkish government, even though he was uneducated. The right-wing Macedonians considered him "less successful as an official than as a propagandist of the doctrines of Sandansky and Panitsa."[402] They were also angered by him because they claimed he was trying to extort money from IMRO rebel leaders.[403]

Thus, they invited Jovanovich to one of their homes one night, where a gang of men stabbed him to death and then cut his body into several pieces. The Turkish courts sentenced eight men to death over the killings because they found that the real motive for his murder was not his attempt to extort money, but was instead part of the right-wing's assault to rid Macedonia of its autonomist leaders who would not cave into their leaders.[404]

Macedonia's neighbors realized that the time was ripe to take advantage of the anarchy in Macedonia. In 1912, Bulgaria, Greece, Montenegro and Serbia teamed up with Macedonia's revolutionaries to remove the Ottoman Empire from Europe. On the eve of this war, a famous Macedonian leader named Todor Lazaroff killed himself. He had desired to enroll into the ranks of the Bulgarian army so he could help free Macedonia from the Ottoman grip, but the military doctors denied him this opportunity because he was battling a severe case of tuberculosis. In his suicide note he wrote that he "could not remain behind to die in bed while his brothers were fighting for liberty."[405]

Many of his Macedonian brothers fought and died for that liberty in the battalions of the Bulgarian army, as well as in the Serbian and Greek armies. The Macedonians thought that – despite their previous attempts to take over Macedonia – their neighbors would secure

Macedonia's freedom and liberation. The Ottoman Empire was defeated within a few months, and now several Balkan armies controlled Macedonian territories. After the Bulgarian army's victory near Solun, Sandanski gave a toast to the army in which he said he hoped Macedonia would now be able to achieve its final goal of independence. Prince Ferdinand of Bulgaria had different plans and ordered him killed.[406] Bulgaria now maintained control of a portion of Macedonia, and the Prince did not want the concept of an independent Macedonia to take root, lest it ruin Bulgaria's chances of acquiring the rest of Macedonia from Greece and Serbia.

Prior to this First Balkan War, Bulgaria's negotiations for a Balkan Union, and her treaties with Greece and Serbia to divide Macedonia, went by unknown to the Macedonians. After concluding in March of 1912 a treaty with Serbia, Bulgaria decided to enter into a treaty with Greece. Even though the Greeks had been an age-old enemy, Bulgaria needed Greece's navy in the Mediterranean to fight off Turkey. Essentially, they agreed on no boundaries, only agreeing that the first to reach a town in Macedonia would be allowed possession of that town.[407]

The Macedonians contributed eighteen battalions of volunteers to the Bulgarian army, not suspecting that Bulgaria had secretly made arrangements for the partition of Macedonia.[408] IMRO's leaders soon learned about this partition and sent a note of protest to the Bulgarian government, who chose to ignore it.[409] The Macedonian legionaries of General Ghenev began accusing the Bulgarian government of having deceived the people in order to "sell Macedonia."[410] Minister Gueshov of Bulgaria wrote about why Bulgaria came to an agreement without involving the Macedonians:

Deeply convinced that the Macedonian question ought to be taken out of the hands of the Macedonian Revolutionary Committee as Cavour took the question of Italian unity out of the hands of the Italian revolutionists, I hasted to open negotiations.[411]

Serbia and Greece, for their parts, had their own visions of expanding their territories and would not cede their parts of Macedonia to an independent republic. They further feared that Bulgaria would move in and sweep Macedonia into its sphere of dominance. This was Bulgaria's desire, which led to the Second

Balkan War in 1913, with Bulgaria primarily warring against Greece and Serbia. Macedonians found themselves torn and divided, once again, and demoralized that they had traded in one grand tormentor for three smaller ones. Some Macedonians fought with Bulgaria, putting their bets that she had the best intentions for them, but most were scattered and willingly did not participate in the consumption of their land.

But Bulgaria was dealt a resounding loss. Greece and Serbia ended up with the bulk of Macedonian territory. With the ending of the Second Balkan War in 1913, the Macedonian blame-game picked up again. The Macedonian Scholarly and Literary Society in St. Petersburg sent a memorandum out against the partition and division of Macedonia, and stated that Macedonians made up two-thirds of the population while the rest were Turks, Greeks, Jews, Albanians and Vlachs.[412] They said that the Macedonian movement should focus on keeping Macedonia as a unit and should not be subjected to the interests of their neighbors. The IMRO right-wing, however, went back to focusing on how to eliminate Sandanski. It was not long before Sandanski met his predicted fate.

Sandanski had embarked on a short trip through Macedonia by himself in April of 1915 in Bulgarian occupied Macedonia (Pirin Macedonia). His friends offered to accompany him. Sandanski declined their offer, saying: "Once I made two mothers weep (a reference to the mothers of Mitso Vransky and Tancho, who were killed in Salonika) and I don't want to make any more weep. Let whatever happens happen." Sandanski dined with some friends the night before the tragedy. That evening, one of his friends asked him why he had never married. He replied, "I have decided that I shall not marry until we see what way Macedonia is going to go." His friends then warned him about travelling solo, saying that were plenty of his enemies just waiting to kill him at the opportune moment. He simply answered: "I know that I am not going to die in my bed. I have killed and I shall be killed."[413]

The next morning, he took off for his final destination. MacDermott writes:

> **As he rode through the April morning, he caught up with a group of carriers taking wine to Nevrokop, but he spurred Mitsa [his donkey] on, overtook them and went ahead. At length, he reached a part of the mountain known as *Blatata* — the marshes.**

He passed the Lower Marsh and, riding above a narrow valley wooded with beeches, he approached the Upper Marsh — a wide meadow, with a brook flowing through it, and countless golden cowslips growing among the lush grass. Here the path turns sharply left to make a horse-shoe detour around the marsh, and, on the bend, rising-ground obscures the view, so that the approaching traveller cannot see what lies beyond. It was here that the first shot rang out.

Yané immediately dismounted, or possibly fell, from his mare, and in so doing, he broke his leg. He was now at a terrible disadvantage. He dragged himself to the bole of a huge beech tree, and began shooting back with his revolver. Thirty spent cartridges were later found in the area. But the murderers were many — seven or eight cowards, armed with Manlicher rifles — and one of them maneuvered himself into a position from which he was able to fire the fatal shot. The body rolled a little way down the steep side of the valley and came to rest on its back, with open eyes fixed on the sunlit sky. Some bravo then boldly advanced and discharged several bullets into the abdomen of the corpse.[414]

Sandanski's camp placed the blame on IMRO's right wing, specifically on Todor Aleksandrov (who had been on the Central Committee of IMRO before the Balkan Wars) and Gligor Nikolov. Both men were backed by Prince Ferdinand. They had supposedly employed Stoyan Filipov and six of his men to commit the murder. At a trial in Bulgaria, in the August of 1915, three of the assassins said this was a "patriotic mission" that Filipov passed on to them; and Filipov stated that Aleksandrov gave him the orders to do so. Filipov also stated that "he was the enemy of Sandansky and that he hated him, and so did the people, because he was a 'Turkish spy'."[415] Sandanski's decision to work with the Young Turks to keep Macedonia intact allowed Macedonia's right-wing to exploit Sandanski's efforts to create a Macedonia for the Macedonians as a Turkish conspiracy rather than a genuine Macedonian movement, allowing the Bulgarian Prince to continue his plans of subverting Macedonia.

After Sandanski's death, the Macedonian independence movement – especially the left-wing movement – essentially faded away. There were pockets of resistance who fought for an independent Macedonia – such as Chupovski's faction – but they were eventually chased out of Macedonia.[416] And Macedonia's right-wing leaders continued eliminating left-wing Macedonians wherever they could find them. On February 25, 1916 in the streets of Sofia, Naum Tiufekchiev was killed. IMRO executioner, Tushe Skachkov, fired six bullets into his chest. The order was given by Todor Aleksandrov.[417]

However, another war – World War I – once again enticed the Balkan peoples into a battle over Macedonian territory. The outcome of this war did not lead to freedom or independence for Macedonia, but rather to the similar subjugation that the Macedonians had faced under the Turks. Macedonians were now in a position to be assimilated into Bulgarians, Greeks and Serbians. This was just the spark that IMRO needed to revive the need of a 'Macedonia for the Macedonians.' Former Macedonian foes of the left-wing and independence movement started adopting that slogan and agenda upon realizing that their savior was not in Bulgaria, but rather in themselves.

VII.

Aleksandrov and a Divided Macedonia

During World War I, Bulgaria told the Allies that they would sever their alliances with Germany and Austria and join the Allies only in exchange for possession of Macedonia. Bulgaria, Serbia and Greece were again engaged in a battle over Macedonia, with similar alliances as in the Second Balkan War. But even before Bulgaria had chosen sides in the war, it had iterated that it would choose sides based on who would promise it possession of Macedonia. Prime Minister Radoslavov said Bulgaria would take arms against the Ottomans within twenty-four hours if Serbia ceded Vardar Macedonia to it. "We will fight for but one end," said Radoslavov. "That is to extend our frontiers until they embrace the peoples of our own blood, but that end must be guaranteed to us beyond all doubt."[418] Bulgaria further felt justified in demanding such because they claimed to have been aggrieved as a result of the Balkan Wars, stating that Bulgaria did "most of the fighting against Turkey over Macedonia...and received the least of the reward, the bulk going to Servia and Greece."[419]

The British refused this proposal of incorporating Macedonia into Bulgaria and instead offered a counterproposal that would make Macedonia an independent country with Solun as its capital. But Bulgaria declined the offer:

> That Bulgaria should have refused this offer is only another illustration of the duplicity of Ferdinand and his governing clique. His hold on the Bulgarian people has been his pretended espousal of the cause of the Macedonian Bulgars. For long years past the Macedonians have strived for an independent Macedonia, but this was made impossible by the policies of the great powers interested. They were, however, on the verge of achieving this ideal after the First Balkan War, when the interference of Austria in Albania caused Serbia and Greece to demand a revision of the treaty which had provided for Macedonian freedom. Against this demand the Macedonians protested, and their leaders were largely instrumental in

precipitating the Second Balkan War. The result was their defeat and the Treaty of Bucharest, which forced the Macedonian patriots under the wing of the Bulgarian government, the only refuge left for them.

That Bulgaria should now have refused terms including an independent Macedonia was, indeed, a matter to be kept secret. Ferdinand, naturally, desires Macedonia as an extension of his own territory, although the Macedonians are very little in sympathy with his Greater Bulgaria imperialism and would only accept it as an alternative between freedom on the one hand and subjection to Greece and Serbia on the other.[420]

Macedonians themselves argued for differing outcomes – some wrote letters for complete Macedonian independence, others for accession to Bulgaria, and others for autonomy but with the Great Powers as temporary protectorates. Bozhidar Tatarchev, a cousin of Hristo Tatarchev, sent a Memoir to the Paris Peace Conference in February claiming that either accession to Bulgaria or an independent Macedonia would be desirable.[421]

During the war, socialist Bulgarians argued that Bulgaria had no right over Macedonia and that their quest to conquest Macedonia would ruin Bulgaria. On December 10, 1917, Bulgarian social democrat Dimitar Blagoev stated in the Bulgarian parliament that Bulgarian aims for wanting Macedonia were not about uniting all Bulgarians, but about access to the Aegean Sea. In 1918, Bulgarian social democrat Hristo Kabakchiev highlighted the same points, saying Macedonia was a foreign territory and that Bulgaria wanted Solun simply to have a better trade route into the Mediterranean.[422]

These Social Democrats of Bulgaria were supporting an autonomous Macedonia, which upset many leading Bulgarians:

> **Such are the views of the Social Democrats. They do not even dare admit that Macedonia is a Bulgarian country: they want autonomy for Macedonia. Was it for this we made so many sacrifices? Is it for this so many brave sons of Bulgaria are perishing? Is it for this we are spending milliards: for the sake of an autonomy for Macedonia?**[423]

Many Bulgarians perished in the fight for Macedonia, but so did many Serbs, Greeks and Turks. But those peoples had their own countries – the Macedonians did not. Several Macedonian refugees found their way into Bulgaria after the Second Balkan War hoping to find some kindred spirits, but the Bulgarians there were not fond of the Macedonians, and the Macedonians reciprocated the ill-feeling. The Bulgarians told the Macedonians:

'My brother is lying dead in Macedonia because of you, and now you come up here to live in my house, eat my bread, and take my job. Get out.' And the [Macedonian] refugee answers: 'Who told you to come down to Macedonia and trample down our vineyards, and then run off and leave our village to be burned? I don't care if your brother is dead in Macedonia. My brother is dead, too.'[424]

It was the case that these Macedonians saw themselves as different than the Bulgarians. "It happens that Macedonians who come to Bulgaria continue to call themselves Macedonians...In Bulgaria, whether they are descended from a Macedonian who traveled eastward in 1878, or whether they are quite recent immigrants, they call themselves Macedonians."[425]

While many Bulgarians were blaming the Macedonians for their problems, Serbia was having an exceptionally hard time keeping the Macedonians pacified and tolerant of their rule. When the First Balkan War ended, and the Serbs had replaced the Turks as the new masters of their section of Macedonia, the inhabitants were not entirely dissatisfied. They saw the Serbian army as liberators and they thought Serbia would do just that – liberate them and let them have their own country. For example, in Bitola, on November 24, 1912, the Macedonians held a "thanksgiving" to show their appreciation to Serbia. A writer noted what that day was like:

One of the ancient churches of the city was crowded with happy worshippers, the Crown Prince and his suite among them... After that a requiem for the souls of the poor soldiers who had been left dead and dying on the distant hills – victims of one of the bloodiest advances ever known in the long and bloody history of Macedonian wars. And after that the loosening of

flags, the ringing of bells, to show the joy of an unshackled spirit.[426]

But three years later, Bitola had "almost forgotten that a day of Thanksgiving ever existed." The Macedonians were back to their "old lives of fear" and Serbians had "become as enemies."[427] Under Serbian rule, the name Macedonia was thrown out and exchanged for South Serbia. After King Alexander's administrative reforms, the 'Vardarska Banovina' was the new name and all "Macedonians were declared to be Serbs."[428]

After military rule was applied to Macedonia, socialist Serbs joined the sentiments of socialist Bulgarians about Macedonians. One socialist Serbian paper wrote:

If the liberation of these territories is a fact, why then is this exceptional regime established there? If the inhabitants are Servians why are they not made the equals of all the Servians; why is the constitutional rule not put in operation according to which 'all Servians are equal before the law'? If the object of the wars was unification, why is not this unification effectively recognized, and why are these exceptional ordinances created, such as can only be imposed upon conquered countries by conquerors? Moreover, our constitution does not admit of rules of this nature![429]

Other Serbian papers shared similar sentiments. Pravda asked, "Are the people of the annexed territories to have fewer rights now than they possessed under Turkish regime?" Another wrote about the Macedonians: "The population has no rights, only duties."[430]

There were also Serbians who acknowledged that the Macedonian language was separate from both Serbian and Bulgarian. In 1919, linguist Aleksandar Belich argued that the Macedonian dialects were neither Serbian nor Bulgarian. He then admitted that politics would decide Macedonia's linguistic fate.[431] Also, during World War I, one Serbian who had traveled to Macedonia claimed that many Macedonians were speaking "no known language."[432] This Slavic language was Macedonian.

During the terrible teens – the period that saw three devastating wars consume the Balkans – the Serbians began forcing the Macedonians to both conscript into the Serbian army and to declare themselves Serbian. "A certain Pano Grantcharov, or Gherov, tried to commit suicide to escape being entered as a Servian volunteer." In villages around Tetovo – such as Zhilche, Raotince and Leshok – the authorities would beat the peasants into declaring they were Serbs.[433]

After the Balkan Wars, the Serbians were still encountering very little success in recruiting Macedonians into the Serbian army. At Ristovac, a battle took place between Serbian police and Macedonian recruits refusing to join the army. Eighteen Macedonians were killed after the Serbians called in field guns to be used on the Macedonians. The Macedonians refused to take the military oath. A similar situation was reported of Macedonians from Shtip refusing to take the military oath and being massacred.[434] One visitor to the region noted:

Serbia was in deadly need of fresh recruits for her woefully depleted army, but these Macedonians were not willing conscripts, many of them being pro-Turk or pro-Bulgar in their sympathies, many more simply hating the thought of being 'called up,' most of them not at all eager to fight for anyone.[435]

Serbia also began colonizing Macedonia with "200 percent Serbs."[436] The Serbians began pouring Serbian teachers into Macedonia, while Macedonian teaching staff were transplanted throughout Serbia and Montenegro. This was to ensure that the language being taught to Macedonians was in Serbian and not Macedonian.[437]

Serbia, including its new addition of Macedonia, was a country of about 13,000,000 people. Although Serbs were the principle element, this 'Yugoslavia' housed plenty of Croats, Slovenes and Macedonians who did not consider themselves Serbs. This reality made the goal of a centralized Serbian government a tough one, and the Serbian authorities would need to assimilate the Croats, Slovenes and Macedonians in order to centralize power in Belgrade.[438]

One consul in the Balkans on News Years Day in 1915 talked about why the Macedonians did not want to be part of the Serbian army: "The average Macedonian is neither Serb, nor Greek, nor Bulgar. He's just whatever suits him at the time. Lord! The Macedonian question! There's going to be a 'small hell' when they rope in the recruits in [Skopje]. The bazaar is seething with revolt already." In the same conversation, another man from the region spoke on the issue of nationality in Macedonia:

> I remember in the old days, that is some five to ten years ago, wandering bands of Komitdagi used to convert whole villages to the Greek, Serb or Bulgar Church by the sword...I know. It sounds almost incredible. But it's true. Those who did not 'vert were simply pillaged or even occasionally slaughtered by their fellow Christians. The Turks looked on and smiled.

The man was asked if the Macedonians were different than Serbs and Bulgars, and he replied: "In a way, yes, and no. They're just Macedonians."[439]

Other observers shared similar sentiments. "The slavophone population of Serbian Macedonia definitely regard themselves as distinct from the Serbs. If asked their nationality they say they are Macedonians, and they speak the Macedonian dialect." The same was said about the Macedonians in Greek Macedonia: "The inhabitants here are no more Serb than the Macedonians of Serbia – they speak Macedonian, and they call themselves Macedonians;"[440] and "those people whom I had met were insistent on calling themselves neither Serbs nor Bulgars, but Macedonians."[441]

The Macedonians thus continued with assaults against the Serbian army. On March 20, 1915 Panajot Karamfilovich participated in what is known as the Valandovo Action. Along with captains Vane Stojanov, Peter Ovcharov, Petar Chaulev and Lubomir Vesov – with a total of 1,000 rebels – the Macedonians defeated Serbian troops in the three towns of Valandovo, Pirava and Udovo. They eliminated 470 Serb soldiers and captured over 350, thus temporarily conquering Valandovo.[442]

However, these events caused an international sensation. Bulgaria had still not entered the First World War (they would not until the summer), but Serbia and the Allied Powers considered this attack by IMRO as a Bulgarian plot. However, its plans had went unknown to the Bulgarian leaders – IMRO acted on its own to contest Serbian domination. The head of the Strumica section of IMRO, Kosta Cipushev who was a central figure in the Valandovo Action, was summoned by Bulgarian Prime Minister Radoslavov to explain IMRO's actions.[443] Cipushev was a well-known Macedonian during his time, and he was married to Todor Aleksandrov's sister, Ekaterina, while Goce Delchev was his best man and Dame Gruev was his matchmaker.[444]

Greece during this period was also campaigning to assimilate Macedonians into Greeks. By the end of the First World War, Greece and Bulgaria signed a treaty for the voluntary exchange of populations. This treaty was finalized on September 29, 1919. Over 30,000 Macedonians from Aegean Macedonia (Greek Macedonia) left, and the Bulgarian government sold these Macedonians' homes, businesses, churches and cemeteries to Greece.[445]

Furthermore, the Macedonian lands that Greece had captured were primed to be the best in the Balkans for agricultural purposes. By 1921, Aegean Macedonian production was dramatically increasing: there were 1.5 million okes of cotton per year; its large production of opium supplied the United States and the United Kingdom; its wool remained in Greece, being used as socks for the peasants and khakis for the soldiers; its tobacco was the finest in the world and essentially all of it went to the United States; and the silk was produced and shipped to the Dutch.[446]

In the 1920s, Greece devised a strategy for the Hellenization of Aegean Macedonia: the government settled 600,000 Christian refugees from Turkey into Aegean Macedonian villages where primarily Turks and other Muslims were once abundant. This was secured in the "Treaty of Lausanne." One observer noted that League of Nations loaned Greece so much money for the settlement of these refugees that they were at least "housed and settled in comfort if not in luxury."[447] The native Macedonians were discontent that the newcomers were being better treated than they had been treated by the Greek government. Furthermore, most ethnic Macedonians in the border zones and near railway lines were deported to Thessaly and the Greek Islands, as Greece became afraid these Macedonians would collaborate with Turkey in the event of a war. Macedonian men who did not either serve in the Greek army or who deserted the Greek army were deported to other parts of Greece[448]

Furthermore, in the 1920s, Greek organizations started to terrorize the Macedonian population into becoming Greeks. One of these was called the Greek-Macedonian Fist, founded in 1927. It "ordered the Greek language to be spoken in all public places, at restaurants, during trade negotiations, at meetings, during meals, and weddings." Those who did not comply would be deemed traitors and punished.[449] Moreover, Macedonians' names were changed to Greek. Macedonians living in the United States who wrote to relatives in Aegean Macedonia had their letters returned if they used the Macedonian version of their names. A note appeared on the returned letters saying, "such person or persons are not found."[450]

The Macedonians, however, continued striving for good governance, fundamental rights and freedoms, and safety and security. The Chairman of the League of Nations Mixed Commission on Greco-Bulgarian relations wrote in 1923:

> **But in the evenings in their own houses or when we had given the officials the slip, we encouraged them [the Macedonian peasants] to speak to us. Then we in-variably heard the same story as "Bad administration. They want to force us to become Greeks, in language, in religion, in sentiment, in every way. We have served in the Greek army and we have fought for them: now they insult us by calling us 'damned Bulgars'" ... To my question "What do you want? an autonomous Macedonia or a Macedonia under Bulgaria?" the answer was generally the same: "We want good administration. We are Macedonians, not Greeks or Bulgars...We want to be left in peace."[451]**

The Greek Communist party, for its part, was not going along with the Communist International Party's (Comintern) established solution for the Macedonian Question, which aimed to create an independent Macedonia under a Balkan Confederation. In 1924, the reason given by the Greek Communists centered around the new refugees that had infiltrated into Macedonia. Here is a Greek Communist Party representative's remarks:

> **It is true that we sent a letter to the Balkan Federation protesting...the slogan of the Macedonian autonomy[.] After the Treaty of Lausanne, all the Turkish inhabitants of Macedonia were obliged to leave, and the Greek bourgeoisie installed 700,000 refugees in their place...But the fact remains that there are 700,000 Greek refugees in Macedonia. The workers and peasants of Greece were therefore not prepared to accept the slogan of autonomy of Macedonia.[452]**

After that, though, by the end of 1924, there were mixed ideas within the Greek Communist Party on the Macedonian autonomy. They officially accepted it and supported it, but many of their party leaders risked their lives by supporting self-determination of Macedonian and Thracian minorities. For example, Pouliopoulos, who was secretary of the Greek Communist Party since 1922, broke away from the Greek Communists over this issue and started his own newspaper, *The New Course*. He opposed autonomy for Macedonia.[453]

Meanwhile, the Greek fascists were continuing with their efforts of Hellenizing the Macedonians. On October 21, 1926, Greece announced a law that required the obligatory change of the names of all settled places in Aegean Macedonia. Most of these were Macedonian names, some were Turkish and Vlach. Regardless, by 1928, "the names of 1,497 inhabited places were changed."[454]

As Macedonia's neighbors were striving to assimilate and denationalize the Macedonians, the Macedonians response was to revive IMRO based on old ideals adapted to modern times. Many familiar faces from the past showed up – along with many new faces – and along with many old and new divides and allegiances. If a quote was needed to sum up IMRO between the two World Wars, it would be difficult to find only one. Many authors described and detailed the terror and reign of what IMRO became during the 1920s and 1930s. *The Carp Review* wrote in 1928:

> **Trains are blown up, bombing plots revealed and the world is told that this or that Macedonian committee or political faction is waging war against another faction or against the Serbs or Greeks.**[455]

The Pittsburgh Press reported in 1934:

> **America has its mountain feuds, Italy has its cruel vendettas and many other nations have ruthless secret societies, but none of these is stronger or more fierce than the Inner Macedonian Revolutionary Organization…For 50 years, various governments have tried to stamp out the IMRO. Still it goes on, maintaining its secret army, law courts, secret service, educational system and tax collection system. The IMRO is a small but fearsome and highly important factor in Europe.**[456]

And the *Spokane Daily* simply described the IMRO in 1934:

The Internal Macedonian Revolutionary Organization -- the 'invisible empire' of the Balkan Mountains.[457]

Who were the initiators of this new brand of IMRO? IMRO regenerated at the end of the World War I in its familiar left and right wing factions. Both factions sent representatives to the Paris Peace Conference in April of 1919. The left-wing called themselves the Temporary Representatives of the IMRO, while the right-wing called themselves, initially, the Executive Committee of the Macedonian Brotherhood in Bulgaria. The left-wing was led by Popchristov as a delegate to the conference, while the right wing was led by Aleksandrov and Protogerov, supposed conspirers of the Sandanski murder. The left-wing advocated for an autonomous Macedonia on behalf of the Macedonian people and not for Bulgaria's or the Bulgarian peoples' interests. The right-wing argued for an autonomous Macedonia as part of Bulgaria. Several Macedonian organizations worldwide also submitted statements and requests about the future of Macedonia. A submission from Switzerland, for example, desired a completely independent Macedonia. However, no results were reached and the status quo prevailed: Macedonia remained divided mostly between three countries, and Albania obtained a tiny sliver.[458]

At the Second Congress of the Macedonian Brotherhood (the right-wing Macedonians, who eventually assumed the IMRO name) in 1920, old divisions were already surfacing. Over five dozen delegates left the meeting before it concluded. A year later in 1921, on December 4th, over two dozen local Macedonian Brotherhood Committees organized their own conference called the Macedonian Federative Organization (MFO). They wanted an autonomous Macedonia with geographical and economical borders following the example of Switzerland.[459] A central figure to MFO was Hristo Tsvetkov. As a member, he spent much time in western Aegean Macedonia and Albania, establishing contacts and fighting fascist propaganda. While in Tirana, he and other MFO members, such as Filip Athanasov and Pavel Hristov, met Protogerov in 1923 and decided to cooperate in their struggle against Greek authorities. Tsvetkov also used Albania as a base of operations during this time.[460]

Aleksandrov's IMRO was the MFO's main opposition. Its center was in Bulgaria and it primarily carried out its activity in Pirin and Vardar Macedonia. On June 11th, 1920, the new IMRO constitution was established. Between 1919 and 1924, over 500 people were killed belonging to MFO, IMRO and the Serbian and Bulgarian authorities. In this same period, no less than five dozen separate raids by MFO and IMRO armed bands into Vardar Macedonia took place.[461] One of the left-wing Macedonian movement's biggest loss happened in the early summer of 1921, when right-wing Bulgarian government associates of Todor Aleksandrov murdered Gjorche Petrov in the streets of Sofia.[462]

The ensuing violence often inspired Serbian and Bulgarian authorities to react harshly against the Macedonians. One notable instance was recorded in the village of Garvan, just south of Shtip, where the Serbian authorities massacred many Macedonian men:

Dobritza Matkovitch [the Commander in charge] dismounts from his charger in the little open space in the center of the village and orders the assistant mayor to call in the men form the fields...Twenty-eight of them have come. Some others have crept away to hide in the near-by woods. Says Dobritza Matkovitch: "By the will of God and His Majesty King Alexander I am the Grand Jupan Dobritza Matkovitch, and I order you to tell me where the comitadjis are, and who of you are giving them shelter and food. If you do not tell me I shall kill you like a pack of dogs!" "We neither know nor have seen any comitadjis!" reply the villagers..." I shall take you to Shtip," he says to the menfolk. The latter beg to be set free and refuse to leave the village. But the whips, the straps and the butt ends of the rifles drive them ahead...The men, their hands tied at their backs, stumble ahead upon the road...

At a place upon the road about two miles from the village, Matkovitch orders his troops to turn the peasants away from the road and drive them toward the fields...So they fall down on their knees and plead for their lives. But the whip lashes come whistling down upon their heads, and the butt ends of the rifles ram at their backs, and so the cringing, groaning bodies move away from the road through the fields toward the foothills of the mountain. In a field some distance from the roadside the

twenty-eight men are stopped. "Tell me where the comitadjis are, and who of you have given them food and shelter!" Again the villagers deny knowing the whereabouts of comitadjis. "You do not know where the comitadjis are! Then you yourselves are comitadjis!" shouts Dobritza. And he orders his soldiers to stand off and shoot.

The soldiers withdraw a few paces and make ready to aim. But one among them begins to grunt, and another starts fidgeting, and still another hisses his disapproval. They refuse to shoot. They are the sons of just such old, simple villagers as these. They have not the heart to shoot down these innocent men. There are youngsters too among these twenty-eight men from Garvan. There is one who is twelve and another thirteen years of age. The boys look pleadingly at the soldiers, and tears run down their cheeks...

Jupan Matkovitch curses his troops for disobeying him. He threatens them with court martial and again and again issues stern commands to them to carry out his orders. But the soldiers refuse. There is the machine gun standing by obediently. It has no tongue to refuse and no soul to rebel. Matkovitch himself bends down to the machine-gun. The poor villagers wail out; they touch the earth with their knees and beg for mercy...But the racket from the machine-gun drowns the cries. The soldiers turn their heads away, from shame and grief. The fire-belching machine-gun rattles off bullets, and the bodies tumble, huddling and hugging one another as if for protection. The bodies in their agony squirm and wiggle and the blood drenches them and their earth...

For six days the twenty-eight corpses lie in the field, while the women in the village, informed of the tragedy by the troops, keep crying and groaning in their houses. On the seventh day peasants from the neighboring village come to the scene and bury the corpses. An old woman, a grandmother of sixty-five, seeing the pile of dead bodies, drops dead on the spot, making the total number of victims twenty-nine.[463]

Similar horrors were not yet possible in Bulgaria. One reason Bulgaria had difficulties in initially dealing with IMRO is because, as part of the peace treaty of World War I, Bulgaria was not allowed to have a conscript army and possessed only an all-volunteer army of 33,000 soldiers.[464] Another reason was that Aleksandrov often had several allies inside the Bulgarian government. The Bulgarian leaders and politicians allied with Aleksandrov for good reason – he had built a fierce and loyal Macedonian following.

Aleksandrov was born in Shtip in 1881. He graduated from high school in Skopje in 1897, and his professional calling – as was many IMRO members of the time – was to be a teacher. He was arrested in 1903 for his IMRO activity and imprisoned by the Turks in Skopje. He escaped in 1904 and fled to the mountains, leaving his mother and six younger sisters alone. He eventually became a secretary for the revolutionary committee in Shtip under the leadership of Mishe Razvigorov. Eventually, he was elected as a member of IMRO's Central Committee in 1911. When he helped to revive IMRO in 1919, he was thrown into prison by the Bulgarian authorities, but he managed to escape soon after.[465]

He crossed back into Macedonia and along with Protogerov and Peter Chaulev, he became one of the three Central Committee members. Aleksandrov originally wanted IMRO's base to be in Vardar Macedonia, but the Serbian government sent a large army into Vardar Macedonia to eradicate the Macedonian revolutionaries. Aleksandrov then shifted the headquarters of IMRO to Pirin Macedonia, where the Bulgarian army was absent.[466]

Aleksandrov's IMRO was well-organized and very efficient in revolutionary activity. They combined the old system of revolutionary strategy with new technology and fresh methodology:

> **[Aleksandrov] never wrote a decree, never an order. All his commands were transmitted by word of mouth throughout the country, and even to foreign capitals, in most of which he had agents watching and ready to execute his orders. His couriers were said to be the most efficient in the world...[H]is wanderings have established cohesion among 150,000 veterans of the world war, whom he would be able to mobilize in a few days. Of the total, 60,000 are now on active service, being distributed in small bands, which can quickly unite if one is attacked. He has no artillery, but at various secret places has established arsenals of rifles and bombs, with plenty of**

> ammunition and uniforms, all of which are said to be transmitted without trouble through Salonika...
>
> The person charged with [an] execution is given a certain time in which to carry out his task. If he fails, he is killed himself. The death sentence is usually preceded by at least one letter of warning, but in certain cases it is carried out immediately...Perhaps the reason of their success lies in the exceptional form of idealism which animate the members of the organization. Each person has a role assigned to him or her, and the signing of a death warrant by Todor Alexandroff is the signal for the whole machine to begin its work.[467]

Even the Serbian authorities noted IMRO's exceptional organization under Aleksandrov. In one instance, near Shtip, Aleksandrov's band engaged in a battle with the Serbian garrison. Belgrade said that the Macedonians attacked the colonists settling there, and several people were killed or injured. The Serbians noted the revolutionaries for being very disciplined, well-organized and for being proficient in rapid firepower, such utilizing hand-held throwing bombs. The Serbian government put a 250,000 *dinar* reward for Aleksandrov's head.[468]

Aleksandrov's greatest weakness, however, was the difficulty he had in building a uniform and consistent approach to Macedonia while he was the leader of IMRO. When he assumed control, the directive was "the liberty of Macedonia, in a form of autonomy or independence within its ethnographical and economical borders." However, he often changed that directive. For example, while he did not necessarily demand independence of Pirin Macedonia from Bulgaria, he did hope that Vardar Macedonia would at least gain status as an equal member among the Yugoslav republics. Regarding the Macedonians in Greece, he strived only for local self-administration and linguistic and cultural rights. He faced severe criticism for such discrepancies and differences in policy, so less than three weeks after giving the new directive, he revised it to finally gain the support of most Macedonians. His new directive was like the original direction: "The struggle of liberation for Macedonia will continue until we acquire autonomous administration for all three parts of Macedonia."[469]

Bulgaria, of course, was not the only base of operations for IMRO and the Macedonians. IMRO's reach spread throughout Europe. In particular, IMRO created many initiatives and made many connections in Vienna:

> **The Macedonians have two revolutionary organizations here. One is pacifist, hoping to attain autonomy for Macedonia by diplomatic methods. The other is the thorough-going Balkan comitatje type, which think that the only way to persuade your enemy is to kill him, and that the only way to achieve a program is to terrorize your opponents into it. The latter group has its headquarters in one café; the former in another. And they hate each other as much as either hates the Greeks or Turks or Serbs or present Bulgarian administration…**
>
> **Macedonian comitatje are not always true to type. Some of them look what one imagines them to be; fierce dark eyes, boorish manners, European clothes worn with a Balkan clumsiness. But the leader of the committee in Vienna is a smartly dressed man, quiet, and well-bred, speaking excellent French and German.**[470]

The news correspondent who visited the warring Macedonian factions at their café headquarters in Vienna highlighted that he liked the left-wing Macedonians better than the right-wing Macedonians:

> **I like the revolutionaries of the other café better. Their leader is Dr. Athanasoff, and he looked like a Balkan peasant for all his European dress. Dr. Athanasoff believes in revolution by argument and diplomacy. He doesn't seem to be getting very far with it, but I was interested in meeting with this new type of comitatje. When I saw him last, he was very bitter over Jurokoff's death. He made me angry, too. Why should these revolutionaries kill a man who had the same aims as they, only different methods? Idiots, I thought.**[471]

Moreover, in the meantime, Aleksandrov's IMRO had become more than a nuisance for Bulgaria, Greece and Serbia. IMRO's violent disturbances had both social and political consequences for those three countries, and IMRO was known around Europe as the troublemaker of the Balkans. Aleksandrov explained why this course of action and reputation was necessary:

> **We are not revolutionaries by profession and more than anybody else we are thirsty and hungry for peace because no other country in the world has suffered more from disorder than Macedonia has suffered. But we are forced to use revolutionary methods simply because Serbia and Greece do not allow us to use other methods in order to defend our human rights and nationality. We will cease to fight as revolutionaries as soon as we are given the possibility of fighting as citizens.**[472]

Aleksandrov's revolutionaries were thus branded as among the most passionate and dedicated to their cause. They were "fiery eyed men… who live for nothing else than Macedonia, and who, if they thought all hope of freeing it were lost, would scarcely hesitate, like passionate and despairing lovers, to destroy themselves, life having lost for them its sole purpose."[473]

These revolutionaries, often labeled as terrorists and gangsters in the world's eyes by the late 1920s and 1930s, were not what one generally envisions in today's gangsterdom, where money, pleasure and excess are the motivators for violent pursuits. These IMRO pursuits were for one cause and one cause only: autonomy and unification of Macedonia. Those who did not desire that could not join. Moreover, those who wanted to live a decent and enjoyable life, could not join. Albert Londres wrote:

> **Above all, these rebels are men of principle. If you wish to enjoy the good things of life, it is no use joining them. They mostly drink water; many of them are vegetarians; and when they pass a woman in the street they do not heed her. In Macedonia the men in general are not dissolute, but they wish to be absolutely beyond reproach. They put purity of the heart and denials of the flesh before any of their unreasonable claims. Lies, hypocrisy, boasting, drunkenness, debauchery, prodigality and the use of firearms – all are forbidden. Chasity, humility, modesty, love of family life and of their neighbors, though these are natural virtues, are imposed upon them.**[474]

The one exception to the above description was that weapons were employed, but only for killing enemies and traitors to the Macedonian Cause. They were "not made for domestic use."[475]

Like the IMRO of old in the 1890s and early 1900s, this new IMRO was a state within a state, having its own police, postal service, tax-collectors, government and courts. On the local level, IMRO courts heard all matters of cases. If a man tried to court a married woman and the husband proved his case in court, the guilty party would get "nineteen rapid blows with a road and six given slowly and deliberately."[476] This was not much different than the old system of justice.

Throughout the early 1920s, IMRO initiated plenty of rebellions in Bulgaria and Pirin Macedonia. In December of 1922, Aleksandrov, along with his assistant plotters, Ivan Mihajlov and Athanasov, led an uprising in Kyustendil, where "many persons who were prominent were assassinated[.]" The Bulgarian government then declared martial law, shutting down all restaurants, cafes and theatres.[477] In the early months of 1923, IMRO staged a revolt in Nevrokop. They "drove a number of government officials out of the town" and explained "that their movement was simply a warning that the government should send better functionaries to that region" and stop ill-treating the Macedonian refugees who came from Greece and Serbia.[478]

IMRO had also forced the Bulgarian authorities to relinquish control on taxation matters. Todor Aleksandrov's IMRO now controlled and dictated that business, which contributed to IMRO's war chest. In response, the Bulgarian Minister for War, Mouraveiff, ordered the mobilization of a volunteer army of 20,000 Bulgarians to reassert Bulgaria's control in Pirin Macedonia. "They may kill me and other members of the party," said Mouraveiff. "[B]ut that will not alter our policy to put an end once and for all to the Macedonian disturbers of the peace."[479]

Then, in June of 1923, it was reported that Aleksandrov led a band of 7,000 Macedonian rebels into Sofia and began "conducting a reign of terror." These Macedonians, described as "fierce hill tribesmen," "roughly clad," and "hard-riding," joined Bulgarian right-wing organizations in taking down Stamboliski, a Bulgarian left-wing leader, who famously advocated for a Balkan Confederation and proclaimed that he was not a Bulgar nor a Serb, but rather a

Yugoslav.[480] However, Stamboliski knew how to infuriate Macedonians and appease Serbs. He made a speech in Belgrade saying "he would pile up all the Macedonians on freight cars and dispatch them to Belgrade for the Serbs to do with them as they please."[481]

What happened to Stamboliski at the hands of IMRO executioners will go down as one of the most notorious and grueling killings of a prime minister, similar to the Macedonian assassination of Bulgarian Prime Minister Stambolov nearly 25 years prior. Albert Londres described:

> **During the morning of the 9th June, 1923, while at his country house at Slivnitza, Stambouliski was visited by soldiers who, under the orders of one of the demobilized officers, had been sent to arrest him. His bodyguard opened fire and the soldiers retired. Stambouliski gave orders that the village bells should be rung and rockets fired. At these signals the peasants from the outlying districts took up their arms and gathered, about a thousand strong, at Pazarzic. Detachments of soldiers attacked them, but the peasants had the upper hand. Stambouliski spent the night at home.**
>
> **Next day the rebels were reinforced and the peasants beaten. Left unprotected, Stambouliski was arrested and taken to Pazarzic, where the military commander arranged to send him to Sofia. Late at night an officer under secret orders arrived, and under an escort of four members of IMRO, the dictator was taken back to his home. The officers having cornered the bull, the Komitadjis seized him. By their orders Stambouliski was made to dig his own grave. The four 'specialists' cut off his ears and nose and one – who rejoiced in the title of the 'Vovoid of the Black Mountains of Uskub' – felled and slaughtered him.**[482]

The reason for the killing – and as to why Aleksandrov issued death warrants for four Bulgarian ministers – was because Bulgaria and Yugoslavia signed the Nish Convention, which had called for better relations between those two countries and for dealing with the Macedonian problem. Those ministers staunchly opposed the independence of Macedonia. Aleksandrov's IMRO was still adamantly advocating for an independent Macedonia and not for

Macedonia joining Serbia and Bulgaria in a separate federation. An IMRO member, Atanas Nikolov, was given the responsibility of assassinating one of these Macedonian opponents: Daskalov, the Bulgarian ambassador to Czechoslovakia. Nikolov committed the deed in August of 1923. He was acquitted by a jury, on a vote of eight to four, because it was claimed he was ordered to kill Daskalov by the IMRO and faced death if he did not.[483]

In the first few months of 1924, the Bulgarian authorities had arrested over 400 Macedonian leaders. A Macedonian, who was a former attorney general in Bulgaria, made an appeal to the Bulgarian parliament that the arrests were illegal because they were "made without the legal procedure provided in the constitution." The Minister of Interior acknowledged this, but said that such actions were necessary to "safeguard the life of the country."[484]

In the spring of 1924, Aleksandrov began to seriously reconsider his methods and aims. He traveled to London to meet with Soviet officials to collaborate on revolutionary struggles. He met Rakovsky of the Russian delegation and had many secret conversations with him. They talked about how the Soviets could assist the Macedonians with the Yugoslavs and how the Macedonians would in turn help the Soviets with the Bulgarian government:

> **The arbitrary arrests of Macedonians carried out by the Bulgarian Government under Yugoslav pressure, the Yugoslav measures in Macedonia, and the failure of all hope of obtaining support for the aims from among the big Powers led to a complete change in the attitude of the Macedonian leaders: it was decided to accept the Soviet offer to help them to throw off the Yugoslav yoke, and Alexandroff himself was deputed to conclude an agreement with the Soviet Government. He refused to go to Moscow, so it was agreed that he should come to London, where he could meet M. Rakovsky.**
>
> **M. Rakovsky is understood to have told the Macedonian leader that the Soviet Government did not demand the establishment of a Bolshevist regime in Macedonia; it was prepared to assist the Macedonian organization by all possible means – supply of arms and money, diplomatic support and so on – to deliver its country from Yugoslav domination on one condition only: that the Macedonian organization should remain strictly neutral in**

the struggle of the Bulgarian Communists and Agrarians against the Tsankoff Government. Todor Alexandroff accepted this condition.

All that remained to happen was for the Macedonian Central Committee to ratify this agreement.[485]

This agreement, known as the May Manifesto, was signed on May 6th, 1924. It had concluded that "Macedonia today is again enslaved and divided among the three Balkan states: Serbia, Bulgaria and Greece." It also stated that none of those countries were "considering giving the Macedonian people autonomy or the right for cultural development as a national minority." For Aleksandrov to agree to this was shocking to some Macedonians because he had been a fierce opponent of the left-wing Macedonians' aims, and the left-wing Macedonians were strong supporters of this document. The Manifest – with Protogerov's, Chaulev's and Aleksandrov's signatures – appeared in the first issue of Dimitar Vlahov's Macedonian publication based in Vienna, *Federation Balcanique*, on July 15th, 1924.[486] However, Aleksandrov was worried that his life was now in jeopardy when news circulated that he signed it, or had it signed on his behalf, as it upset the right-wing Bulgarian Government. "Probably Alexandrov and Protogerov received a stern warning, particularly from the War Minister, Volkov."[487] Thus, Aleksandrov dismissed it as a communist fiction.[488]

The Manifesto was critical of all Balkan governments. In part, it stated:

None of the Balkan Governments think of the liberation and reunion of the divided parts of Macedonia; none of them thinks or acts on behalf of the right of self-disposal of the Macedonian people in an independent political unit...For these reasons I.M.R.O. finds itself forced to declare that the policy of all the present Balkan Governments is hostile to the political independent existence of Macedonia...

As regards Greece, I.M.R.O. will fight against every effort for the restoration of the monarchy...and against every Government which supports the present partition of Macedonia, denationalizes the population of Greek Macedonia, and forcibly changes the ethnographical character of the area by

evicting the indigenous population in order to replace it by settlers from Asia Minor and Thrace.

As regards Yugoslavia, I.M.R.O. will fight determinedly against all the Belgrade Governments, without distinction of party, which support the present Serb policy of arbitrary centralism, the denationalization and oppression not only of the Macedonian people...

As regards Bulgaria, I.M.R..O. declares that...the present Bulgarian Government of Tsankov is following, contrary to the interests of its own people, an openly anti-Macedonian and anti-Bulgarian policy...[489]

Aleksandrov echoed many of these views in an article he wrote that was published in a Serbian newspaper in August of 1924. In it, he pointed out that the Macedonian agitation was not simply about incompetent Serbian rule, Bulgarian provocations, or restless and cruel Macedonians. Rather, the only solution to the problem, he said, was self-determination for all the peoples of Yugoslavia, including the Macedonians:

All oppressed nationalities who jealously guard their nationality are struggling shoulder to shoulder to attain their right to self-determination. After they have won their autonomy, they will be in a position to organize a great federated state with equal rights for all nationalities. Neither a powerful government able to repress the activities of the revolutionary bands, nor a good administration, can prevent the dissolution of imperialist Jugoslavia. The oppressed nationalities in Serbia are struggling neither for the attainment of a strong chauvinistic government nor for a wise Serbian administration (two incompatible terms) for their liberty...'That you govern well is not what we desire, but that you depart.'[490]

But for his varying stances and allegiances, Aleksandrov would pay with his life. An IMRO Congress was scheduled for September 1st in Lopovo. The Congress was to decide on whether or not IMRO would join the Communists and vote for a new Central Committee.

Aleksandrov and Protogerov traveled together, along with their escorts, to the Congress. Two days before the Congress was scheduled to start, the men arrived in Gorna-Sushitza where they met four couriers commissioned by Aleko Pasha and Georghi Athanasov. Pasha was a bandit chief before becoming an IMRO revolutionary, and Aleksandrov was very wary of Pasha's tendency to mix opportunism and commercialism with his revolutionary work. Athanasov, on the other hand, was the IMRO governor of the Petrich District in Pirin Macedonia. He was relatively new to the IMRO movement and was extremely ambitious, believing he should be in a position of equal power to Aleksandrov.[491]

The next day the men took off for Lopovo. As Aleksandrov and Protogerov took a mid-afternoon rest in the fields to let their horses graze, three of the couriers fired at them, instantly killing Aleksandrov and his bodyguards before they could react. Supposedly, Protogerov fainted. When Protogerov eventually reached Lopovo with his bodyguard, he claimed that the killers escaped into the woods before he could react. At Lopovo, Pasha and Athanasov demanded a resolution be passed to declare the killers outlaws and ordered them shot to death.[492]

There were three different theories of who masterminded Aleksandrov's murder. First, some suggested that the communists or federalists must have ordered it because Aleksandrov repudiated his signature on the May Manifesto. Second, Ivan Mihajlov suggested, four years after Aleksandrov's assassination, that it was ordered by Protogerov (which was eventually used by Mihajlov as a justification to kill Protogerov and assume complete control of IMRO). Third, and perhaps most likely, some Macedonians argued that the Bulgarian War Office could no longer trust Aleksandrov after his flirtation with the communists and federalists, so they instigated or encouraged Mihajlov to order the killing of Aleksandrov.[493]

Shortly after Aleksandrov's death, his followers initiated a "reign of terror" in Sofia, where at least 50 people were killed.[494] Eleven days after Aleksandrov's murder, Mihajlov organized a plot to take revenge on those who he proclaimed ordered the murder. He requested Protogerov, Pasha and Athanasov to meet him and his followers on September 24th in Gorna Djumaja. Mihajlov did not appear, but the messenger that came opened fire, killing Pasha and

Athanasov. Protogerov was roughed up and denounced publicly.[495] On the same, Chudomir Kanardzhiev was assassinated. He was a Bulgarian but also a close partner of Sandanski. Along with Gjorche Petrov, Kanardzhiev had tried to reestablish the left-wing of IMRO after World War 1. He was killed in Plovdiv.[496]

After King Boris of Bulgaria learned about Aleksandrov's death, he revealed his thoughts regarding Aleksandrov's death and the Macedonian situation:

> "I warned Stambolisky not to involve the Macedonians in our political life...I said the same thing to Tzankov. On June 9 in Vrana I told the coup's leaders: 'I hope that what you did today is for the good of Bulgaria, but the fact that the army and the Macedonians are involved is not a good thing!' And I said the same thing to Todor Alexandrov himself when I saw him shortly after June 9: 'Don't involve the Macedonians in our internal politics! It will end badly: you'll be contaminated by the vices of our partisanship, and our partisans will adopt your surgical methods.' But he did not listen. He thought that I was talking out of fear. Poor man, he paid for this mistake with his head!"[497]

Still, even though his reign was short, Aleksandrov left a legacy in Macedonia that had almost rivaled that of IMRO's founders:

> You can tell when you are in Macedonia to the fraction of an inch. In northern Jugoslavia on every wall is a picture of King Alexander, in central Bulgaria everywhere are pictures of King Boris. The moment you step across the invisible border of Macedonia it is the gruff, bearded face of Todor Alexandrov which faces every corner.[498]

Professor Dr. Hans Uebersberger said this of Aleksandrov:

> The Macedonian leader, Todor Alexandroff belongs to an unusual type of men that live a life not of their own, but for the sake of their people. Alexandroff was unassuming, modest, and of cool judgment, but otherwise with a firm disposition, having always at heart the greatest good of his people. Though ten years have passed since I last saw and spoke to him, for the first

and last time, I still clearly see this exceptional man standing before me serene. With the exception of Leo Tolstoi no one has left such inextinguishable impression upon me as Todor Alexandroff.[499]

Aleksandrov paid for his life likely because he interjected himself so willfully in Bulgarian politics. Instead of simply focusing on a solid course for Macedonia, he decided to make allies and enemies in the Bulgarian political scene. He was now dead and his right-wing successor was even more ferocious, changing the Macedonian organization from a revolutionary one to a network of gangsters. As one author would proceed to note about the end result of the Macedonian organization: "IMRO has changed its skin. It is now a hidden retreat of terrorists – from the skin of the lion it has changed to the skin of a wolf."[500]

VIII.

Mihajlov's Reign and IMRO's Demise

Ivan Mihajlov was now on his way to usurping control of IMRO. The organization was still divided into two factions: the Federalists and the Mihajlovists. Both groups believed in, and worked toward, a united and autonomous Macedonia. The essential differences revolved around control and methodology. In particular, Mihajlov's policy was "to stop at no crime or terrorism to achieve" an independent Macedonia.[501] The Federalists "genuinely aimed at creating an autonomous Macedonia within a South Slav Federation" and "thus represented the more truly 'Macedonian' tradition of the earlier I.M.R.O."[502] The men leading the Federalists were Todor Panica and Filip Athanasov; and they had a program similar to the Communists, even though they had no connection to them.[503]

But around this time, there was a split within the Federalist faction between those with tendencies toward communism and those who were opposed to communism.[504] Mihajlov's IMRO began targeting both factions. In 1924, IMRO member Dimitri Sefanov stalked the Macedonian journalist Peter Shankev for several months before executing him in Milan, Italy. The Macedonian Committee had met in central Macedonia to declare Shankev a communist traitor and gave Stefanov money to perform the deed.

> [Stefanov] visited Rome and learned that Shankeff had gone to Milan. Following him to this city, he saw Shankeff for the first time in Cathedral Square. There, he declared, he might have killed him, but refrained from making the attempt because of the fears his shots might miss and injure innocent people. Stefanoff shadowed the journalist for several days…becoming well acquainted with his habits. He learned that every day at a certain time Shankeff went to a public bar for a drink. Yesterday, Stefanoff found his quarry seated at a table drinking. He approached him…and looking him straight in the eyes, and without a word, drew his automatic pistol and shot him five times, killing him instantly.

Stefanov tried to commit suicide, but his pistol did not fire. Asked why he did it by police, Stefanov replied: "I am a Macedonian nationalist and I love my mother country intensely. It was only to serve her that I executed this renegade."[505]

These actions did not slow down the communist Macedonians' momentum. IMRO (United) was eventually established in Vienna in October 1925, under the direction of the Comintern. This new Macedonian group split from the Federalist faction and served as another rival to Mihajlov's IMRO.[506] More importantly, however, they wanted to at least win over Macedonians from Mihajlov's IMRO to the Communist side, which promoted an independent and united Macedonia among equals of other Balkan countries. IMRO (United) had little significant political or revolutionary clout in Bulgaria, but managed to make headway in Vardar Macedonia, until they "were expunged completely by the Serbian authorities in 1929."[507]

For its part, the Bulgarian Communist Party wanted to unite the left-wing Macedonians under its umbrella. They attempted this by criticizing any Macedonian communist view that refused to join the Bulgarian Communist Party. For example, Panko Brashanov and Rizo Rizov were criticized by Georgi Dimitrov, the eventual Prime Minister of Bulgaria, for insisting to form a new Macedonian organization within Macedonia. Still, IMRO (United) remained true to its aims. It had a central committee and also separate regional leadership for all three divided Macedonian parts. The regional offshoots were active during different times: in Vardar from 1926 to 1929, and in Pirin from 1929 to 1936, while only being sporadically active in Aegean Macedonia.[508]

Mihajlov's IMRO, however, never stopped thirsting for Federalist blood. In May of 1925, Todor Panica, the Macedonian left-wing revolutionary responsible for the murders of Boris Sarafov and Ivan Garvanov nearly two decades earlier, was living with his compatriot Filip Anastasov in Vienna. Panica had fled to Austria in the early months of 1925 because he had made enemies with the right-wing Bulgarian Prime Minister Alexander Tsankov.[509] Furthermore, Ivan Mihajlov, as the new leader of the right-wing IMRO, had sentenced Panica to death the previous year for corroborating with the communists and allegedly serving foreign interests.[510]

On the evening of May 8th, Panica, his wife and their bodyguards were watching a performance of "Peer Gynt," a popular Norwegian play whose main character, ironically, is forced to live as an outlaw.[511] They were sitting in a theatre box with some other Macedonians.[512] Behind them sat Menka Karnecheva, the 26-year-old daughter of a wealthy Macedonian. Menka was a frail woman with black hair and dark eyes[513] and was born to Vlach parents in Krushevo. Eventually, she would marry Ivan Mihajlov.[514]

Menka, whose body was riddled with disease, had been a schoolteacher in Macedonia and taught there until she moved to Vienna. As a teacher, she "drum[med] into her pupils how the Balkan province had been butchered by the Turks, Serbs, Bulgars and Greeks." She instilled into her students her dream of an independent Macedonia with Solun as its capital. When she arrived to Vienna, she met many Macedonians who wanted the same thing but insisted that Todor Panica stood in the way. Not knowing much about Panica, Menka was willing to partake in the 'revolutionary' fight:

Menica offered to do the job. Her request met with blunt refusals. A woman to murder this powerful gangster? Such an idea was obviously absurd. But Menica explained she only had a few months to live. If she failed, she would be dead before she could be sentenced. If she succeeded, well, one more traitor would be out of the way. Regretfully, her conspirators saw her point and agreed to the plan. She was to pose as a student of Vienna University, interested in Macedonian history. She would attempt to interview Panizza to get his ideas. She would become his friend, and then – [515]

Another source claims, however, that when Menka was studying in Munich, she became friendly with Panica's sister-in-law. One of her university friends was living with Panica and he offered her hospitality. She stayed with them for several months. She returned their hospitality by getting them tickets to see 'Peer Gynt.'[516]

So Menka, awaiting the most opportune time to strike at her new friend, when the main character was "shipwrecked in the midst of a thunderstorm,"[517] she pulled out her revolver and shot him in the head. She continued shooting, but Panica's wife jumped in the path of the incoming bullets, suffering a critical head wound herself,[518] as "one bullet entered her mouth and passed through her tongue."[519] One of Panica's guards, Bagatinov, drew his pistol but Menka shot him before he could respond. Menka had her orders and had executed them perfectly. She had even taken all precautions to blend in with others and visited the theater beforehand to get a sense of its layout.[520]

At her trial, Menka claimed she killed Panica out of "patriotic reasons."[521] But IMRO was not the only one out to assassinate Panica. "For nearly 20 years a price has been on his head" as governments and political organizations in Bulgaria, Serbia, Greece and Turkey had been trying to track him down and bring him to justice for a variety of reasons.[522] Yet, Menka got to him first and she was sentenced to eight years in prison for her crime. But the day after her imprisonment she was released because the doctors believed she had less than two months to live, due to her tuberculosis. On her way to Macedonia, many IMRO leaders greeted her, among them Ivan Mihajlov, and Menka found a new hero in the man who had ordered the Viennese Macedonians to murder Panica.[523]

After Todor Panica was killed, the Federalists stepped up their efforts to destroy Mihajlov's reign. On October 31st, 1927, in Shtip, Mihajlov's father and brother were taking a stroll over the Vardar Bridge when they were murdered by Federalists. "Five revolver shots were fired by the assassins in the presence of many witnesses and the two men were killed instantly." This was the same spot where a Serbian general was assassinated the year prior.[524] While IMRO Federalists could not reach Mihajlov directly, they targeted those closest to him in hopes of frightening him.

But Mihajlov did not let these deaths go unanswered. General Protogerov was assassinated by three Macedonians on a summer Saturday night in Sofia on July 9th, 1928. Although born a Macedonian and considered by many an important revolutionary figure, he had served as a Bulgarian general in the first World War and was accused of war crimes by Yugoslavia for his actions in that war.[525] His followers, however, saw him as one of the greatest Macedonian leaders:

> **As for Protogeroff: ask about this almost legendary figure, this man whose mark never fails, who always avoids capture, who slips in and out of the hands of his many and various enemies, and they will brag about him for an hour.**[526]

Protogerov was also a Mason and a vegetarian. He had heeded the call of Todor Aleksandrov to fight for a free and united Macedonia when Aleksandrov resurrected IMRO in 1919.[527]

Protogerov had succeeded Aleksandrov as a leader. But Mihajlov, upon becoming a member of the Central Committee, quickly schemed to obtain more power. Protogerov had the reputation of a kind but weak man, completely different from the ruthless and unscrupulous Mihajlov. "However, Mihajlov allowed Protogerov to survive until he had consolidated his own grip on I.M.R.O. He was helped by the replacement of the Tsankov Government by that of the Macedonian, Liapchev, who was remarkably tolerant of I.M.R.O." After Protogerov's assassination, the IMRO Congress met on July 22nd, 1928. Protogerov's followers were excluded. IMRO approved of Mihajlov's decision and IMRO thus became divided into Mihajlovists and Protogerovists. And the war began.[528]

Some speculated that Protogerov was assassinated because "he refused to disturb the present good relations between Bulgaria and Jugoslavia" by leading a military insurrection against Yugoslavia. Protogerov had noted that, even though Yugoslavia had been an enemy of Bulgaria and Macedonians, it was the first country to send aid to Bulgaria after a huge earthquake there. "We cannot cut off the hand that feeds us," he said.[529]

At his funeral, "ceaseless lines of fierce looking Comitadjis passed the body and gave a last salute to the uncrowned monarch of the Macedonian irregulars."[530] Whether crowned or not, with Protogerov dead, Mihajlov was the only Macedonian leader left with any significant power. Most people inside IMRO knew it, too.

At that time, as had always been the case, there was a three-person Central Committee technically in charge of IMRO. These Committee leaders were elected at IMRO conventions by the IMRO Congress, which was composed of 36 chiefs. The three Central Committee members possessed equal rights and responsibilities, and it was "against all statute rules that one member of the committee should pass judgment on either of his comrades." Mihajlov violated this by assassinating Protogerov, a member of the Central Committee of three. The other Committee member was Georgi Popchristov, who was an ally to Protogerov.[531]

Mihajlov's faction was the strongest and most organized, as he had inherited (much by force) the followers, funds and organization of Todor Aleksandrov.

> His 'cabinet colleagues' are a dozen in number. Each is an outlaw; each has a price on his head. 'Cabinet meetings' are held now in rocky fastnesses, then in deep forest grades, now in 'safe' villages, then in quiet wayside inns. Never for more than a couple of days does the government stay in one place. Yet it is a government with an army, thoroughly organized and mobile, and with reserves, every man of which knows where to 'join up.'
>
> Arms and ammunition are manufactured in the IMRO's private and secret arsenals. It has its codes of laws and courts of justice, with executioners to do their dread bidding. This remarkable government even prints its own postage stamps for its secret postal system. Scattered all over Europe – if you know just where to look – the accredited representatives of Ivan Michailov. Up in the wildest Bulgarian mountains he maintains an intelligence and propaganda department which is as efficient as anything of its kind in Eastern Europe... And throughout Macedonia, the teachers in the schools obey an invisible education department which insists on scholars being taught to be patriotic Macedonians.[532]

IMRO had already become a mighty force in the Balkans before Mihajlov's rise, but Mihajlov's methods changed it into a criminal enterprise:

> How does IMRO feed its servants? This is how! The owners of the cafes, restaurants and hotels; the grocers, bakers, sausage makers and stall holders of the district occupied by the conspirators – all of them taxpayers of the official Bulgarian Government – could not open their shutters or pitch their stalls unless they paid, in addition, a tithe to Mihailoff.
>
> At Vantche's [Mihajlov] orders the hotel-keepers must reserve five rooms in their hotels; two on the first floor for voivods, three higher up for the rank and file. To every man who presents himself with a card bearing Mihailoff's seal, every baker, every

butcher, every dairyman, tailor, hatter, shoemaker and chemist must supply bread, meat, cheese, clothes and medicines. Any who refuse will, for the first offence, have their shops closed for a month. If they refuse a second time, their shops will be rifled; a third time, they will be set on fire; a fourth, and the offender will be seized and taken before the tribunal of IMRO.[533]

Using his network, Mihajlov was determined to rid IMRO of non-conformers. In November of 1928, the different factions of IMRO engaged each other in an especially destructive bloodbath. Among the dead was Belev, an IMRO leader of the Macedonian committee in Ohrid[534] who had also been a Bulgarian police chief. "Beleff and his committee had severely denounced the internal Macedonian struggle, and accused the group led by Gen. Ivan Michailoff of ordering the murder of Gen. Protogueroff."[535] Belev was a close friend to Protogerov.[536] Mihajlov ordered the death sentence for all "foes of his faction within the revolutionary organization" and his supporters immediately sought out and killed several Macedonians,[537] including Belev.

Protogerov's supporters threatened to "publish all the past misdeeds and plots of the Macedonian revolutionary organization" despite the fact that doing so "would be tantamount to signing their own death warrant, since they had been involved in many of these acts." This threat came after Mihajlov threatened to "march on Sofia" after fighting and disputes with the ruling Bulgarian government in November of 1928. The Bulgarian government had sent troops to Pirin Macedonia to seek out Mihajlov and gave him an ultimatum to stop the terrorism. Mihajlov replied that the "federal members of the Bulgarian government deserved death" and classified them as the greatest threat to the Macedonian people.[538] Mihajlov declared war on the Bulgarians, in addition to his rival Macedonians.

Financing this war was not easy. But Mihajlov's IMRO exploited whoever they wanted, whenever they wanted:

In 1927 IMRO dragged 20,000,000 *levas* out of the Jews of Sofia. They also took 4,000,000 from the Armenians. The organization knows the assets of every Jew, Armenian and Greek in Sofia. It knows how much each one possesses in cash, the value of his real estate and of his goods. When one of them receives an inheritance IMRO is there for its share before the government authority. If a father is giving a dowry to his daughter, IMRO is present at the signing of the deeds. Its collectors are chosen from the most burly of the conspirators; having seen them one can understand everything."[539]

Before the 1920s were over, Mihajlov considered Pirin Macedonia to be an independent country under his control and not a part of Bulgaria.[540] Only his IMRO enforced laws and executed justice in the region. By the beginning of the summer of 1930, over one-hundred left-wing Macedonians were killed by Mihajlov's faction in the Pirin region since Protogerov's death. The murders happened everywhere, from "public highways" to "inside their homes."[541]

Two of these killed were Bogdarov and Naum Tomalevski, two men close to Protogerov. Bogdarov was killed on January 13th, 1931 while Tomalevski was killed a month earlier on December 3rd, 1930. However, IMRO had tried to make attempts on their lives before. Once, when Tomalevski and Bogdarov were together in October of 1930, IMRO wanted to seize the moment to kill them. However, the two appointed assassins for the job could not be found. IMRO thus appointed two others on the spot who had no time to study the pictures of their victims. The IMRO member who dealt with the pictures indicated that they kill the tall and the short one when they walked out of the house. When the tall one and short one came out, the IMRO operatives killed both the tall one and the short one. However, it was soon discovered that the tall one and the short one they killed were tailors and that Bogdarov and Tomalevski were either still inside or left through another door.[542]

Tomalevski had been very active in the Macedonian revolution throughout the 1920s and was staunchly against Mihajlov's domination. He was one of a few Macedonians who had joined Aleksandrov and Protogerov in February of 1920 in organizing rebel activity in Serbian occupied Macedonia. He had helped form the Macedonian Scientific Institute in 1923; collected evidence of the conditions of and abuses against Macedonians; and after Aleksandrov's assassination wrote actively about the desire to see an autonomous Macedonia within a Balkan Confederation. In part, he wrote to the League of Nations in the late summer of 1923 about how IMRO would desire Macedonia to be a part of a Yugoslavia that treats Macedonians as equals. He warned, however, that if Macedonians' rights continued to be violated, IMRO would redouble its efforts to stop the suppression of Macedonians. In January of 1924, Tomalevski and Protogerov had a meeting in London with the Croatian politician, Stjepan Radic, where they discussed the possibility of joint Macedonian-Croatian opposition in the Yugoslav Parliament. He toured Europe with other Macedonians in 1925, and convinced Austrian, Hungarian and Italian government representatives to collaborate against Yugoslav intolerance of Macedonians. After Protogerov's murder in 1928, he became a marked man by Mihajlov for siding with the Protogerov faction.[543]

Another IMRO member that Mihajlov tried to eliminate was Vapcarov, who had been a supporter of Sandanski. Vapcarov participated in the 1919 revival of IMRO and even sided with Mihajlov over Protogerov when Aleksandrov was assassinated. He was elected to IMRO's Central Committee in 1926. When Protogerov was assassinated, however, he openly opposed Mihajlov. Mihajlov then ordered him killed, but Vapcarov escaped to New York. He returned to Bulgaria in 1930 and was kidnapped by Mihajlovist's faction.[544]

Of course, the Protogerov faction would not back away from the Mihajlov faction. On February 8th, 1931 it was reported in the news that Jordan Gorkov, Mihajlov's second in command, was killed:

Jordan Gourkoff, second in command to the terrorist Mihailoff, was assassinated to-day by members of the Protogueroff group. The crime was committed in one of the busiest streets of Sofia. M. Gourkoff, a lawyer and a man of considerable note, was riddled with bullets. He was alone on this occasion, having dispensed with the usual bodyguard. The murder was decreed as a reprisal for the recent killing of an important Protoguerovist.[545]

Gorkov was a lawyer and strong supporter of Ivan Mihajlov. Foolishly, he had been roaming the streets without bodyguards or a revolver:

Our young lawyer suddenly realized where so much conceit had led him: a shower of bullets whistled round his ears. Wounded, he staggered down the street and took refuge in a grocer's shop where he thought he would be safe. His assassins followed him and there Gourkoff, representative of the bar of his country, fell,

between a box of prunes and a barrel of treacle, and died on the sawdust.[546]

In February of 1931, a band of Mihajlov's followers "swept down on a rival rebel camp and kidnapped a number of their most prominent members." This camp that Mihajlov's faction obliterated was that of the other chief of the Macedonian Central Committee who had been aligned with Protogerov: Georgi Popchristov.[547] With Popchristov as Mihajlov's prisoner, along with Parlitchev, Mihajlov had managed to make himself in charge of nearly every aspect of IMRO.

Mihajlov did not kill Popchristov or Parlitchev. Rather, he forced them into signing a declaration to bring about peace and unification of the warring Macedonian parties. They did not want to, but had little choice:

> One Sunday morning Madame Parlitcheff went to church with her child. Her bodyguard accompanied her, listening reverently to the service as they stood on either side of her...The service over, Madame Parlitcheff was persuaded by her bodyguard that it would be unwise to return on foot. Precaution had been taken and a car was waiting. Together with the child and bodyguard she got in and was driven – about thirty-five miles, to Gorna-Djoumaya, in Bulgarian Macedonia. They bodyguard, as you may have gathered, had been bought over by Ivan Mihailoff.
>
> That night, in the very heart of Sofia, the houses of Parlitcheff and Popchristoff were surrounded by Komitadjis...Here also the bodyguard had succumbed to the lure of gold. The doors were opened and the apartments invaded. Parlitcheff, in great distress, was on the watch. The leader of the invasion handed to him a paper – the text of the reconciliation between the Mihailovists and the Protoguerovists. "Sign it! If you don't your wife and child..."[548]

The gang warfare continued throughout the decade. In December of 1932, the editor of Mihajlov's magazine was targeted:

> Two Protoguerovists, disguised as sportsmen and armed with guns, attacked M. Simeon Eftimoff, the Mihailovist editor of

Makedoniya, who was being escorted by his three bodyguards. Many shots were exchanged. The editor and his guards were all seriously wounded, a policeman who tried to restore order was killed, and three members of the public were also wounded, two of whom afterwards died. The crowd seized the two Protoguerovists, one of whom tried to escape by throwing a bomb into the thick of the crowd, but an officer shot him dead, and some plucky individual picked up the bomb and extinguished the fuse.[549]

Eftimov would die of his wounds in early January. Christo Trajanov, the other Protogerovist involved in the shootout with Eftimov and his bodyguards, was sent to a hospital to recover from his wounds, where he met his doom:

Trajanoff lay in ward with nineteen others, and as the authorities had received letters threatening him he was guarded by two policemen. Soon after midnight the nurse, Katharina Konstantinoff, in making her last round for the night, approached the assassin's bedside, adjusted his pillow, then drew a revolver from under her apron, and with great calmness fired three shots into his head. Trajanoff was killed outright. The nurse, who was immediately arrested, told at her examination of how she had been visited earlier in the day by a Macedonian who had given her the revolver and ordered her to shoot Trajanoff. As a good Macedonian, she had done so.[550]

In February 1933, Mihajlov realized that this campaign of extermination of the left-wing Macedonians – along with the Bulgarian suppression of Macedonian activity – was not aiding the Macedonian cause. Many Macedonians refused to cave into his terroristic ways. Thus, he helped organize the Great Meeting at Gorna Djumija in February. There, he and Macedonians vowed to break the Bulgarian chain and work toward the political aspirations of the Macedonians. The Bulgarian authorities responding by clamping down harder on IMRO and Mihajlov.[551]

This Great Meeting, however, also determined to settle accounts with Yugoslavia and stated that the Yugoslav dictatorship would soon be gone. However, a unified front of Mihajlovists and Protogerovists and other Macedonians evaporated. Mihajlov announced a merciless fight against the Communists, "a term that was now being used to cover the non-Mihailovist factions in the militant group."[552]

In July of 1933 Mihajlov then declared "he would abandon his campaign against the Protoguerovists" as long as they submitted to recognizing his faction of IMRO as the supreme authority and that they would no longer conspire against him. The Protogerovists replied that the feud began five years ago when Mihajlov ordered the assassination of Protogerov and proclaimed they only were acting in self-defense. They further stated that "they did not believe in the argument of the gun and wished to stop bloodshed." They would stop reprisals as long as they were not attacked or provoked. They would not abandon their views, but they would make sacrifices for the general good of the Cause so long as Mihajlovists made sacrifices. Mihajlov rejected this and, while not reigniting an armed campaign against them, accused them in the newspapers of being spies and traitors.[553]

Despite the war raging between the Macedonian parties, the different Macedonian factions still put up a fierce resistance against their subjugators. In the spring of 1925, the Bulgarian government outlawed all communists and began dismantling their organizations. Mihajlov's IMRO aided the fascist Bulgarian state, "giving the government great assistance, providing large bands of fighting men where they are most needed."[554] The Prime Minister of Bulgaria at this time was Tsankov. By the 1930s, Tsankov would proceed to embrace fascism and become a supporter of Hitler and the Nazi regime.[555] But for the time being his extreme right-wing views were still being fine-tuned as he dealt with the left-wing Macedonians.

Even though Mihajlov was working with the Bulgarians when it suited him, the majority of Macedonians had no faith in Bulgaria's will to help the Macedonians achieve independence and unity. For Macedonians, Bulgaria was as much of an obstacle to their cause as Serbia and Greece. For example, in the spring of 1924, Nikola Guenov (a former Macedonian official in Bulgaria) entered a U.S. consulate office in Bulgaria and asked Vice-Consul Leroy Spangler to confirm his understanding of certain laws, such as whether the U.S. consulate office was considered foreign soil. Upon confirmation, he whipped out a revolver, shouted "this is American soil" and killed himself with a bullet to the head. It happened to be that in Bulgaria, unless a

Bulgarian citizen died on foreign soil, a person without legal heirs forfeited his estate to the Bulgarian state upon his death. Guenov, who had no heirs, desired his life savings to be donated to the Macedonian Cause. Thus, killing himself at the U.S. consulate office permitted his fortune to be directed as stated in his will,[556,557] which was found on his corpse along with $4,000 in US currency and 50,000 *levas*.[558] A natural death on Bulgarian territory would have given his estate to an enemy of the Macedonian cause, the Bulgarian government.

The Macedonians tolerated Bulgaria more than Serbia and Greece, but they still held the Bulgarians accountable for wrong-doings. The left-wing IMRO Federalists, for their part, were bent on exacting revenge on Bulgarian leaders who had often participated in the murder of 200 of their compatriots under Aleksandrov's leadership and Mihajlov's new reign. In the middle of April 1925, "a small group of anarchists cooperating with Macedonian federalists" were accused of bombing a Sofia cathedral in an attempt to kill Bulgaria's Premier Tsankov, who managed to narrowly escape the bombing. However, the bomb killed 150 people at the church. The Macedonians targeted Tsankov because he had helped finance and protect Aleksandrov's and now Mihajlov's right-wing IMRO.[559]

It became evident that the differing IMRO factions would not let their factional rivalry dissuade them for their crucifixion of Bulgarian, Greek and Yugoslav authorities. The Macedonian assassin, Ivan Montchilov, targeted the Yugoslavian police chief Lazitch in Belgrade just a few days after Protogerov's death in 1928. Lazitch "had placed a price of 500,000 Serbian *francs*" on Protogerov's head. Even with Protogerov dead, Lazitch was still one of IMRO's leading enemies in Yugoslavia; so Montchilov shot him in the head and then attempted to commit suicide. Moreover, Lazitch survived the assassination attempt.[560]

Ivan Montchilov had been living as an exile in Belgrade. He became a spy for Serbia and monitored Macedonian and Bulgarian activities for many years. In 1928, he was offered a job by Lazitch, who was the Yugoslavian Director of Public Security at the time, to kill Mihajlov. He was to receive 200,000 *dinars* for the deed. He told Lazitch he would do it, but then confided in Minchinov, a man of IMRO, about what Lazitch wanted him to do. Mihajlov then met with Montchilov. The IMRO concocted a scheme:

Nine days later, the official Serbian agency, Avala, announced that Ivan Mihailoff had been assassinated. The newspapers in Belgrade published the news with full details...Meanwhile, the victorious Ivan Montchiloff returned to Serbia. He was received like a Saint Michael after slaying the dragon. The man of the moment entered Belgrade. As the head of the police force, the man who for years had been fighting Ivan Mihailoff, Jica Lazich, received the hero. Then the paid traitor tore off his mask. "In the name of the Macedonian Revolutionary Committee!" he exclaimed, firing three shots at Lazich.[561]

Before, during and after the height of the internal feuds of IMRO, the answer to any anti-Macedonian activity by outsiders was a death warrant for the perpetrators. Both factions of IMRO were initially very skeptical of a possible union between Serbia and Bulgaria, potentially creating a "dual monarchy," which would impede the Macedonians' "chances of forming an independent government." IMRO's aims were to create divisions and hatred between Serbia and Bulgaria so a union would not happen,[562] but eventually the left-wing of IMRO began advocating for an autonomous and united Macedonia within such a union. The problem was that, aside from the socialists and communists – who were still a small but growing minority – the Serbian and Bulgarian regimes were not ready to tolerate an autonomous Macedonia in any sense.

So IMRO continued issuing death warrants. Such warrant was issued for a Serbian general named Michael Kovachevitch. On October 6th, 1927, IMRO members assassinated Kovachevitch in Shtip. He "was shot down at the door of his home...and the assassins left a lighted bomb behind them to cut off pursuit."[563] Another of these death warrants was issued for Velimir Prelich, who, as a legal adviser to the Skopje Prefect, ordered the investigation and arrest of Macedonian students there in November of 1927. The responsibility for killing him was passed down to Hora Bujrev. Two months later, Bujrev shot him in the streets of Skopje. The bullet severed his spine, paralyzing him, but not killing him. Bujrev, on the other hand, committed suicide right after attempting to kill Prelich.[564]

However, Prelich met his death in 1928. Mara Buneva, who was from Skopje, acquainted herself with him before carrying out the deed. Because Buneva was a hat maker, IMRO helped her open a shop in Skopje where she would make hats. Serbian and Macedonian women bought her latest models, which served as a funding source for the IMRO. Buneva's purpose there, however, was to kill Prelich for the way he had been treating Macedonian students – the store was her cover. Prelich had even stopped by her shop once and exclaimed to his wife: "My dear, how clever this woman is with her hands."[565] One day, she met him on the most populous street of Skopje, drew her revolver, shot and killed him, and then took her own life.[566] She killed herself with a bullet to the heart.[567]

In December of 1928, IMRO managed to execute a notorious Yugoslav band leader who was raiding Pirin and Vardar Macedonia and harassing Macedonians. His name was Sekulitchki. Just before his death, he had attempted to blow up a statue of Todor Aleksandrov. However, his plot was thwarted and IMRO loyalists captured him. In Kyustendil, "the inhabitants woke up to find his body suspended from a tree in the public square, near the monument of the Macedonian chief, Theodor Alexandroff."[568] His body was facing Aleksandrov's statue and pinned to his body was a note that read: "Such is the fate of all traitors."[569]

IMRO also aimed to create hostilities between Serbia and Greece and use those hostilities to the advantage of the Macedonian Cause. Two Macedonians attempted to dynamite Serbian banks, buildings and the Serbian consulate in Solun in September of 1927. Their plot was foiled and, after a trial, the two were executed in the spring of 1928.[570]

But foiled plots didn't hamper the Macedonian Cause. One writer explained why the IMRO was so difficult to suppress:

People have been trying to stamp them out, to suppress them for 30 years. Apparently, it cannot be done. Half a dozen Jugoslav governments, half a dozen Bulgarian governments, have tried and failed. The committeemen are of the people; they live in small, mobile bands and the people – their people – protect them. It is hard enough to catch a simple thief or robber in these barren hills. To catch a comitadji – when you keep in mind that about nine-tenths of the population sympathize with the comitadji – is almost impossible. They are fanatical nationalists – the Irishmen of the Balkans – and they know how to hide…'All members of the organization make it a point of

honor to know just what is necessary to know and not one other thing.'[571]

Albert Londres described the inner-workings of this network of the 'Irishmen of the Balkans'. Here is one description of IMRO's establishments in Sofia:

> The Makedonska is a large café. Seventeen customers occupy thirteen tables. On another table is an empty pyrogen. Poor proprietor! Not one of them is taking any refreshment. The place is silent. Like pawns, these men give the room the appearance of a chessboard on which the game has been abandoned. They are waiting to be called. At a sign from a voivode they will get up, perhaps to be sent to 'travel' in Yugoslavia, perhaps to assassinate the last remaining friend of Protogueroff.
>
> ...'L'Italie' is successful in this quarter. It is a restaurant situated at the corner of Mariza Street and Serdika Street. It is one of Vantche's arsenals. It would be of no use asking for a job as a cellarman there, even if you were fully qualified to do the work. The cellar does not contain bottles, it is a depot for rifles, bombs, and 'paklenamachina.'[572]

One IMRO revolutionary who worked tirelessly to put a dent into Serbia's rule over Vardar Macedonia was Felix Sarcovich, who operated with a band of 50 IMRO members along the Albanian frontier with Vardar Macedonia. Throughout the 1920s he had gained such notoriety for his actions that the Serbian government put a bounty on his head for $180,000. One of his bands' most vicious acts took place in the summer of 1928, when they locked nine Serbians – including four Serbian policemen – into a hut and burned them alive. After that event, the Serbian government "declared a war of extermination against Sarcovitch and his band."[573]

The most extraordinary assassination ordered and executed under Mihajlov's reign, however, was that of Yugoslavia's King Alexander and French Foreign Minister Louis Barthou in late 1934. Mihajlov would start another global war if he believed it were necessary to free Macedonia,[574] and many believed this assassination would be just that catalyst. In October, King Alexander had arrived in Marseille, France by boat and was greeted by Minister Barthou. They proceeded through the streets in a formal procession, where crowds had gathered to cheer the King's arrival. Amongst the crowd, with a bouquet of flowers in his hands, stood IMRO loyalist Vlado Czernozemski, "a notorious Macedonian terrorist and associate of Ivan Mihailov."[575]

Czernozemski was known in Balkan circles for assassinating those who opposed independence for Macedonia[576] and those from other IMRO factions. In 1921, he murdered a Bulgarian agrarian leader who opposed IMRO, and in 1930 he assassinated Ivan Tomalevski, "one of the leaders of the Protogerov" faction of IMRO,[577] in front of Tomalevski's home.[578] "Tomalevski had gone into his garden…when he saw a window curtain in a neighboring house move. He told his son to run for his revolver. But it was too late. Two shots rang out. Tomalevski fell dead."[579] That neighbor's house belonged to police officer. Tomalevski's bodyguards were drinking in a nearby bar instead of attending to their duties and thus were not there to witness two men enter Tomalevski's neighbor's house two nights before the murder. The men vowed to remain in the house until Tomalevski gave up his guard. Tomalevski's father decided to plant a bush in the garden on December 3rd and Tomalevski went to help him. Four shots rang out, two of those hitting Tomalevski.[580]

Czernozemski served some prison time; but after escaping, he eventually landed a new role as Mihajlov's bodyguard, messenger and chauffer.[581] But Czernozemski was destined for greater tasks. He was a Macedonian fanatic, but he was as principled and focused as any Macedonian loyalist:

He was a silent, moody person, always keeping to himself, his nose perpetually buried in a book. He neither drank, smoked, nor ate meat. Incredible as it may seem, he once said that he would not eat meat because it was cruel to kill animals.[582]

In Marseille, as King Alexander's car approached Czernozemski's position, Czernozemski sprung forward shouting "long live the King!" Then, in a matter of a few seconds, three bullets fell the king. An eye witness described the event:

> The procession had covered only 150 yards when I saw clearly on my right a man emerge from the cheering crowd on the sidewalk and leap with a single bound on the right footboard of the automobile. A series of cracks followed and in the twinkling of an eye the scene of vibrant enthusiasm, so ordered and beautiful, had turned into a wild panic. People dashed from the official car or else hurled themselves upon it, seemingly gone mad. I saw a Colonel rain furious blows with his saber upon a man struggling against the side of the car. I saw policemen rushing up with revolvers and firing at the man who now fired wildly in the surging crowd. I saw police showering blows upon a bleeding mass which no longer resembled a human being, and drag it off the square, while the crowd fell upon it, trampling it under foot.[583]

The entire scene was chaotic. Onlookers and guards immediately pounced on Czernozemski. The chauffeur of the King's car grabbed Czernozemski by the neck and began choking him. Colonel Piollet began slashing the assassin with his sword. After firing off his rounds, Czernozemski tried to kill himself with his pistol, but the police thwarted this suicide attempt.[584]

Some speculated that Foreign Minister Barthou could have survived, except a traffic jam in the streets of Marseille prevented him from getting to a surgeon. His severed artery bled out and he passed away. Those with him at the time of his death told Barthou that the King and others escaped injury. "I am so glad," said Barthou. "I am happy to know that I was the only one wounded."[585]

The assassinations, however, did not only inflict damage to the two officials. Sixteen bystanders and officials were injured in the shootings and two, Madame Dubrec and a police officer, eventually succumbed to their injuries. Czernozemski's intention was to only assassinate King Alexander, but his automatic pistol was so powerful that it "fired ten shots at one pressure of the trigger."[586] Still, "most of the spectators who were injured were hit by bullets aimed by police at the murderer."[587]

Czernozemski's assassination of King Alexander and Minister Barthou was not the work of a lone-wolf or solely a Macedonian contraption. IMRO worked closely with the Croatian Ustashi, as both were opposed to the fascist Yugoslavian King and Serbian domination of their peoples. Many Croats felt disdain for King

Alexander because he "kept their leaders imprisoned, suppressed their party, and denied them their dearest wish – to become a unit with equal rights in federal Yugoslavia."[588]

One of Czernozemski's Croatian partners, Mio Kraj, declared to authorities, "I am a Croat. What I did and what I wanted to do were for Croatian liberty." Although he claimed to be a "Croat patriot" and that he had come to France on the orders of Ustashi leader Dr. Ante Pavelic, Kraj could not execute his duties. He fled at the last minute because the thought of shooting into the crowd "made him quail" and was scared that Czernozemski would shoot him down for hesitating to act.[589]

This was not the first attempt by the Ustashi to assassinate King Alexander. In December of the previous year, three Croats failed to kill him during a visit to Zagreb, "which was intended to be a Christmas gift to the Croat people."[590] Although the passion was on the Croats' side, the Ustashi's main obstacle was their lack of organization and training. They had found their lucky break in Mihajlov's IMRO, whose organization had been specializing in revolution, terrorism and assassination for four decades. IMRO had been seeking to kill King Alexander for the past decade. In 1928, the Serbian authorities discovered one of these failed plots:

> **The plot was revealed by a recent police investigation of the recent murder of the Macedonian leader Christovitch. Police said they discovered a paper, on which details of the plan to kill the king were written, sewed in the lining of Christovitch's coat. The paper indicated that King Alexander and a number of raditch (peasant party) leaders were to be slain. The murders were then to be blamed on the Serbians and the Croats would be influenced to revolt against the government. The plan, it was stated, was merely to open the way for a Macedonian revolt.[591]**

More collaboration between the two organizations and better planning was needed to be successful. Thus, beginning in 1932, Mihajlov sent Czernozemski to Hungary "as a courier of secret messages" to the Croatian Ustashi organization operating there. By 1933, Czernozemski was living in Budapest and serving as a "liaison officer" between IMRO and the Ustashi. He soon began instructing the Croats in weaponry and military tactics, such as how to construct and use bombs and firearms.[592]

The Croats produced for Czernozemski a forged Czech passport, and as he traveled to France, he used the name Petrus Kamelen.[593] But the French and Yugoslav authorities discovered this was simply an alias and hurried to identify him. On Czernozemski's right arm was a tattoo of a skull and bones, the signature IMRO symbol; and printed underneath it was "Liberty or Death." "IMRO" was tattooed above the skull and bones.[594] Initially, the authorities thought that these tattoos were "a trick to throw them off the right track."[595] They knew that the Macedonians had grievances with the Serbs, and that the Macedonians were a constant nuisance, but all reasonable suspicions were that only the Croats, along with maybe the Italians, would scheme to pull off such a grand gesture of hatred. The authorities even briefly looked into whether Czernozemski was connected with the Macedonian revolutionary group "Ochrid," a group that was striving for the independence of Macedonians but had no connection to IMRO. The authorities, however, quickly downplayed any link between "Ochrid" and Czernozemski.[596]

It was then discovered that a pretty, brown-haired woman named Marie Vjoudroch had carried the assassin's gun into France and that there were more than just a few members of the "assassin squad." Most of them started with Hungarian passports and made it into France by the way of Switzerland. Two suspects named Ivan Rajtich and Zvonemer Pospschil gave authorities most of this information. These two Croats had said that four assassins met a man in Lausanne simply known as "the doctor" who brought them new clothes to wear on the day of the assassination. It was a Balkan tradition that a revolutionary would be dressed in new clothes before a major assassination, as such an act was tantamount to suicide. In Fontainebleau, the assassins obtained fake Czech passports. They came to Paris by motorbus, two stayed in one hotel and two in another. Marie arrived with the four handbags of guns at a hotel and gave them to one man who then distributed them to the assassins. The "doctor" had instructed the four assassins to wait in front of the opera to await his final orders.[597] There they met the delegate, Egon Kvaternik, who told them: "You know the king is arriving. You also know what you must do – go to Marseille and fire on the king."[598]

As with any most assassinations of high public officials, Europe was on edge over the possibility that either similar-scale assassination attempts would follow or that a European war would ignite, as was the case when a Bosnian Serb's assassination of the Austrian Archduke Franz Ferdinand triggered World War I.[599] At King Alexander's funeral in Belgrade, both "foreign and native newspaper men and photographers had their rooms and their baggage searched for fear they had explosives concealed."[600] Days before, as the King's body was being transferred through Yugoslavia to Belgrade, "police rigidly enforced orders to householders to keep their shutters tight closed, lest a sniper's bullet aimed from a window pick-off any of the high officials accompanying the body homeward."[601]

Meanwhile, in France, the police were searching for all the homes of Yugoslavian refugees living in Paris for any connections to the assassination.[602] France especially "was striving desperately to keep the Marseille murders from becoming another Sarajevo,"[603] and the sentiment around Europe was that "the Balkans are more Balkanic than ever."[604] Foreign Minister Barthou himself said, just a few months before his assassination, said that he could "no longer prophecy that we shall not have war in 1934."[605] Thus, it was not just the assassination, but events preceding the assassination along with the assassination that combined to paint an imminent doomsday scenario for Europe.

Even though their fears of a world war eventually began to dissipate, the authorities were convinced that the assassination would at least change the present course of events in Europe. Perhaps an overreaction, but they barred French theatres from showing the assassination, caught on film, to not stir emotions.[606]

As the IMRO had now transitioned from a thorn in the heel of the Balkan nations to a European ticking time bomb, the Bulgarian government felt heavy international pressure to eliminate the Macedonian agitation for independence. In the early years after World War I, Bulgaria was hesitant and incapable of checking IMRO. "Because of the power of the Macedonians in Bulgaria, the government ha[d]not dared to take action against them." Bulgaria eventually entered into border agreements with Yugoslavia to deal with Macedonian "terrorism." While Bulgaria and Yugoslavia were technically on friendly terms, the countries were separated by barbed wire. Anyone trying to illegally cross the border was immediately shot. IMRO members were notorious for committing raids into southern Serbia and then escaping back into Bulgaria and Pirin Macedonia to hide.[607]

Bulgaria's first ever charge against an IMRO leader for acts of violence came in the spring of 1930, when Mihajlov was charged with the murder of "two political enemies."[608] Over the next few months, hundreds of Macedonians were arrested.[609] Bulgaria arrested Macedonians suspected of being involved with IMRO and deported these patriots to the interior of Bulgaria.[610] In the summer of 1934 the government captured Krem Kiro, an infamous executioner responsible for at least fifty murders. Police claimed they obtained a confession from him linking him to the murders as part of "efforts to establish an autonomous Macedonia."[611] By October of 1934, after the assassination of King Alexander, the Bulgarian government gave every citizen the right to kill Ivan Mihajlov and five of his associates.[612] Mihajlov had been accused of being responsible for 3,500 assassinations during his reign[613] and the Bulgarian authorities were aiming to end his rule and finally establish control over Pirin Macedonia.

By then, Bulgaria had partitioned Pirin Macedonia between two different prefectures in Bulgaria in order to lessen the influence of IMRO and to get a grip on the Macedonian resistance. Even though the Bulgarian right-wing government shared similar ideologies as Mihajlov, the control of Macedonia was now a power struggle and a national matter.[614] King Boris named a new Prime Minister, who intended on transferring Bulgaria into a true fascist state. Bulgaria had previously only been annoyed with the Macedonians, and had only taken lukewarm measures in quelling IMRO. But that was about to change:

> **If the Macedonian revolutionists choose to fight, they will now have three governments against them instead of only Greece and Yugoslavia as formerly. The new government of Bulgaria is frankly anti-Macedonian...In the new scheme...Petritch [Pirin Macedonia] territory will be divided between Sofia and Plovdiv provinces. Another hint of the anti-Macedonian character of the new government was seen in the prompt removal of General Ivan Volkof, Bulgarian Minister to Italy. Volkof, the only active army officer in the diplomatic service, was friendly to the Macedonian movement, as a result of which the restless province had become almost a state within a state.[615]**

Still, in 1935, IMRO (United) in Pirin Macedonia had enough energy left to push their agenda. They issued this statement:

The Greeks call us 'Slavophone Greeks' and the Serbs 'correct Serbs'. Why? So as to justify their rule and their oppressive aspirations toward Macedonia. The Bulgarian chauvinists act in the same way. They exploit the relationship between the Macedonians and the Bulgarians and characterize us as an 'indivisible section of the Bulgarian nation.' The Bulgarian imperialists have always aspired to conquer and enslave Macedonia, not liberate it…We must state it so that all hear, that we are not Serbs, nor Greeks, nor Bulgarians. We are Macedonians, a separate Macedonian nation. Only in this way can we best defend the independence of our movement and our right for an independent Macedonian state.[616]

As a result of this proclamation, Bulgarian authorities began arresting scores of Macedonian IMRO (United) members in Sofia and Petrich. These wide-scale arrests "paralyzed" IMRO (United) activity in Bulgaria. The members were tried and most, under the promise of lenient sentences, declared they were Bulgarians. But some still declared themselves as Macedonians, such as Asen Karakchiev, who also demanded the right of Pirin Macedonia to secede from Bulgaria. Prison sentences for such proclamation ranged from 5 years to nearly 13 years, while many of those declaring themselves Bulgarian were found innocent.[617]

As far as the right-wing IMRO, Mihajlov and his wife were forced to seek refuge in Turkey once Bulgaria's new prime minister assumed power. Turkey would not extradite him to Bulgaria or Yugoslavia, both having placed orders to capture or kill him.[618] Mihajlov was also said to have been seeking a safe refuge in the United States; but regardless of where he resided, he insisted on continuing the Macedonian struggle, stating: "As long as Macedonia is not free and independent, the Balkans will not be peaceful."[619] But while in exile, three of his closest loyalists were sentenced to death. In addition, "[s]ix other Macedonians were sentenced to life imprisonment and 16 to prison terms up to 15 years."[620]

Mihajlov's reign as an unchecked king in Macedonia, and in Bulgaria, was coming to an end even without Bulgaria's threat on his life. Most Macedonians were tired of his rule. His criminal enterprise reached deep into the lives of most Macedonians who were simply trying to survive. For example:

> **Macedonia produces the best tobacco in the world. The harvest is gathered in and the lorries are ready to leave for the railway station from which the tobacco leaves will be dispatched to Egypt. They do not leave until the arrival of the envoy of the revolutionary organization. The owners of the tobacco, the important ones as well as the smaller merchants, have to pay five per cent of their turnover to Ivan Mihailoff. Suppose they refused to pay? The lorries with their loads would be confiscated and next season the Macedonians would be forbidden to work in the fields of such 'unconvinced' patriots. You might think that these 'patriots by compulsion' need only go to the police. Here, IMRO is the police. If the owners have not the ready money they pay with a post-dated cheque. Mihailoff at once releases the goods and gives them the receipt signed 'Liberty or Death.'**[621]

Many Macedonians feared and harbored disdain for Mihajlov's rule of IMRO, which had become as tyrannical the rule of Bulgaria, Serbia and Greece. One Macedonian in Petrich was flogged for simply reading a document that was considered to be anti-IMRO. An old man talking ill of Mihajlov's reign, also in Petrich, was bludgeoned to death in public. Five men in Delchevo who had been holding secret meetings were discovered, arrested and killed. Four Macedonians from Skalava were temporarily detained, abused and threatened with death for listening to "treasonable speeches." In Ploski, the tax-collector and his clerk said that the Macedonians there did not have to pay their tax to Mihajlov. Both were hanged over a pile of manure. Nearly two dozen young men in Mitinov refused to enlist in Mihajlov's army and were whipped.[622] Mihajlov's IMRO had turned Macedonia into everything that the original IMRO founders had fought against.

IMRO, for many Macedonians, no longer became the ideal that it once had been. Mihajlov's gangsterdom usurped ideological tendencies:

In the nineteen-twenties it became more of a financial racket, selling its services to the highest bidder – the Bulgarian Government, the Italians, possibly for a brief period Soviet Russia. It also became an extortion racket, forcing the Macedonian emigrants in Bulgaria and the inhabitants of the Petrich Department (Bulgarian Macedonia) to buy immunity from economic blackmail and terrorization at a heavy price, through 'voluntary' patriotic subscriptions on 'taxes'...In the early nineteen-thirties it trafficked illegally in drugs: the League of Nations Opium Advisory Committee at one time reported that there were ten factories in the Petrich Department and Sofia manufacturing acetic anhydride.[623]

Further, many of the Macedonians in Vardar Macedonia eventually turned against the right-wing IMRO bands:

I.M.R.O.'s organization of komitadji attacks over the frontier from Bulgaria, and of terrorist acts in Yugoslav Macedonia, inevitably provoked the Yugoslav authorities to repressive measures and reprisals against the local Macedonian populations. These heightened the resentment of the people of Yugoslav Macedonia; but in the end they grew tired of I.M.R.O. and accepted arms from the Yugoslav authorities to protect their villages against komitadji attacks.[624]

IMRO under Mihajlov had lost much of its support among the population. This is why IMRO had to resort to "terrorist acts, assassination, and bomb outrages" on its own people. Mihajlov's IMRO had "no serious economic or social ideas other than the catch-phrases of Macedonian revolution and liberation." Moreover, "it suffered from a fatal ambiguity over the question whether it was aiming at Macedonian autonomy or at annexation to Bulgaria."[625]

As his reign crumbled, Mihajlov turned to other methods to promote his views on Macedonia. While in exile in 1935, he wrote:

We want...to establish a completely independent Macedonia which would reach from the Albanian frontier in the west to the Mesta River (in Greece) in the East, from the Shar Mountains (on the borders of Albania and Yugoslavia) in the north to about

the 40th of latitude (the Aegean Sea coast of Greece) in the south.[626]

If Greece or Yugoslavia were to give Macedonia a large degree of cultural autonomy, Mihajlov said:

> In such a case our official programme would be that terroristic warfare should cease and we would return to legal methods for obtaining our aims, which would continue to be the complete independence of Macedonia... When in 1919...at the time of the Treaty of Neuilly, [and the] whole world was against them, the Macedonians did not lose faith in their just cause. The fact that I am abroad at present does not make the slightest difference to our cause... [W]e have known worse than this. What does it mean that 500 Comitadjis are confined in concentration camps in Bulgaria, that I am abroad, that my friend, Kosteff, second member of the Macedonian Executive Committee is interned, while Nasteff, the third member, is being sought by the Bulgarian police? We have survived other persecutions. Do you not remember that thousands of our adherents have been killed in Yugoslavia, that seven villages were destroyed by gunfire, and that 2000 Comitadjis were detained at one time in concentration camps? Did our activities abate then? No, they did not."[627]

Just because Mihajlov was exiled from Bulgaria, it did not mean that the Macedonian threat had evaporated. In the fall of 1938, a Macedonian named Stoil Kirov assassinated Ivan Peeff in Sofia. Ivan Peeff had been a general and chief of staff of the Bulgarian army. Before committing suicide, a revolutionary named Josifov also wounded Major Stoyanoff, "an aide accompanying the general[.]"[628] But Bulgarian authorities responded within a few days by arresting 3,000 Macedonians and IMRO affiliates in search for the remaining IMRO leaders responsible for the continuing outrages and revolutionary activity in Bulgaria. The Bulgarian police raided "hotels, cafes and private dwellings" in their crackdown. Before Kirov died, he admitted that "he used pistols supplied by the outlawed IMRO."[629]

Bulgaria had completely entered a new phase in their quest for eradicating the Macedonian fight for independence, and IMRO was no longer a viable force in the Balkan drama. In a few years, Bulgaria would find itself in another massive war, fighting against Serbs, Greeks and Macedonians in an attempt to annex Macedonia. IMRO's right-wing faded away into irrelevancy; the Macedonian left-wing, however, saw a resurgence. These Macedonians eventually formed massive resistance movements in Vardar Macedonia and Aegean Macedonia during the 1940s. Vardar Macedonia became a constituent republic of Yugoslavia in 1944, and Aegean Macedonians had nearly defeated the Greek royalists in securing their freedom; but the intervention of British forces and betrayal by communist allies flung the Macedonians of Greece into several decades of destitution.

These 1940s Macedonian movements were no longer spearheaded by IMRO, which had lost its credibility amongst a Macedonian population who was sick of exploitation and violence. Moreover, unlike the admired IMRO before the onset of the First World War, the new IMRO was not viewed as an idealistic group of patriotic Macedonian men fighting for liberty and equality, even though they espoused a 'Macedonia for the Macedonians'. Instead, they were viewed as power-hungry men who let politics divide them instead of uniting under a patriotic common struggle. IMRO evaporated from the Balkan landscape as new Macedonian patriots began reviving the old ideals of Macedonian unity, freedom and equality.

ENDNOTES

[1] http://www.mn.mk/makedonski-legendi/6398-Dimitar-Popgeorgiev---Berovski, *Macedonian Nation – Macedonian Legends, Dimitar Popgeorgiev-Berovski*.
[2] *Macedonian Nation – Macedonian Legends, Dimitar Popgeorgiev-Berovski*.
[3] http://www.mn.mk/makedonski-legendi/4410-Dedo-Iljo-Malesevski , *Macedonian Nation – Macedonian Legends, Dedo Ilyo Maleshevski*.
[4] *Macedonian Nation – Macedonian Legends, Dedo Ilyo Maleshevski*.
[5] *Macedonian Nation – Macedonian Legends, Dimitar Popgeorgiev-Berovski*.
[6] Дойнов, Дойно. *Кресненско-Разложкото въстание, 1878-1879*, (София, 1979), 37.
[7] Krste Bitkovski, *Macedonia in the XIX Century*, in Todor Chepreganov, ed., *History of the Macedonian People*, (Institute of National History, 2008), 165.
[8] *Macedonian Nation – Macedonian Legends, Dimitar Popgeorgiev-Berovski*.
[9] Laura B. Sherman, *Fires on the Mountain: The Macedonian Revolutionary Movement and the Kidnapping of Ellen Stone*, (Columbia University Press, New York, 1980), 5.
[10] *Macedonian Nation – Macedonian Legends, Dimitar Popgeorgiev-Berovski*.
[11] Bitkovski, *Macedonia in the XIX Century*, 166.
[12] Дойнов, *Кресненско-Разложкото въстание*, 54-58.
[13] http://polacywmacedonii.net/wywiady/ludwik-wojtkiewicz/ . *Polish people in Macedonia*, Accessed 12-12/2016.
[14] Magdalena Turkowska, *Polacy a sprawa macedońska. Polscy powstańcy jako działacze polityczni w Imperium Osmańskim* - http://biuletynmigracyjny.uw.edu.pl . Accessed 12/13/2016.
[15] Turkowska, *Polacy w Imperium Osmańskim*
[16] Клейн, Збигнев. *Полски следи в изграждането на нова България 1877-1914*, София, б.г., издателство „Парадигма".
[17] Дойнов, *Кресненско-Разложкото въстание*, 35-36.
[18] Дойнов, *Кресненско-Разложкото въстание*, 54-58.
[19] *Енциклопедия „Пирински край". Том 1*, (Благоевград, 1995), 409.
[20] Дойнов, *Кресненско-Разложкото въстание*, 35-36.
[21] Дойнов, *Кресненско-Разложкото въстание*, 47.
[22] Дойнов, *Кресненско-Разложкото въстание*, 61-65.
[23] Костенцев, Арсени. *„Спомени"*. Издателство на Отечествения фронт, (София, 1984)
[24] Дойнов, *Кресненско-Разложкото въстание*, 61-65.

[25] http://www.mn.mk/makedonski-legendi/12377-Vojvoda-Georgi-Zimbilev . Macedonian Nation – Macedonian Legends, Vojvoda Georgi Zimbilev, 9/21/2016. Accessed December 2016.
[26] Bitkovski, *Macedonia in the XIX Century*, 166.
[27] Bitkovski, *Macedonia in the XIX Century*, 167.
[28] *Macedonia: Documents and Materials*, Ed. Voin Bozhinov and L. Panayotov, (Bulgarian Academy of Science, Sofia, 1978) 368, 369.
[29] Bitkovski, *Macedonia in the XIX Century*, 167, 168.
[30] Macedonian Nation – Macedonian Legends
[31] Hadži-Vasiljević (1928). *Četnička akcija u Staroj Srbiji i Maćedoniji* (in Serbian). (Belgrade: Sv. Sava 1933) 1.
[32] Hadži-Vasiljević *Četnička akcija u Staroj Srbiji i Maćedoniji*, 2.
[33] Hadži-Vasiljević *Četnička akcija u Staroj Srbiji i Maćedoniji*, 3.
[34] Hadži-Vasiljević *Četnička akcija u Staroj Srbiji i Maćedoniji*, 3.
[35] Doklestić, Ljubiša, *Srpsko-makedonskite odnosi vo XIX-ot vek: do 1897 godina*. (Nova Makedonija, 1973), 163-166.
[36] Društvo sv. Save, *Brastvo*. (1908) 12-13.
[37] Hadži-Vasiljević *Četnička akcija u Staroj Srbiji i Maćedoniji*, 10,11.
[38] Mercia MacDermott, *Freedom or Death: The Life of Gotse Delchev*, (The Journeymen Press,London, 1978) 55-57.
[39] Кънчов, Васил. *Избрани произведения, Том I*, (София, 1970), 186.
[40] Баждаров, Георги. *Горно Броди*. (София, 1929), с. 49.
[41] "Документи за българското Възраждане от архива на Стефан И. Веркович 1860-1893", (София, 1969), 609.
[42] Баждаров, *Горно Броди*, 51.
[43] Mercia MacDermott, *For freedom and perfection: a biography of Jane Sandanski*, (1987), 44.
[44] A. Hulme Beaman, *M. Stambuloff*, (London, Bliss, Sands and Foster, 1895), 40.
[45] Beaman, *M. Stambuloff*, 40.
[46] Beaman, *M. Stambuloff*, 145.
[47] Beaman, *M. Stambuloff*, 171-174.
[48] Duncan Perry, *The Politics of Terror: The Macedonian Liberation Movements, 1893-1903*, (Duke University Press, U.S.A. 1988), 33, 34.
[49] Duncan Perry, *Stefan Stambolov and the Emergence of Modern Bulgaria, 1870-1895*, (Duke University Press, USA, 1993) 160-168.
[50] Perry, *Stefan Stambolov* 160-168.
[51] Yosmaoglu, *Blood Ties* 26

[52] Perry, *Stefan Stambolov* 160-168.
[53] Perry, *The Politics of Terror* 33, 34.
[54] Perry, *Stefan Stambolov* 160-168.
[55] Yosmaoglu, *Blood Ties* 26. Note 30.
[56] Perry, *Stefan Stambolov* 167.
[57] Beaman, *M. Stambuloff,* 171-174.
[58] http://www.krumblagov.com/fifty/32.php , Accessed 12/12/2016.
[59] Beaman, *M. Stambuloff,* 171-174.
[60] Perry, *Stefan Stambolov* 175.
[61] *История на България*, (1991) 261, 266, 438.
[62] Perry, *Stefan Stambolov* 180, 181.
[63] Perry, *Stefan Stambolov* 180, 181.
[64] Perry, *Stefan Stambolov* 181.
[65] Perry, *Stefan Stambolov* 227, 228.
[66] "For a Political Murder", *Sunday Morning Herald, Baltimore*, Dec. 23, 1986, 1.
[67] Perry, *Stefan Stambolov*, 229.
[68] "For a Political Murder", 1.
[69] Perry, *Stefan Stambolov* 224.
[70] "For a Political Murder", 1.
[71] Gardev, Borislav, *Mihail Stavrev: Revolutionary and Assassin*, July 2014, http://afera.bg. Accessed, 12/13/2016.
[72] "For a Political Murder", 1.
[73] See Sinadinoski, Victor, *Anarchy in Macedonia* for a description of this.
[74] http://www.krumblagov.com/fifty/32.php Accessed 12/12/2016.
[75] http://www.mn.mk/makedonski-legendi/12570-Evtim-Sprostranov .
[76] Bitkovski, *Macedonia in the XIX Century*, 174.
[77] Perry, *The Politics of Terror* 37,38.
[78] Bitkovski, *Macedonia in the XIX Century*, 174.
[79] Perry, *The Politics of Terror* 38.
[80] Anastasoff, *The Tragic Peninsula* 23-28.
[81] Bitkovski, *Macedonia in the XIX Century* 175.
[82] Anastasoff, *The Tragic Peninsula* 23-28.
[83] Bitkovski, *Macedonia in the XIX Century* 175, 176.
[84] Anastasoff, *The Tragic Peninsula* 29-34.
[85] Hristo Andonov-Poljanski,*Goce Delchev and His Views*, in the Epic of Ilinden, (Macedonian Review Editions, Skopje, 1973), 81.
[86] Anastasoff, *The Tragic Peninsula* 29-34.
[87] Bitkovski, *Macedonia in the XIX Century* 175, 176.
[88] MacDermott, *Freedom or Death*, 97.
[89] Bitkovski, *Macedonia in the XIX Century* 175, 176.
[90] *Sho Stava*, Vol. 2, Iss. 12. Pg. 4.
[91] Laura B. Sherman, *Fires on the Mountain: The Macedonian Revolutionary Movement and the Kidnapping of Ellen Stone*, (Columbia University Press, New York, 1980), Pg.9.
[92] *Sho Stava*, Vol. 2, Iss. 12. Pg. 4.

[93] "General Tsoncheff", The Macedonian Question, Geelong Advertiser, Mar. 12, 1904, 5.
[94] Anastasoff, *The Tragic Peninsula* 23-28.
[95] Anastasoff, *The Tragic Peninsula* 29-34.
[96] Anastasoff, *The Tragic Peninsula* 35, 36.
[97] Anastasoff, *The Tragic Peninsula* 36-39.
[98] Maurice Kahn, Temps, Mar. 28, 1903, in Draganof, *Macedonia and the Reforms*, (London, 190),10.
[99] Bitkovski, *Macedonia in the XIX Century* 180.
[100] Anastasoff, *The Tragic Peninsula*, 47.
[101] Nigel Carlyle Graham, "Macedonia as I Saw It", *Good Words,* ed. Donald Macleod, 1905, 140.
[102] Bitkovski, *Macedonia in the XIX Century* 184.
[103] Carnegie Endowment for International Peace, Division of Intercourse and Education, Publication No. 4, *Report of the International Commission to Inquire into the Causes and Conduct of the Balkan Wars*, (1914, Washington, D.C.), 33.
[104] Anastasoff, *The Tragic Peninsula* 46.
[105] "The Bulgarian-Macedonian Movement and What the Trouble with the Turkish Government Is All About", The Deseret News, Mar. 7, 1903, 2.
[106] "Macedonia", Mercury, Hobart, Mar. 18, 1903, 7.
[107] Anastasoff, *The Tragic Peninsula* Pg. 17.
[108] Mary Edith Durham, *The Burden of the Balkans,* (Edward Arnold, London, 1904), 114.
[109] Albert Sonnichsen, *Confessions of a Macedonian Bandit,* (Duffield & Company, New York, 1909), 37,38.
[110] H.N. Brailsford, *Macedonia; Its Races and Their Future*, (Methuen & Co., London, 1906, Reprint edition by Arno Press, 1971), 133.
[111] Keith S. Brown, *Loyal Unto Death: Trust and Terror in Revolutionary Macedonia*, (Indiana University Press, Bloomington, 2013), 84.
[112] Draganof, *Macedonia and the Reforms* 15.
[113] Anastasoff, *The Tragic Peninsula* 47.
[114] Brailsford, *Macedonia* 113.
[115] "Delay in Macedonia", Boston Evening Transcript, Mar. 20, 1903. 2.
[116] "An Underground Republic: An Adventure in Macedonia", Blackwood's Magazine,Volume 179, 1906, 310.
[117] Anastasoff, *The Tragic Peninsula* 44, 45.
[118] "Macedonia", Mercury, Hobart, Mar. 18, 1903, 7.
[119] Vladimir Audreiff Tsanoff, "Macedonia In Revolution: An Eloquent Defence of the Insurrection", Boston Evening Transcript, Aug. 15, 1903, 20.
[120] *Sho Stava*, Vol. 2, Iss. 12. Pg. 20.
[121] Sonnichsen, *Confessions of a Macedonian Bandit* 172 – 174.
[122] Sonnichsen, *Confessions of a Macedonian Bandit* 152.
[123] Sonnichsen, *Confessions of a Macedonian Bandit* 152.
[124] MacDermott, *Freedom or Death,* 269.

[125] Arthur D. Howden Smith, *An American's Adventures with the Macedonian Revolutionists*, (G.P. Putnam's Sons, New York, 1908), 28.
[126] Albert Londres, *Terror in the Balkans*, translated by L. Zarine, (Constable & Co., London. 1935), 146.
[127] Anastasoff, *The Tragic Peninsula* 52.
[128] Londres, *Terror in the Balkans* 27,28.
[129] Boston Evening Transcript, Mar. 1, 1902, 16.
[130] "Salonika Celebrating: How Macedonia's Big City Welcomed the Sultan's Constitution", The Montreal Gazette, Sep. 3, 1908. Pg. 10.
[131] "Macedonians Demand, Levy Tolls on Turks," The Pittsburgh Press, Dec. 24, 1904, 1.
[132] Nick Anastasovski, *The Contest for Macedonian Identity, 1870-1912*. (2005), 237.
[133] "Macedonians Demand, Levy Tolls on Turks" 1.
[134] Yosmaoglu, *Blood Ties* 224.
[135] Sonnichsen, *Confessions of a Macedonian Bandit* 35,36.
[136] Perry, *The Politics of Terror* 58,59.
[137] Perry, *The Politics of Terror*, 58,59.
[138] *Sho Stava*, Vol. 2, Iss. 12. Pg. 4.
[139] Anastasoff, *The Tragic Peninsula* 48.
[140] Perry, *The Politics of Terror* 61, 62
[141] Perry, *The Politics of Terror* 76.
[142] Brown, *Loyal Unto Death* 154.
[143] "Bulgarian Minister Assassinated Today," Press and Horticulturist, Riverside, Feb. 7, 1902, 1.
[144] Noel Buxton, *Europe and the Turks*, (John Murray, London: 1907) Pg. 37.
[145] *Correspondence Respecting the Affairs of South-Eastern Europe*, (Harrison & Sons, Printed for His Majesty's Stationery Office, 1903), 10.
[146] *Correspondence Respecting the Affairs of South-Eastern Europe* 29.
[147] *Correspondence Respecting the Affairs of South-Eastern Europe* 38.
[148] "Discovered Deep Plot for a Great Revolt", The Pittsburgh Press, Apr. 9, 1901, 2.
[149] Brailsford, *Macedonia* 127.
[150] William Le Queux, *The Near East: The Present Situation in Montenegro, Bosnia, Servia, Bulgaria, Roumania, Turkey, and Macedonia* (New York: Doubleday, Page and Company: 1907), 293.
[151] "Macedonia", Mercury, 7.
[152] *Correspondence Respecting the Affairs of South-Eastern Europe* 111.
[153] *Correspondence Respecting the Affairs of South-Eastern Europe* 166.
[154] Brown, *Loyal Unto Death*, 166.
[155] Anastasoff, *The Tragic Peninsula* 73-75.
[156] "Rebels Fought Boldly", The Pittsburgh Press, Aug. 15, 1902.
[157] MacDermott, *Freedom or Death*, 234.

158 Sonnichsen, *Confessions of a Macedonian Bandit* 108.
159 Andonov-Poljanski, *Goce Delchev and His Views*, 83.
160 MacDermott, *Freedom or Death*, 161.
161 MacDermott, *Freedom or Death*, 102.
162 Randall B. Woods, "Terrorism in the Age of Roosevelt: The Miss Stone Affair, 1901-1902", (American Quarterly, Vol. 31, No.4, 1979), 480.
163 James Krapfl, *The Ideals of Ilinden: Uses of Memory and Nationalism in Socialist Macedonia* (Columbia University: March 1996).
164 Carnegie, *Report of the International Commission* 32, 33.
165 http://www.krumblagov.com/fifty/32.php Accessed 12/12/2016.
166 Perry, *The Politics of Terror* 47, 48.
167 Силянов, Христо. *Освободителните борби на Македония*, (София, 1933), 83.
168 Perry, *The Politics of Terror*, 47, 48.
169 Енциклопедия „Пирински край", том II. (Благоевград, Редакция „Енциклопедия", 1999), 203.
170 http://www.mn.mk/makedonski-legendi/12570-Evtim-Sprostranov .
171 Perry, *The Politics of Terror*, 52-54.
172 Anastasoff, *The Tragic Peninsula* 56-62.
173 Anastasoff, *The Tragic Peninsula* 56-62.
174 "The Macedonian Leader", The Reading Eagle, Aug. 23, 1903, 6; The American Monthly Review of Reviews: Vol. 28, ed. Albert Shaw, 1903, 92.
175 Perry, *The Politics of Terror* 54, 55.
176 Perry, *The Politics of Terror* 54, 55.
177 Andonov-Poljanski, *Goce Delchev and His Views*, 86.
178 Perry, *The Politics of Terror* 54, 55.
179 MacDermott, *Freedom or Death*, 133.
180 Perry, *The Politics of Terror* 62, 63.
181 Sherman, *Fires on the Mountain* 20.
182 Sherman, *Fires on the Mountain* 20.
183 Andonov-Poljanski, Goce Delchev and His Views, Pg. 86.
184 Perry, *The Politics of Terror* 68.
185 Perry, *The Politics of Terror* 68.
186 Lape, *The Life and Work of Gjorche Petrov* 150-151.
187 Perry, *The Politics of Terror* 82, 83.
188 MacDermott, *Freedom or Death*, 219, 220.
189 Anastasoff, *The Tragic Peninsula* 62.
190 Smith, *An American's Adventures* 23.
191 Perry, *The Politics of Terror* 89-95.
192 Perry, *The Politics of Terror* 89-95.
193 Perry, *The Politics of Terror* 89-95.
194 Perry, *The Politics of Terror* 89-95.
195 Perry, *The Politics of Terror* 87.
196 Perry, *The Politics of Terror* 88.
197 MacDermott, *Freedom or Death*, 254.
198 Brown, *Loyal Unto Death* 186.

[199] Perry, *The Politics of Terror* 97,98.
[200] Perry, *The Politics of Terror* 98-100.
[201] Gardev, Borislav, *Mihail Stavrev: Revolutionary and Assassin*, July 2014, http://afera.bg. Accessed, 12/13/2016.
[202] *Спомени на Симеон Радев*, в: Борбите в Македония и Одринско. 1878 – 1912. (София, 1981), 251.
[203] Литературна история, (БАН, том 10, 1983) 45.
[204] Елдъров, Светослав. *Генерал Иван Цончев. Биография на два живота*, (София, 2003), 82.
[205] Sonnichsen, *Confessions of a Macedonian Bandit* 105, 106.
[206] Perry, *The Politics of Terror* 89.
[207] Manol Pandevski, *Yane Sandanski – Revolutionary*, The Epic of Ilinden, (Macedonian Review Edition, Skopje, 1973), 159-163.
[208] MacDermott, *For freedom and perfection*, 58.
[209] *Correspondence Respecting the Affairs of South-Eastern Europe* 81.
[210] "The Macedonian Agiation", The Times, London, April 12, 1901,. 3-4
[211] *Correspondence Respecting the Affairs of South-Eastern Europe* 8.
[212] Anastasoff, *The Tragic Peninsula* 63-65.
[213] Woods, "Terrorism in the Age of Roosevelt" 482
[214] Anastasoff, *The Tragic Peninsula* 63-65.
[215] Sonnichsen, *Confessions of a Macedonian Bandit*. 257, 258.
[216] Sonnichsen, *Confessions of a Macedonian Bandit* 257, 258.
[217] Anastasoff, *The Tragic Peninsula*, 66.
[218] Perry, *The Politics of Terror* 113, 114.
[219] "Turkey's Troubles: The Macedonian Rising," The Age, Melbourne, Oct. 22, 1902, 5.
[220] Perry, *The Politics of Terror*, 115,116.
[221] "Macedonian Situation," The Deseret News, Oct. 10, 1902, 5.
[222] A.T. Christoff, *The Truth about Bulgaria*, 1919, 35.
[223] Bitkovski, *Macedonia in the XIX Century* 187.
[224] Perry, *The Politics of Terror* 117,118.
[225] Andonov-Poljanski, *Goce Delchev and His Views*, 91.
[226] Perry, *The Politics of Terror* 117,118.
[227] Bitkovski, *Macedonia in the XIX Century* 187.
[228] MacDermott, *Freedom or Death*, 1978: 320.
[229] Bitkovski, *Macedonia in the XIX Century* 188, 189.
[230] "Terror in Macedonia: Turkish Troops fill the Town of Monastir," Boston Evening Transcript, Apr. 7, 1903, 1.
[231] "The Macedonian Leader", 6.
[232] "Latest News from the Old World", The Pittsburgh Press, Apr. 15, 1902, 1.
[233] *Correspondence Respecting the Affairs of South-Eastern Europe* 15.

[234] *Correspondence Respecting the Affairs of South-Eastern Europe* 15.
[235] *Correspondence Respecting the Affairs of South-Eastern Europe* 16.
[236] Macedonia, Mercury, Hobart, Mar. 18, 1903. Pg. 7.
[237] *Correspondence Respecting the Affairs of South-Eastern Europe* 26-28.
[238] Durham, *The Burden of the Balkans* 113.
[239] Sonnichsen, *Confessions of a Macedonian Bandit* 104, 105.
[240] *Correspondence Respecting the Affairs of South-Eastern Europe* 120.
[241] http://www.mn.mk/makedonski-legendi/3024-Boris-Sarafov
[242] "Macedonians Would Force War," Boston Evening Transcript, Oct. 8, 1903m 3.
[243] Vladimir Adreieff Tsanoff, "The Menace of Bulgaria", Boston Evening Transcript, Jan. 17, 1903, 16.
[244] Perry, *The Politics of Terror* 170.
[245] Perry, *The Politics of Terror* 171.
[246] Sherman, *Fires on the Mountain*.15, 16.
[247] Sherman, *Fires on the Mountain* 17.
[248] Sonnichsen, *Confessions of a Macedonian Bandit* 256 – 262.
[249] "Brigands of the Balkans," Press and Horticulturalist, Riverside, Feb. 4, 1902, 3.
[250] "Consul Dickinson Refuses Ransom to Bulgarian Brigands," The Pittsburgh Press, Oct. 17, 1901, 1.
[251] Sonnichsen, *Confessions of a Macedonian Bandit* 256, 262.
[252] Sonnichsen, *Confessions of a Macedonian Bandit* 258 – 262.
[253] Boston Evening Transcript, Mar. 1, 1902, 16.
[254] Boston Evening Transcript, Mar. 1, 1902, 16.
[255] Boston Evening Transcript, Mar. 1, 1902, 16.
[256] "Wellesley's Appeal for Miss Stone," Boston Evening Transcript, Oct. 16, 1901, 3.
[257] Woods, "Terrorism in the Age of Roosevelt" 489, 490.
[258] Woods, "Terrorism in the Age of Roosevelt" 488.
[259] Woods, "Terrorism in the Age of Roosevelt" 488.
[260] Boston Evening Transcript, Mar. 1, 1902, 16.
[261] "Is Miss Stone Alive: Well Known Brigand Instructed to Find Out", The Lewiston Daily News, Nov. 5, 1901, 5.
[262] Boston Evening Transcript, Mar. 1, 1902, 16.
[263] "Miss Stone's Release: Graphic Thinks it will be Long Delayed," Boston Evening Transcript, Feb. 13, 1902, 12.
[264] The Age, Feb. 7, 1902, 5.
[265] Woods, "Terrorism in the Age of Roosevelt" 492.
[266] Boston Evening Transcript, Feb. 24, 1902, 14.
[267] Perry, *The Politics of Terror* 105.
[268] Sonnichsen, *Confessions of a Macedonian Bandit* 256.
[269] Sonnichsen, *Confessions of a Macedonian Bandit* 266.
[270] Boston Evening Transcript, Feb. 24, 1902, 14.

[271] Perry, *The Politics of Terror* 105.
[272] Sherman, *Fires on the Mountain* 13.
[273] "Demand $5,000 Ransom", Boston Evening Transcript, Oct. 10, 1905. 8.
[274] "Mutilated by Brigands," Express and Telegraph, Adelaide, Nov. 16, 1905, 4.
[275] "Macedonian Bandits Want Hostage: Plot to Kidnap an American Millionaire in Bulgaria", The Evening News, San Jose, Oct. 29, 1903, 1.
[276] Perry, *The Politics of Terror* 171.
[277] MacDermott, *For freedom and perfection,* 153.
[278] "An American Aided Rebels", The Pittsburgh Press, Sep. 3, 1903m 1.
[279] The Dawson Record, Oct. 18, 1903, 4.
[280] Bitkovski, *Macedonia in the XIX Century* 188, 189.
[281] MacDermott, *Freedom or Death,* 326-328.
[282] MacDermott, *Freedom or Death,* 326-328.
[283] Anastasoff, *The Tragic Peninsula* 81-85.
[284] Anastasoff, *The Tragic Peninsula* 81, 82.
[285] Mazower, *Salonica, City of Ghosts* 249-252.
[286] Stoyan Christowe, *Heroes and Assassins,* (Robert M. McBride & Company, New York, 1935), 77-80.
[287] Mazower, *Salonica, City of Ghosts* 249-252.
[288] Frederick Moore, *The Balkan Trail,* (The MacMillan Company, New York, 1906). 119; Mazower, *Salonica, City of Ghosts* 249-252.
[289] Moore, *The Balkan Trail* 119; Mazower, *Salonica, City of Ghosts* 249-252.
[290] Mazower, *Salonica, City of Ghosts* 249-252.
[291] Moore, *The Balkan Trail.* 120
[292] [292]Mark Mazower, Salonica, City of Ghosts, Pg. 249-252.
[293] Moore, *The Balkan Trail* 122-124.
[294] Mazower, *Salonica, City of Ghosts* 249-252.
[295] Mazower, *Salonica, City of Ghosts* 249-252.
[296] Moore, *The Balkan Trail* 132, 133.
[297] Mazower, *Salonica, City of Ghosts* 249-252.
[298] The Balkans: Pacifying Macedonia, The Age, Melbourne, May 6, 1903. Pg. 5.
[299] The Balkans: Bulgarian Dynamiters, The Age, Melbourne, May, 5, 1903. Pg. 5.
[300] The Balkans: Bulgarian Dynamiters, The Age, Melbourne, May, 5, 1903. Pg. 5.
[301] Moore, *The Balkan Trail* 105.
[302] Moore, *The Balkan Trail* Pg. 118.
[303] Anastasoff, *The Tragic Peninsula* 29-34.
[304] Anastasoff, *The Tragic Peninsula* 29-34.
[305] Anastasoff, *The Tragic Peninsula* 29-34.
[306] MacDermott, *Freedom or Death,* 361,362.
[307] MacDermott, *Freedom or Death,* 361,362.
[308] Anastasoff, *The Tragic Peninsula* 83-85.
[309] *Sho Stava,* Vol. 2, Iss. 12. Pg. 37.
[310] Anastasoff, *The Tragic Peninsula* 23-28.
[311] Anastasoff, *The Tragic Peninsula* 83-85.

[312] "A Terrible Threat", St. John Daily, Sun, Jun. 9, 1903, 6.
[313] The American Monthly Review of Reviews: Vol. 28, ed. Albert Shaw, 1903, 421.
[314] *Sho Stava*, Vol. 2, Iss. 12. Pg. 20.
[315] *Sho Stava*, Vol. 2, Iss. 12. Pg. 20.
[316] *Sho Stava*, Vol. 2, Iss. 12.
[317] *Sho Stava*, Vol. 2, Iss. 12. Pg. 38.
[318] Brown, *Loyal Unto Death* 106.
[319] "15 Villages Destroyed," The Daily Star, Fredericksburg, Aug. 12, 1903, 2.
[320] "Towns Burned: Turks Destroy Fourteen Villages in the District of Uskub and Veleze," The Pittsburgh Press, Aug. 14, 1903, 7.
[321] *Sho Stava*, Vol. 2, Iss. 12. Pg. 7.
[322] *Sho Stava*, Vol. 2, Iss. 12. Pg. 14, 15.
[323] Alexander W. Hidden, *The Ottoman Dynasty: A History of the Sultans of Turkey from the earliest authentic record to the present time, with notes on the manners and customs of the people*. (Nicholas W. Hidden, New York, 1912), 422.
[324] *Sho Stava*, Vol. 2, Iss. 12. Pg. 8.
[325] *Sho Stava*, Vol. 2, Iss. 12. Pg. 9.
[326] *Sho Stava*, Vol. 2, Iss. 12. Pg. 9.
[327] *Sho Stava*, Vol. 2, Iss. 12. Pg. 33.
[328] Orde Ivanovski, *Nikola Karev - Organizer of the Krushevo Republic*, The Epic of Ilinden,(Macedonian Review Edition, Skopje, 1973), 137, 138.
[329] Ivanovski, *Nikola Karev* 141.
[330] James Krapfl, *The Ideals of Ilinden: Uses of Memory and Nationalism in Socialist Macedonia* (Columbia University: March 1996).
[331] Krapfl, *The Ideals of Ilinden*
[332] *Sho Stava*, Vol. 2, Iss. 12. Pg. 34.
[333] *Sho Stava*, Vol. 2, Iss. 12. Pg. 34.
[334] 15 Villages Destroyed, The Daily Star, 2.
[335] "The Rebellion in Macedonia," The Sydney Mail, Aug. 26, 1903,. 15.
[336] "Outrages Occur All Over Turkey," The Carroll Herald, Sep. 9, 1903, 7.
[337] "Macedonians Hold Their Own," The Evening News, San Jose, Sep. 16, 1903, 1.
[338] "They Want to Fight," The Evening News, San Jose, Sep. 24, 1903, 5.
[339] Major David S. Anderson, *The Apple of Discord: Macedonia, The Balkan League, and The Military Topography of The First Balkan War*, (School of Advanced Military Studies, Fort Leavenworth, 1993), 23.
[340] William E. Curtis, *The Turk and His Lost Provinces*, (Flemming H. Revell Company, 1903), 17.
[341] "Fight for Macedonia: Many Members of the Illinois Militia Volunteer to Go Against the Turks", Lewiston Sunday Journal, Sep. 18, 1903, 1.

[342] "Help for Macedonia," New York Daily Tribune, Apr. 27, 1904.
[343] See Victor Sinadinoski, Anarchy in Macedonia: Life Under the Ottoman, 1878-1912, for an indepth description and analysis of the crimes of the Turks against the Macedonians during this time.
[344] Londres, *Terror in the Balkans* 31,32.
[345] Durham, *The Burden of the Balkans* 6.
[346] The American Monthly Review of Reviews: Vol. 28, ed. Albert Shaw, 1903, 422.
[347] The American Monthly Review of Reviews: Vol. 28, ed. Albert Shaw, 1903, 600.
[348] "Macedonian Women Fighting," The Day, New London, Aug. 14, 1903, 11.
[349] "Native are Tortured by Insurgents", The Pittsburgh Press, Aug. 26, 1903, 1.
[350] Katrin Bozeva-Abazi, *The Shaping of Bulgarian and Serbian Identities: 1800s-1900s*. 2003 Thesis for McGill University,. 36, 165.
[351] Krste P. Misirkov, *On The Macedonian Matters*, 1903, ed. Boris Vishinski, tr. Alan McConnell (Macedonian Review, 1934), 9.
[352] Misirkov, *On The Macedonian Matters* 26.
[353] Anna Geifman, *Thou Shalt Kill: Revolutionary Terrorism in Russia, 1894-1917*, (Princeton Unviersity Press, 1993), 200,201.
[354] See Sinadinoski, Anarchy in Macedonia, Chapter v.
[355] MacDermott, *For freedom and perfection*, 165.
[356] MacDermott, *For freedom and perfection*, 473.
[357] "An Underground Republic", 308.
[358] "An Underground Republic", 308.
[359] The American Monthly Review of Reviews: Vol. 28, ed. Albert Shaw, 1903, 476.
[360] MacDermott, *For freedom and perfection*, 42.
[361] MacDermott, *For freedom and perfection*, 45,46.
[362] Smith, *An American's Adventures* 93-95.
[363] MacDermott, *For freedom and perfection*, 223.
[364] Dimitar Bechev, *Historical Dictionary of the Republic of Macedonia*, (The Scarecrow Press, Lanham, 2009), 230.
[365] "An Underground Republic", 310,311.
[366] Bitkovski, *Macedonia in the XIX Century* 195-197.
[367] Bitkovski, *Macedonia in the XIX Century* 195-197.
[368] http://www.mn.mk/makedonski-legendi/12570-Evtim-Sprostranov .
[369] Lape, *The Life and Work of Gjorche Petrov* 153-154.
[370] Bitkovski, *Macedonia in the XIX Century* 197, 198.
[371] Woods, "Terrorism in the Age of Roosevelt" 482.
[372] "Terrible Vengeance, World's News", Sydney, May 26, 1905, 2.
[373] John Foster Fraser, *Pictures from the Balkans*, (Cassell and Company, London, 1912), 13,14.
[374] Bitkovski, *Macedonia in the XIX Century* 186.

[375] The American Monthly Review of Reviews: Vol. 28, ed. Albert Shaw, 1903, 92.
[376] Anastasoff, *The Tragic Peninsula*, 56-62.
[377] Brailsford, *Macedonia* 73,74.
[378] Londres, *Terror in the Balkans* 44,45.
[379] "A Clockwork Bomb", The Age, Melbourne, Jul. 27, 1905, 5.
[380] "A Girl Becomes a Soldier to Avenege Her Parents' Death," Harbor Grace Standard, Montreal, Nov. 17, 1906, 5.
[381] "Girl Fights Turks to Free Macedonia", The Pittsburgh Press, Sep. 12, 1905, 11.
[382] Anastasoff, *The Tragic Peninsula* 23-28.
[383] Smith, *An American's Adventures* 32-34.
[384] Le Queux, *The Near East* 294, 295.
[385] Yosmaoglu, *Blood Ties*. 230.
[386] Yosmaoglu, *Blood Ties* 238-240.
[387] Yosmaoglu, *Blood Ties* 230.
[388] Yosmaoglu, *Blood Ties*. 220
[389] "Salonika Celebration: How Macedonia's Big City Welcomed the Sultan's Constitution," The Montreal Gazette, Sep. 3, 1908, 10.
[390] "Lived by Murder for Twenty Years," Observer, Adelaide, Sep. 19, 1925,46.
[391] "National Hero Shot Dead," Evening Journal, Adelaide, Jan. 18, 1908, 4.
[392] "New Revolt Averted by Assassin's Bullet",The Pittsburgh Press, Dec. 30, 1907, 5.
[393] Smith, *An American's Adventures* 30.
[394] MacDermott, *Freedom or Death,* 284.
[395] Bitkovski, *Macedonia in the XIX Century* 198.
[396] http://www.mn.mk/makedonski-legendi/12570-Evtim-Sprostranov .
[397] "Bulgaria's Fight to be Free," The Sun, Oct. 11, 1908, 3.
[398] Elisabeth Barker, *Macedonia: Its Place In Balkan Power Politics*, (Royal Institute of International Affairs, 1950), 40.
[399] "Macedonian Assassin Shot: By Rival Factionists," The Sydney Morning Herald, Aug. 30, 1909, 8.
[400] Anastasoff, *The Tragic Peninsula* 165.
[401] Ernst Christian Helmreich, *The Diplomacy of the Balkan Wars, 1912-1913*. (Cambridge, Harvard University Press, 1938), 37.
[402] "A Macedonian Murder," Perth, Feb. 24, 1910, 7.
[403] "A Macedonian Murder," Perth, Feb. 24, 1910, 7.
[404] "A Macedonian Murder," Perth, Feb. 24, 1910, 7.
[405] "Bulgarians Move to Front", Boston Evening Transcript, Oct. 14, 1912, 3.
[406] Ivan Katardziev, *Macedonia in the Period from the Balkan Wars to the Beginning of World War II (1912 to 1941)*, in Todor Chepreganov, ed., History of the Macedonian People, (Institute of National History, 2008), 211, 212.

[407] Carnegie, *Report of the International Commission* 47.
[408] *Balkan Locarno and the Macedonian Question*, Central Committee of the Union of the Macedonian Political Organizations, (Indianpolis,1928), 9.
[409] *Balkan Locarno and the Macedonian Question*, 9,10.
[410] Carnegie, *Report of the International Commission* 50-69.
[411] Ernst Christian Helmreich, *The Diplomacy of the Balkan Wars, 1912-1913*. (Cambridge, Harvard University Press, 1938), 38.
[412] Anastasovski, *The Contest for Macedonian Identity* 171.
[413] MacDermott, *For freedom and perfection*, 476-480.
[414] MacDermott, *For freedom and perfection*, 476-480.
[415] MacDermott, *For freedom and perfection*, 476-480.
[416] Katardziev, *Macedonia* 211, 212.
[417] Mantov Dimitar. *Pantheon black immortality*. (1995), 35.
[418] "Ask Bulgaria to Join With Allies," The Milwaukee Sentinel, Aug. 11, 1915, 2.
[419] "Link to the Orient Lies in the Balkans," Reading Eagle, Nov. 13, 1915, 6.
[420] Ed. Francis J. Reynolds, Allen I. Churchill, Francis Trevelyan Miller, *The Story of the Great War: History of the European War from Official Sources*, Vol. VII. (P.F. Collier & Son, 1919, New York),251,252.
[421] http://www.mn.mk/makedonski-legendi/12526-Bozidar-Tatarcev .
[422] Turkkaya Ataov, *The Bulgarian Quashing of its Minorities*, (1989), 6.
[423] George Clenton Logio, *Bulgaria: Problems and Politics*, (William Heinemann, Longond: 1919),183.
[424] David Starr Jordan and Harvey Ernest Jordan, *War's Aftermath: A Preliminary Study of the Eugenics of War*, (Houghton Mifflin Company, Boston, 1914),88, 89.
[425] Henry Baerlein, "What is Happening in Macedonia" in Fortnightly Review, 123, May 1928, 627.
[426] J. Walter Smith, "Serbia at the Second Thermopylae", Boston Evening Transcript, Nov. 24, 1915, 20.
[427] J. Walter Smith, "Serbia at the Second Thermopylae", Boston Evening Transcript, Nov. 24, 1915, 20.
[428] Barker, *Macedonia: Its Place In Balkan Power Politics* 22, 23.
[429] Carnegie, *Report of the International Commission* 158-165.
[430] Carnegie, *Report of the International Commission* 158-165.
[431] Victor A. Friedman, *Macedonian Language and Natinoalism During the Nineteenth and Early Twentieth Centuries*. (Balcanistica. Vol. 2. 1975. Reprinted in the Macedonian Review, 1986.Vol 16 (3)),. 288.
[432] Fortier Jones, *With Serbia Into Exile: An American's Adventures with the Army that Cannot Die*, (New York, The Century Co., 1916), 59.

[433] Carnegie, *Report of the International Commission* 169-171.
[434] "A Balkan Quarrel: Reported Massacre of Macedonians", The Glasgow Herald, May 9, 1914, 9.
[435] J. Johnston Abraham, *My Balkan Log*, (E.P. Dutton & Company, New York, 1922), 173.
[436] "Macedonia is Still Balkan Troublemaker", Berkeley Daily Gazette, Aug. 10, 1923, 4.
[437] Katardziev, *Macedonia* 218.
[438] Ferdinand Schevill, *The History of the Balkan Peninsula: From the Earliest Times to the Present Day*, (Harcourt, Brace and Company. New York. 1922), 508.
[439] Abraham, *My Balkan Log* 137, 138.
[440] British Foreign Office, FO 371/11245, pg. 2 and 3. Statements by Oliver C. Harvey.
[441] British Foriegn Office, FO 371/11405, Kennard (Belgrade) to A. Chamberlain, 21 April, 1926. Enclosure, R.A Gallop, 'Conditions in Macedonia', 19 April, 1926, p1.
[442] Гоцев, Димитър. *Национално-освободителната борба в Македония 1912 – 1915*, (Издателство на БАН, София, 1981), 147.
[443] Гоцев, Димитър. *Национално-освободителната борба в Македония 1912 - 1915*, (Издателство на БАН, София, 1981), 148.
[444] Ристески, Стојан. *Судени за Македонија (1945 - 1985)*, (Полар, Охрид, 1995), .282.
[445] Katardziev, *Macedonia* 212, 213.
[446] E.C.D. Rawlings, *General Report of the Industrial and Economic Situation in Greece*, Deparatment of Overseas Trade. 1921 – 1923. See gererally.
[447] "Rebirth of Salonika; A Changed Land," Maitland Daily Mercury, Jan, 6, 1927, 8.
[448] Kontogiorgi, Elisabeth, *Population Exchange in Greek Macedonia : The Forced Settlement of Refugees,n1922-1930*, 206-7 (2006).
[449] Katardziev, *Macedonia* 223.
[450] Anastasoff, *The Tragic Peninsula* 247.
[451] http://www.qate.net/~manqo/Rossos_British_FO.htm , FO 371/8566, Bentinck (Athens) to Curzon, 20 August 1923, Enclosure, Colonel A.C. Corfe, *"Notes on a Tour Made by the Commission on Greco-Bulgarian Emigration in Western and Central Macedonia,"* in Rossos, Andrew, Slavic Review, vol. *53*, no. *2, 1994, The British Foreign Office and Macedonian Ntioanl Identity, 1918-1941*.
[452] Barker, *Macedonia: Its Place In Balkan Power Politics* 61,62.
[453] Barker, *Macedonia: Its Place In Balkan Power Politics* 64,65.
[454] Katardziev, *Macedonia* 220,221.
[455] The Carp Review, Feb. 2, 1928. 4.
[456] The Pittsburgh Press, Oct. 12, 1934, 2.

[457] "Arrest Alleged Terrorist Chief," Spokane Daily Chronicle, Oct. 29, 1934, 1.
[458] Katardziev, *Macedonia* 215, 216.
[459] Katardziev, *Macedonia* 235, 236.
[460] Macedonian Nation – Macedonian Legends.
[461] Katardziev, *Macedonia* 235, 236.
[462] Lape, *The Life and Work of Gjorche Petrov* 157.
[463] Christowe, *Heroes and Assassins* 147-152.
[464] J. Walter Collins, "The Macedonian Tangle", The Contemporary View, Vol 125, 1921, 447.
[465] Anastasoff, *The Tragic Peninsula* 272-275.
[466] Anastasoff, *The Tragic Peninsula*, 272-275.
[467] "Rebel Chief Killed: Leader of Macedonians," News, Adelaide, Sep. 16, 1924, 1.
[468] "Bandits Wage Guerrilla War in Macedonia", Constantine Stephanov, The Deseret News, Jan. 27, 1923, 2.
[469] Katardziev, *Macedonia* 237.
[470] "Hunted Rebels Sit in Cafes of Vienna", Berkeley Daily Gazette, Jun. 29, 1923, 12.
[471] "Hunted Rebels Sit in Cafes of Vienna," 12.
[472] Balkan Locarno and the Macedonian Question, 15, 16.
[473] Paul S. Mowrer, *Balkanized Europe: A Study in Political Analysis and Reconstruction*, (EP Dutton & Company, New York, 1921),193.
[474] Londres, *Terror in the Balkans* 79,80.
[475] Londres, *Terror in the Balkans* 79.
[476] Londres, *Terror in the Balkans* 8, 81.
[477] "Sofia Reports Bulgar Revolt", Madera Tribune, Dec. 7, 1922, 1.
[478] "Macedonians in Bulgaria Restive", The Quebec Daily Telegraph, Jan. 27, 1923, 1.
[479] "War Clouds: Macedonians and Bulgarians Agrarian Dispute," Northern Star, Lismore, May, 15, 1923, 5.
[480] J. Swire, *The Bulgarian Conspiracy* (London: R. Hale, 1939), 142.
[481] Christowe, *Heroes and Assassins*. 159.
[482] Londres, *Terror in the Balkans* 42,43.
[483] "Bulgarian Youth Admits Killing, Is Acquitted by Jury", The Owosso Argus Press, Nov. 14, 1923, 1.
[484] "Bulgars Jail Macedonians", Reading Eagle, Mar. 5, 1924, 2.
[485] "Bolshevists and Balkans: Agreement with Macedonians", Telegraph, Brisbane, Sep. 30, 1924, 7.
[486] Barker, *Macedonia: Its Place In Balkan Power Politics* 42.
[487] Barker, *Macedonia: Its Place In Balkan Power Politics* 42.
[488] Katardziev, *Macedonia* 237, 238.
[489] Barker, *Macedonia: Its Place In Balkan Power Politics* 55,56.
[490] "With Price on His Head, Rebel Writes Newspaper", Madera Mercury, Aug. 6, 1924, 4.
[491] Christowe, *Heroes and Assassins* 180, 181.

[492] Christowe, *Heroes and Assassins*, 182-185
[493] Barker, *Macedonia: Its Place In Balkan Power Politics* 42.
[494] "Most Important News of World", Lake Benton Valley News, Sep. 26, 1924, 2.
[495] Stephane Groueff, *Crown of Thorns*, Madison Books, Lanham, 1987, 120.
[496] Bechev, *Historical Dictionary of the Republic of Macedonia*, 112.
[497] Groueff, *Crown of Thorns*, 122,123.
[498] "Mountaineers Fight for Free Macedonia", The Milawukee Journal, Jan. 22, 1928, 4.
[499] Anastasoff, *The Tragic Peninsula* 276.
[500] Londres, *Terror in the Balkans* 40.
[501] "Outlaw's Defiance," South Eastern Times, Millicent, Jun. 17, 1930, 1.
[502] Barker, *Macedonia: Its Place In Balkan Power Politics* 39.
[503] Barker, *Macedonia: Its Place In Balkan Power Politics* 38.
[504] Barker, *Macedonia: Its Place In Balkan Power Politics* 40.
[505] "Traitor Shot in Milan by Agent from Macedonia", The Montreal Gazette, Dec. 25, 1924, 9.
[506] Spyros Sfetas, *The Birth of Macedonianism in the Interwar Period*, Pg. 286.
[507] Sfetas, *The Birth of Macedonianism in the Interwar Period*, 286.
[508] Katardziev, *Macedonia* 239-241.
[509] The Washington Post, May 10, 1925, 2.
[510] *Macedonia and the Macedonians: A History*, Andrew Rossos, Hoover Press, 2008.
[511] http://runeberg.org/peergynt/. Accessed July 6, 2016.
[512] "Murder in a Theatre", The Age, Melbourne, May 11, 1925, 10.
[513] The Washington Post, May 10, 1925, 2.
[514] "Mountaineers Fight for Free Macedonia", The Milawukee Journal, Jan. 22, 1928, 4.
[515] Alfred Tyrnauer, "Nazi's Deadlies Led by Assassin Queen", World's News, Sydney, Nov. 29, 1941, 2.
[516] Londres, *Terror in the Balkans* 47.
[517] "Murder in a Theatre" 10.
[518] The Washington Post, May 10, 1925, 2.
[519] "Lived by Murder for Twenty Years", Observer, Adelaide, Sep. 19, 1925,46.
[520] The Washington Post, May 10, 1925, 2.
[521] Tyrnauer, *Nazi's Deadlies Led by Assassin Queen*, 2.
[522] "Lived by Murder for Twenty Year",.46.
[523] Tyrnauer, *Nazi's Deadlies Led by Assassin Queen*, 2.
[524] "Double Assassination: Macedonian Revolutionary Leaders Murdered", The Montreal Gazette, Nov. 2, 1927, 13.

[525] "Bulgarian Chief Assassin Victim", Spokane Daily Chronicle, Jul. 10, 1928, 2.
[526] "Hunted Rebels Sit in Cafes of Vienna", Berkeley Daily Gazette, Jun. 29, 1923, 12.
[527] "Mountaineers Fight for Free Macedonia", The Milawukee Journal, Jan. 22, 1928, 4.
[528] Barker, *Macedonia: Its Place In Balkan Power Politics* 43.
[529] "King of the Balkan Bandits Assassinated", Lewiston Evening Journal, Jul. 9, 1928, 4.
[530] "King of the Balkan Bandits Assassinated", Lewiston Evening Journal, Jul. 9, 1928, 4.
[531] "Struggle for Power Threatens Bulgaria," Prescott Evening Courier, Aug. 29, 1928, 2.
[532] "Outlaw's Defiance," South Eastern Times, Millicent, Jun. 17, 1930, 1.
[533] Londres, *Terror in the Balkans* 62.
[534] "Bulgaria Cries Out to America", The Spokesman Review, Nov. 23, 1928. Pg. 1.
[535] "Bulgars Fight in Streets as Revolt Grows", The Milwaukee Sentinel, Nov. 23, 1928, 2.
[536] "Bulgaria Cries Out to America", The Spokesman Review, Nov. 23, 1928, 1.
[537] "New Macedonian Chief Executes 11", The Milwaukee Sentinel, Nov. 18, 1928, 12, Sec. 1.
[538] "Macedonian Rebel Defies Government," The Montreal Gazette, Nov. 24, 1928, 15.
[539] Londres, *Terror in the Balkans* 75.
[540] "Bulgar Leader Brands, Hangs," Spokane Daily Chronicle, Nov. 22, 1928, 3.
[541] "Over 100 Assassinated in Macedonian Feuds," Reading Eagle, Jun. 14, 1930, 3.
[542] Londres, *Terror in the Balkans* 92-94.
[543] From Macedonian Legends.
[544] From Macedonian legends.
[545] Londres, *Terror in the Balkans* 6.
[546] Londres, *Terror in the Balkans* 98,99.
[547] "Balkan Rebels Abduct Rivals," The Milwaukee Sentinel, Feb. 15, 1931, 2.
[548] Londres, *Terror in the Balkans* 101, 102.
[549] Leonide Zarine in Albert Londres, *Terror in the Balkans* 173,174.
[550] Leonide Zarine in Londres, *Terror in the Balkans* 174,175.
[551] Katardziev, *Macedonia* 238.
[552] Leonide Zarine in Londres, *Terror in the Balkans* 185, 186.
[553] Leonide Zarine in Londres, *Terror in the Balkans* 178, 179.
[554] "News Review of Current Events", The Polk County News, May 28, 1925, 2.
[555] Phillip Rees, *The Biographical Dictionary of the Extreme Right Since 1890* (Simon & Schuster, New York: 1990

[556] "Kills Self on "American Soil" so Estate Would Go to Macedonia," Portsmouth Daily Times, Apr. 17, 1924, 1.
[557] "Suicide Gives Estate to Country", The Daily Star, Fredericksburg, Apr. 17, 1924,1.
[558] "Suicide Selects U.S. Consulate for His Purpose", The Day, New London, Apr. 17, 1924, 1.
[559] "Sofia Government to Fall as a Result of Bombing Outrage", The Delmarvia Star, Wilmington, Apr. 19, 1925, 6.
[560] "Avenger's Bullets Fail", The Spokesman Review, Spokane, Jul. 14, 1928, 2.
[561] Londres, Terror in the Balkans 129-132.
[562] "Shooting of General Stirs Balkan Fires," The Milwaukee Journal, Oct. 7, 1927, 2.
[563] "Shooting of General Stirs Balkan Fires" 2.
[564] "Assassin's Victim Will Probably Be Paralyzed", The Reading Eagle, Jan. 15, 1928, 17.
[565] Londres, Terror in the Balkans 127-129.
[566] Anastasoff, The Tragic Peninsula, 277.
[567] Londres, Terror in the Balkans 127-129.
[568] "Ignominious Death," The Daily News, Perth, Dec. 11, 1928, 7.
[569] "Bandit Chief Hanged", West Australian, Perth, Dec. 12, 1928, 20.
[570] "Two Dynamiters Executed," The Reading Eagle, May 7, 1928, 2.
[571] "Mountaineers Fight for Free Macedonia," The Milawukee Journal, Jan. 22, 1928, 4.
[572] Londres, Terror in the Balkans 64, 65.
[573] "Notorious Bandit Burns Men Alive", Spokane Daily Chronicle, Jul. 18, 1928,. 1.
[574] The Pittsburgh Press, Oct. 12, 1934, 2.
[575] "Police Intensify Search for 2 Terrorist Chiefs," The Lawrence Daily Journal-World, Oct. 15, 1934, 2.
[576] "Alexander's Body Back in Homeland," Pittsburgh Post Gazette, Oct. 15, 1934, 4.
[577] "King's Assassin Was a Macedonian," Lewiston Daily News, Oct. 15, 1934, 5.
[578] "Macedonian Feud Flares," Lawrence Daily Journal-World, Dec. 2, 1930, 2.
[579] "IMRO Terrorism in the Balkans," Sunday Mail, Brisbane, Jun. 25, 1939, 11.
[580] Londres, Terror in the Balkans 95,96.
[581] "King's Assassin Was a Macedonian", Lewiston Daily News, Oct. 15, 1934, 5.
[582] Christowe, Heroes and Assassins 218.
[583] "Yugoslavia's Queen Comes to Claim Dead", The Telegraph, Nashua, Oct. 10, 1934, 5.
[584] "The Assassin Lynched", West Australian, Perth, Oct. 11, 1934, 17.
[585] "Yugoslavia's Queen Comes to Claim Dead," 5.
[586] "Yugoslavia's Queen Comes to Claim Dead," 5.

[587] "Powerful Pistol Used By Assassin of Balkan Ruler," The Evening Independent, St. Petersburg, Oct. 12, 1934. 1.
[588] H.R. Knickerbocker, "Alexander was Regarded as Strong Man of Europe", The Deseret News, Oct. 10, 1934. 2.
[589] "Terrorist Admits Being Sent for Murder Purpose," The Spartanburg Herald, Oct. 17, 1934, 1,2.
[590] "Alexander's Body Back in Homeland," Pittsburgh Post Gazette, Oct. 15, 1934, 4.
[591] "Plot to Kill King," The Pittsburgh Press, Oct. 26, 1928, 36.
[592] King's Assassin Was a Macedonian," 5.
[593] "Fears Waning for War over Assassination," Pittsburgh Post-Gazette, Oct. 11, 1934, 2.
[594] Prescott Evening Courier, Oct. 10, 1934. Prescott, Arizona, 1.
[595] H.R. Knickerbocker, "Alexander was Regarded as Strong Man of Europe," The Deseret News, Oct. 10, 1934. 1.
[596] "Secret Societies Long Factor in Balkan Life", The Spartanburg Herald, Oct. 15, 1934, 2.
[597] "Terrorist Band Behind Slaying of Balkan King", The Evening Independent, St. Petersburg, Oct. 13, 1934,1.
[598] "Yugoslavia Vigorously Denies That it Plans to Send Ultimatum to Hungary," Spokane Daily Chronicle, Oct. 16, 1934,. 7.
[599] "Fears Waning for War over Assassination," Pittsburgh Post-Gazette, Oct. 11, 1934, 2.
[600] "Terrorist Admits Being Sent for Murder Purpose", The Spartanburg Herald, Oct. 17, 1934. Pg. 1,2.
[601] "Alexander's Body Back in Homeland", Pittsburgh Post Gazette, Oct. 15, 1934, 4.
[602] "Fears Waning for War over Assassination", Pittsburgh Post-Gazette, Oct. 11, 1934. 2.
[603] "Terrorist Admits Being Sent for Murder Purpose", The Spartanburg Herald, Oct. 17, 1934. 1.
[604] "Upset of Peace in Balkans is Feared", Pittsburgh Post-Gazette, Oct. 10, 1934. 1.
[605] H.R. Knickerbocker, "Alexander was Regarded as Strong Man of Europe", The Deseret News, Oct. 10, 1934. P2.
[606] "Fears Waning for War over Assassination", Pittsburgh Post-Gazette, Oct. 11, 1934.. 2.
[607] The Pittsburgh Press, Oct. 12, 1934, Pittsburgh, PA. 2.
[608] "Bulgaria Takes Courage; Names Rebel for Crime", The Milwaukee Journal, Apr. 25, 2.
[609] "Outlaw's Defiance", South Eastern Times, Millicent, Jun. 17, 1930, 1.
[610] "Balkan Rebels Abduct Rivals," The Milwaukee Sentinel, Feb. 15, 1931, 2.
[611] "Bulgarian Fascist Executioner Arrested," Pittsburgh Post-Gazette, Jul. 1934, 2

200

[612] The Milwaukee Sentinel, Oct. 24, 1934. Milwaukee, WI.2.
[613] The Milwaukee Sentinel, Oct. 24, 1934. Milwaukee, WI. 2.
[614] "Fascist State Set Up in Bulgaria", The Glasgow Herald, May 21, 1934, 11.
[615] "Bulgarian Army Seizes Control of National Government," Ottawa Citizen, May 21, 1934, 9.
[616] S. Sfetas, *The Formation of the Slav-Macedonian Identity, A Painful Process*, Thessaloniki, 2003, Pg. 107.Cited in. Spyros Sfetas, The Birth of Macedonianism in the Interwar Period, Pg. 293.
[617] Spyros Sfetas, *The Birth of Macedonianism in the Interwar Period*, 293, 294.
[618] Queenslander (Brisbane, Qld. : 1866 - 1939), Thursday 24 January 1935, 7
[619] "Miahiloff May Seek United States Haven," Schenectady Gazette, Sep. 19, 1934, 11.
[620] "King" Ivan Mihailoff is Sentenced to Death", The Montreal Gazette, Mar. 14, 1935,. 1.
[621] Londres, *Terror in the Balkans* 173.
[622] Londres, *Terror in the Balkans* 115-117.
[623] Barker, *Macedonia: Its Place In Balkan Power Politics* 37.
[624] Barker, *Macedonia: Its Place In Balkan Power Politics* 23.
[625] Barker, *Macedonia: Its Place In Balkan Power Politics* 37,38.
[626] Queenslander (Brisbane, Qld. : 1866 - 1939), Thursday 24 January 1935, 7
[627] Queenslander (Brisbane, Qld. : 1866 - 1939), Thursday 24 January 1935, 7
[628] "Bulgarian Army Chief is Slain", The Evening Independent, St. Petersburg, Oct. 10, 1938, 1.
[629] "Sofia Plot is Smashed," The Montreal Gazette, Oct. 15, 1938, 6.

Printed in Great Britain
by Amazon